Application of Network Function Virtualization in Modern Computer Environments

Živko Bojović

now
the essence of knowledge

Published, sold and distributed by:
now Publishers Inc.
PO Box 1024
Hanover, MA 02339
United States
Tel. +1-781-985-4510
www.nowpublishers.com
sales@nowpublishers.com

Outside North America:
now Publishers Inc.
PO Box 179
2600 AD Delft
The Netherlands
Tel. +31-6-51115274

ISBN: 978-1-63828-358-4
E-ISBN: 978-1-63828-359-1
DOI: 10.1561/9781638283591

Suggested citation: Ž. Bojović. (2024). *Application of Network Function Virtualization in Modern Computer Environments.* Boston–Delft: Now Publishers

Table of Contents

Foreword

This monograph is a comprehensive guide to creating a new network design using network function virtualization (NFV concept), emphasizing application over theory. It is written for teachers, students, network engineers, software developers, and the general public interested in modern ICT trends. It assumes the reader is familiar with basic terminology, has elementary knowledge about computer networking, and possesses fundamental programming skills. The text is divided into the following ten sections:

1. Introduction – bring a detailed review of shortcomings in traditional networks and explain the primary motives that guide network designers and software developers in developing and implementing the NFV concept.
2. Network Function Virtualization – explains the NFV concept fundamentals and describes the key components of the ETSI NFV framework, including the benefits of NFV implementation in network infrastructure,
3. Virtualization techniques – provides a comprehensive review of the virtualization techniques and their application in modern computing environments, with an accent on the characteristics and functionality of virtual entities (virtual machines and containers),
4. Containerization technology – shows more details about motives for creation, characteristics of various containers, and their orchestration. This section also gives a detailed review of the Kubernetes platform and its features.
5. NFV-based network design – describes the basic principles of NFV-based network design and discovers the path for migration from traditional to NFV-based architecture. Also, this section explains the advantages, shortcomings, and challenges of VNF implementation.

6. SDN and NFV – explains the key SDN principles, including architecture, protocols, and use cases, and describes the SDN and NFV integration in modern networks.
7. NFV implementation in the cloud – explains the role of virtualization in the cloud, clouds' architectures, types, and delivery models, and describes OpenStack as an open-source cloud computing platform.
8. Service chaining in modern computer environments – describes key service chaining strategies and explains standardized architecture for SFC deployment and SDN/NFV-based architecture for SFC deployment.
9. Network slicing – describes the current trends in network softwarization, explains the concept of network slicing and its key principles, brings many details related to ONF network slicing architecture, management, and orchestration of network slices, and, finally, explains network slicing use cases in networks with implemented NFV and SDN.

The monograph offers a practical blend of theoretical considerations and the practical implementation of the NFV concept in modern computer environments. It is a valuable resource for the practitioner looking for a comprehensive guide to further network softwarization and building a highly programmable, scalable, and software-based network infrastructure.

We expect that readers' attention moves smoothly from one section to another. Taking all the facts into account, we propose:

- Content for students: Sections 1, 2, 3, 4, 5, and 6
- Content for teachers: Sections 1, 2, 3, 4, 5, 6, 7, 8 and 9
- Content for network engineers: Sections 1, 2, 3, 4, 5, 7, 8 and 9
- Content for software developers: Sections 4, 5, 8 and 9
- Content for the general public: Sections 1, 2, 3, 4, 5, 6, 7, 8 and 9

Preface

The intensive growth of the Internet continues with the increase in the number of users. According to some statistics (https://www.demandsage.com/internet-user-statistics/), in 2023, the Internet had more than 5.3 billion active Internet users, which was about 65.4% of the total planet's population. Many reasons influence this trend, but the real flood of new services and the emergence of new technologies are the key factors. The growth of the Internet has a lot to do with the softwarization of the network. This development trend in network communications began in the late 2010s with the maturity of novel technologies. It caused progress in the whole telecom industry, and crucial changes reflected in a deep transformation of computer networks from traditional, hardware-centric network functions into software-based solutions. The virtualization of network functions and their implementation, together with software-defined networking (SDN) and cloud computing, are key enabling technologies for building more flexible networks that are scalable and adaptable to changing requirements. Current research in this field refers to the resource, service, security, and other orchestration types and further automation of the processes. The main intention is to ensure that different software components work together seamlessly and efficiently, improve efficiency, reduce errors, and enhance the overall agility of the network.

This approach in the further development of network communications brings numerous benefits.

More programmability supports building software-defined networks, which are more adaptable to changing requirements (it is possible to accommodate new services easily) and enable networks to grow based on demand without the need for significant hardware changes. By virtualizing network functions and utilizing cloud infrastructure, it is possible to optimize resource usage and reduce hardware costs. The virtual functions can be deployed more quickly than traditional hardware-based solutions and enable faster service delivery. Overall, previously mentioned technologies and software-based networks are results that align with the more expansive trend of digitalization. Virtualization and other innovative technologies are seen as key enablers for the development of more efficient and dynamic networks.

This monograph is the culmination of years of consideration as to whether providers were ready to implement new technologies and open their architectures. It provides an overview of network softwarization and explains network changes and transformations regarding the convergence to software-defined networking and implementation of virtual functions, as well as pushing the network control to data centers and network edge. The monograph will be an interesting and valuable publication describing the theoretical, methodological, and practical challenges in the usage of advanced computing technologies for providers' and customers' needs. It offers solutions to important issues, shows the road to further work in this field, and represents a solid foundation for the exchange of experiences of students and teachers from various universities and even developers in the professional community.

Acknowledgments

This research has been supported by the Ministry of Science, Technological Development and Innovation (Contract No. 451-03-65/2024-03/200156) and the Faculty of Technical Sciences, University of Novi Sad, through project "Scientific and Artistic Research Work of Researchers in Teaching and Associate Positions at the Faculty of Technical Sciences, University of Novi Sad" (No. 01-3394/1).

The achieved results were published in eminent journals from the Thomson Reuters list and presented at international and national conferences. I owe deep gratitude to all my colleagues for our successful collaboration and dedicated work. Also, it is necessary to highlight the significant contribution of all the reviewers who helped with their suggestions and recommendations to make this material as high-quality as possible.

I owe special thanks to the Faculty of Technical Sciences in Novi Sad (the Dean, Prof. Dumnić, and respected colleagues Prof. Dejan Vukobratović and Prof. Vlada Delić), the companies Levi9 and NetCast Oblak, and Goran Militarov and Ljubica Bojović, who, through their financial donations, helped to provide the necessary budget for the monograph's publication.

I express special gratitude to my mentors, respected professors Vojin Šenk, Vlado Delić, and Emil Šećerov. At this moment, it is not possible to find a more suitable way to describe your support through my career changes. Your counseling outside of our regular sessions has made me a better person and researcher.

Finally, I must emphasize my gratitude to my family for their unwavering support, understanding, and encouragement during the ups and downs of the research and life journey.

DOI: 10.1561/9781638283591.ch1

Chapter 1

Introduction

The goals of improving the quality of existing services and enabling simple implementation of new services have long attracted the attention of telecom operators and inspired the academic and professional community. Despite the huge efforts made to achieve progress in this area, the strict standards that need to be met in terms of hardware and software have significantly slowed down these processes [1]. Great progress was made at the end of the last century with the appearance of the so-called Over-The-Top (OTT) services [2]. Service providers offer new services to users via the telecom operator's Internet network. One of the first examples of providing services via network operators' infrastructure (wired or wireless) was the Voice over Internet Protocol (VoIP) service. Although it could not meet the strict Quality of Service (QoS) initially, this service attracted many users, primarily thanks to its financial benefits [3].

Development in the market has forced telecom operators to change their business policies and urgently start redesigning the network architecture [4]. This redesigning involved the application of advanced technical and technological solutions and the implementation of a new concept of network infrastructure management. Prerequisites for survival in a highly competitive market are prompt responses to all user needs for more complex and resource-demanding services and the construction of a flexible and scalable network environment. Consequently, the computer infrastructure virtualization technology and the network function virtualization concept (NFV) application have emerged as one of the most significant solutions [5]. These technologies enabled seamless network function and new service deployment, a more responsive service provision approach, and greater network management control.

The basis of virtualization technology is the concept of "decoupling" network software from hardware, i.e., making it possible for network software to run on any hardware. This concept allows the designers of computer networks to choose and apply various technical and technological solutions freely, without restrictions such as the requirement for specialized hardware for each network function. It provides telecom operators and users with benefits such as reducing the costs of maintaining the existing and building new network infrastructure, agility in implementing new network functionalities, and others.

The primary motive that guides the designers of computer networks when implementing the NFV concept is the elimination of existing limitations in traditional computer networks. The limitations are mainly related to implementing network functions (such as firewalls, load balancers, or packet gateways), where it is necessary to possess specific software and hardware [6]. For example, in traditional networks, we can meet hardware load balancers. These balancers were loaded with specialized and proprietary built-in software that could handle massive application traffic. Vendors loaded proprietary software onto dedicated hardware and sold it to users as standalone appliances, usually in pairs, to provide failover if one system goes down [7]. This implementation of network functions indicates a high degree of dependence between software and hardware.

To eliminate this dependency, it is necessary to implement network functions, i.e., make the software that provides that functionality independent of the hardware. In other words, instead of using dedicated hardware, the software should be implemented on some general-purpose hardware (so-called Commercial-Off-The-Shelf hardware – COTS), where all operations will be performed by the processor [8]. Implementing such solutions enables new business opportunities on the market, thus attracting the interest of cloud and Internet service providers, mobile operators, and other players in the telecommunications market.

DOI: 10.1561/9781638283591.ch2

Chapter 2

Network Function Virtualization (NFV)

NFV technology develops rapidly, significantly influencing the application of new networking concepts. It implies redesigning traditional, hierarchical, organized networks, implementing more flexible and scalable solutions, and a new concept of network infrastructure management. By operating in a virtual environment such as virtual machines (VMs) and containers, the NFV enables architecture scaling faster, easier, and without extra (specialized) hardware. For example, in the case of system failure on physical devices, the NFV can facilitate disaster recovery. We can relocate a virtual entity to another location in the network so regular functions can be resumed even more quickly. The absence of the need for additional hardware helps operators reduce operational expenses. The new pay-as-you-go business philosophy associated with applying the NFV concept and the cloud also helps clients reduce costs. That is why it can be said with great certainty that organizations are rapidly moving from using dedicated hardware with pre-implemented software to applying advanced software solutions on standard hardware. The significantly wider application of software technologies aims to ensure a substantially higher level of programmability in the network [9].

For the rapid acceptance of NFV technology, it is important to identify contemporary socio-economic trends and analyze the potential problems that follow the implementation of existing and future services in traditional computer networks. Therefore, it must be borne in mind that, besides the numerous advantages of the

NFV concept, certain risks slow down its wider application, primarily in operator networks. One risk refers to multiple standards and open-source initiatives (Open Platform for NFV, Open-Source MANO, Open Network Automation Platform, European Telecommunications Standards Institute – ETSI, and the Metro Ethernet Forum) that encourage NFV development. A clear architectural direction, which would provide acceptable conditions for all providers and operators, is necessary for the wider application of the NFV concept. Another risk is security in complex environments with the implemented NFV concept. Namely, it is essential to apply appropriate solutions to protect the physical layer, the virtualized layer, and the carrier application. This requirement additionally complicates the NFV setup.

Further, when moving from a physical to a virtual infrastructure, the degradation of network function performances may occur. Therefore, it is necessary to continuously monitor the performance of virtualized network functions and avoid potential traffic bottlenecks (e.g., a virtual switch can be a potential bottleneck between virtual machines and network services for different traffic). To correctly comprehend the changes, it is necessary to understand the importance of the transition from a hardware-based approach to a virtualized network approach based on the software [10].

Undeniably, the NFV concept, along with technologies such as software-defined networking (SDN), cloud and edge computing, and others, significantly affects telecom providers, technology vendors, and other players of the connected ecosystems. Widespread use of these technologies leads to further "softwarization" of network environments (5G and 6G networks), resulting in a new value chain for various industries, including public administrations. For example, many administrations implement citizen-centric, data-driven, and performance-focused governance, transforming their e-government system into a smart government [11]. This transformation implied the appliance of different virtualization techniques to solve problems from technical, financial, and privacy perspectives. Operators and providers have become aware of the need to build a more flexible, scalable, and resilient network infrastructure. The main feature of the new infrastructure must be a high degree of agility in responding to heterogeneous user requirements. In most cases, this refers to service requirements based on cloud technologies, new types of communication such as M2M (Machine-to-Machine), or the application of smart Internet of Things (IoT) environments [12]. In such circumstances, the role of NFV and other advanced software technologies is to "introduce" a significantly higher level of programmability into the computer network to create an appropriate basis for implementing and efficiently operating all services.

The rest of this section is organized as follows: Subsection 2.1 provides the characteristics of traditional, hierarchically organized networks and indicates shortcomings, whose solving is the motive for developing and applying the NFV concept.

Subsection 2.2 explains two main principles representing the NFV concept's basics. Further, we explain the ETSI NFV framework, application fields, and the role of VNF in modern computer environments in Subsection 2.3. Subsection 2.4. deals with the concept and the importance of the ETSI NFV framework application for modern ICT (Information and Communication Technology) trends and makes the general picture of the basic building blocks, with more detailed insight into the structure of each of them. Finally, Subsection 2.3.2 highlights the advantages of NFV deployment.

2.1 Computer Networks with the Traditional Architecture

Many computer networks still have the traditional, hierarchical network architecture model. A characteristic of this model (Fig. 2.1) is that numerous functionalities are defined on specially developed hardware, where specialized, proprietary software runs. When manufacturers design and build their equipment, they are guided by a generic set of requirements and offer functionality that combines specific hardware and software. Thus, hardware and software are integrated as a single entity and represent a certain manufacturer's property [9]. Such software remains the manufacturer's property (clients can use it under predefined conditions). Manufacturers want to protect their intellectual property. However, this approach restricts users'

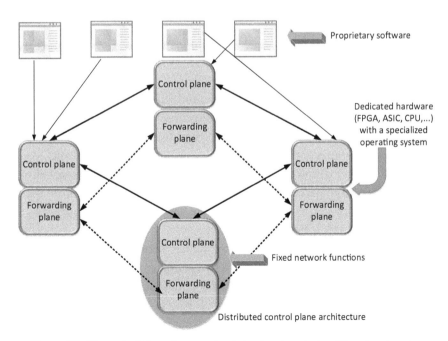

Figure 2.1. Characteristics of computer infrastructure in traditional networks.

rights to modify, distribute, or access its underlying source code, thereby diminishing flexibility and the possibility of rational use of available resources. Moreover, clients can become dependent on the manufacturer, which can produce negative effects from the financial and technical side (they must purchase equipment only from a certain manufacturer).

In real network environments, we meet numerous proprietary solutions, and the problem of establishing connections and communication between them (interoperability problem) is one of many problems we can encounter. Apart from the interoperability problem, the functioning of traditional computer networks is also significantly affected by the need to provide greater bandwidth. The emergence of new and more intelligent services (e.g., video, mobile, and IoT applications), as well as the exponential growth of the number of devices in the network, requires the engagement of significant resources and greater agility in the network. Telecom operators are challenged: How can they expand and scale network resources more effectively without increasing costs?

We must note that traditional networks have certain shortcomings which reduce operational efficiency, such as:

- Limited scalability due to the dependence on physical hardware devices.
- Low level of flexibility in coordinating between fixed-function network devices (require significant manual intervention).
- A single change can have a cascading effect because it can degrade the entire network's performance.
- A rigid, hierarchical architecture that is difficult to modify or adjust to varying user demands.

For example, to implement any hardware, providing a certain amount of electrical power and space for its accommodation is necessary, which can be a problem and an additional cost. Limitations also exist regarding software, as traditional network devices sometimes cannot keep up with changes in data networks (e.g., in terms of the number of routes to be created). In other words, traditional network devices are designed to function in a limited multidimensional space from the perspective of resources, so telecom operators have limited options for upgrading and expanding the network infrastructure.

Managing such a heterogeneous infrastructure is complex because there is no single management interface. For traffic measurement and computer resource load [13], monitoring tools are used with standardized monitoring protocols (e.g., Simple Network Management Protocol, NetFlow, and syslog). Often, more is needed, especially when monitoring parameters specific to certain manufacturers' equipment (e.g., the manufacturer uses a non-standard Management Information Base (MIB) or syslog messages). Work and business organization in this environment represent a serious challenge for telecom providers. They must have highly trained staff capable of maintaining equipment from different manufacturers, which affects operating costs, i.e., increases them.

Traditional computer networks can only sometimes follow the changes in the ICT market and the constant growth of user numbers. The variety of service requests creates a need, initiates a network redesign, optimizes the system, and overcomes difficulties in choosing the appropriate equipment. The upgrade process is burdened with costs related to providing physical access to personnel who need to install new hardware, reconfigure the system, and perform service. Additional training or employment of newly trained personnel represents another cost and slows decision-making on acquiring and installing equipment from another manufacturer. This situation potentially leads to the "lock-in" of telecom providers with one manufacturer's equipment. Every change in network capacity that must be made to satisfy user requirements, even in a longer time interval, requires additional financial resources.

2.2 Fundamentals of NFV Concept

The rapid development of information technologies and the emergence of new forms of communication represent the main driving force behind the development of contemporary society. To enable continuous tracking of these trends, the academic and professional community must find adequate answers to numerous challenges. These challenges are mainly related to allowing the open and flexible implementation of new and increasingly demanding services, which can only be done in a flexible and scalable environment. Building such an environment is only possible through the continuous development and application of advanced software technologies, such as virtualization technology of the computer infrastructure and network as a whole [9].

Today, there is almost no computer network in which there is no virtual (logical) version of at least some devices, whether they are servers, operating systems (Oss), processors, data stores, switches, or routers. The virtualization technology itself has taken root, especially in data centers. Their physical infrastructure, consisting of many independent server systems, has already been largely replaced by virtual servers running on shared hardware. The NFV concept was built on the server virtualization technique, although it has a much larger scope today. It extends to network devices and enables the ecosystem to deploy and manage virtualized network entities. The implementation of the NFV concept in the network is based on two main principles:

- decoupling software from hardware, and

- building network functionalities independent of the network location (e.g., firewalls, load balancers, routers, customer equipment for connecting to the Internet, and even access devices can be implemented at any location with virtualized computing infrastructure).

The NFV concept is a technology that enables the construction of a specific ecosystem. That ecosystem comprises virtual network devices, management tools, and infrastructure that integrate these software solutions with computing hardware. In other words, this technology enables replacing physical devices that perform a network function with one or more software programs that serve the same function running on generic computer hardware (e.g., replacing a firewall with a virtual machine on a standard server). In this way, it is possible to build a suitable environment where network functions can be implemented on any generic hardware that offers basic data processing, storage, and transmission resources. The term COTS hardware is often used in practice and implies hardware that contains the required resources and can run any software (Fig. 2.2) [14].

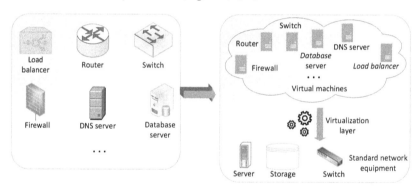

Figure 2.2. The transition from traditional to NFV networking concept.

In traditional computer networks, telecom operators fully control the hardware and software that performs a specific network function. However, the problem arises when user requirements change and when it is necessary to make quick changes in the network. The problem is most pronounced when it is needed to ensure the dynamic establishment of network functions and the rapid realization of the required services. That is why telecom operators, in such situations, opt for the application of NFV technology, with the important assumption that they have standard equipment with the necessary resources at the location [15]. Therefore, virtualizing the computer infrastructure and the network opens some new possibilities regarding configuration and network management. Through the application of open software interfaces, it is possible to create a flexible and scalable environment with the necessary level of agility to solve all user requests, realize certain innovations, and implement new network architectures optimally and efficiently.

2.3   ETSI NFV Framework

In traditional computer networks, where virtualization technology is not applied, the nodes usually contain network functions that represent a combination of software and hardware characteristics of a certain manufacturer. Virtualization technology is emerging as a natural solution to avoid being "lock-in" in specific hardware and software. Bearing in mind the main principles of NFV, it is easy to conclude that this technology represents a step forward in the realization of a more flexible and scalable computer infrastructure because it introduces the following novelties into the traditional network architecture [16]:

- The network element is no longer a set of integrated hardware and software entities because software is developed separately from hardware and vice versa.
- Flexible and scalable deployment of network functions – by separating software from hardware, a high level of flexibility is obtained regarding redistribution and sharing of infrastructure resources, enabling different network functions to be performed simultaneously on shared hardware.
- Dynamic performance of activities in the network – control of operational parameters of network functions takes place through granular control and monitoring of network conditions.

From a strategic point of view, the goal of NFV technology is to enable the implementation of network functions as software entities that run on a virtual infrastructure [17]. In doing so, virtual infrastructure is created on standard hardware (widely used and relatively inexpensive), using various virtualization software (so-called hypervisor tools). In Fig. 2.3, we show the program framework, which represents the basis for work on the standardization of NFV architecture. This programming framework was first presented by the ETSI Industry Specification

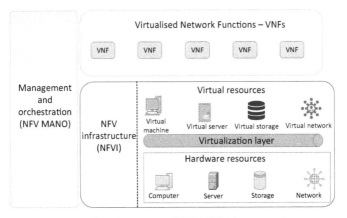

Figure 2.3. Structure of ETSI NFV framework.

Group (ISG) at the "SDN and OpenFlow World" congress, held in October 2012 in Germany [18].

The above mentioned program includes standards defining the management of virtualized network functions (VNF), relationships, mutual dependencies, data flow between VNFs, and allocating required resources. In this regard, the ETSI ISG divided roles within the program framework and categorized three functional blocks [19]:

- NFVI (Network Functions Virtualization Infrastructure) block – the basic building block of the entire architecture in which hardware for hosting virtual machines, software for virtualization, and virtualized resources are grouped.
- VNF block – the block with virtual machines with software-implemented network functions.
- MANO (Management and Network orchestration) block – the block for management and orchestration of network functions through constant inter-action with NFVI and VNF blocks, ensures efficient management and orchestration of all resources in virtualized data centers (physical hardware, networking, and storage devices, resources of virtual machines, etc.), with the focus on the dynamic allocation of resources following the requirements of different services.

2.3.1   Application Fields

To better understand the NFV framework, we must consider that it is possible to apply NFV technology to various functions of packet processing in the control and packet forwarding planes, whether in fixed or mobile networks [20]. In practice, there are numerous solutions in which this technology is actively applied, such as:

- Software-implemented deep packet inspection (DPI) [21] – enables advanced analysis of packet content and traffic, simpler mechanisms for application, updating, testing, and scaling of resources following changing workloads, and multidimensional reporting.
- Functions – include Carrier Grade Network Address Translation (enables Internet access by allowing customers to share a single, public IP address) and Broadband Remote Access Server (a specialized server that enables easier convergence of multiple Internet traffic flows such as digital subscriber line (DSL), Ethernet, cable, and wireless).
- Virtualization of services in network environments [22].
- Virtualization of content delivery networks (CDN) enables easier expansion and scaling of content delivery services and allows reusing hardware to install other service delivery applications [23].

- Virtualization of mobile network core – enables more flexible network management and creates conditions allowing serving a larger amount of traffic with better use of resources (including energy saving, hardware consolidation, support for multi-tenancy access where one software instance with its infrastructure provides service to a larger number of users and faster configuration of new services) [24].
- Coordinated implementation of cloud technologies in organizations – enables on-demand services and network resources to the organization's needs (in general, different versions of a service coexist on shared hardware).

2.3.2 Virtual Network Functions

For an easier understanding of the process and the architecture defined by the ETSI NFV program framework, it is essential to correctly interpret the concept of virtual network functions (VNFs). This concept differs from the traditional concept, where network functions are usually implemented on specially designed hardware (the so-called integrated implementation of hardware and software entities). Instead, it implies a new method of implementation, where network functions shall be implemented as independent software entities on a standard and arguably cheaper computing infrastructure. Therefore, the basic idea on which we base the whole concept rests is the creation of prerequisites for software and hardware to be developed independently [25]. This approach is the only way to enable greater agility and innovation in providing various services in the network.

Industry efforts to articulate and standardize the context of virtual network functions initially took place within the ETSI NFV initiative and later in the open-source context, within projects such as Open Platform for NFV (OPNFV) [26], Open-Source MANO (OSM) [27], and Open Network Automation Platform (ONAP) [28]. Today, a widely accepted definition treats virtual network functions as software applications connected to the network and independent of hardware. That is the basis for the widespread use of microservice architectures, middleware platforms, and distributed applications.

By applying the VNF concept, telecom operators can improve their operations because they implement new services faster in their networks. The programmability that comes with this concept allows network functions to be upgraded and scaled dynamically and in a much more flexible way with a greater degree of granularity, which makes better use of available network resources and thereby reduces operational and capital costs. However, it is important to point out that the implementation level to which the advantages mentioned above will be realized depends primarily on the VNF model implemented in the network. Namely, the basic requirements for designing virtual network functions include ensuring their modularity, portability (transferability to another virtualized resource), independence from hardware, multiple use, and scalability [29]. Implementing the VNF concept can be accelerated if there is already a certain set of hardware (physical) resources at the locations, which is very important from the speed and flexibility needed to, e.g., implement various cloud and network technologies.

We can implement a network service using only one virtual network function (as an independent entity) or by combining several virtual network functions. If different virtual network functions are combined, it must be emphasized that there is communication between them. However, they must know they are not physically connected or work on standard hardware. In Fig. 2.4, we explain the implementation of virtual network functions for security (firewall functionality), encryption, and load balancing.

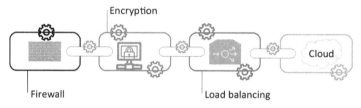

Figure 2.4. An implementation of network services by combining virtual network functions.

To run virtual network functions from Figure 2.4, one can use only one general-purpose hardware device with generic hardware resources (processor, storage, memory, and network interfaces) or multiple devices (so-called integrated hardware solution) that provide the necessary hardware resources to run them [1]. Both solutions have been used in data centers for a long time, whether concerning hypervisor-based virtualization [30] or container-based virtualization [31].

Therefore, virtualized infrastructure (NFVI) is a virtual computing environment. This environment is created when certain subsets of resources are extracted from standard hardware (a common set of resources) and following the technical requirements of the VNF software application. When creating virtual environments, it is imperative to consider the software vendor's recommendations, which refer to the minimum requirements regarding resources to be provided. The virtualization layer plays a key role in this process, which uses physical hardware to create a virtual environment with the resources needed to implement a VNF software application. It is important to point out that any VNF needs to be aware of another with which it may even share physical hardware. In virtualized network architectures (networks with applied NFV programming framework), a functional system must oversee the management, automation, coordination, and interconnection of layers and available blocks.

2.4   Layered Design of the NFV Architecture

To properly understand the concept and the importance of the ETSI NFV frame-work application for modern ICT trends, apart from the general picture of the basic building blocks, it is necessary to have a more detailed insight into the structure of each of them. This point of view implies the need to define elements within these blocks with different roles and responsibilities to realize certain processes [1]. In this sense, in Fig. 2.5, a detailed view of the ETSI NFV framework is given, where functional blocks are grouped into three layers:

- The infrastructure layer (consists of hardware and software components that build the environment for VNFs)
- The layer of virtual network functions (a place where the virtual network functions operate)
- The application layer (consists of many applications/functions, such as net-work management, fault management, configuration management, service management, etc.).

Each layer deals with a certain aspect of NFV implementation.

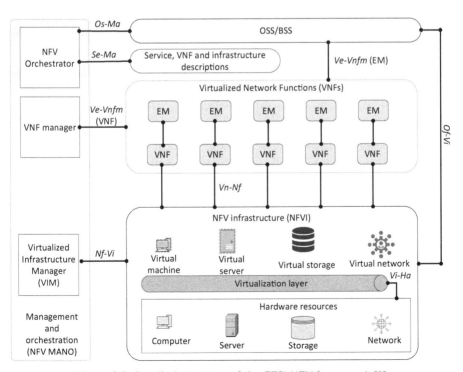

Figure 2.5. Detailed structure of the ETSI NFV framework [1].

2.4.1   Infrastructure Layer

For the functioning of VNFs, virtual resources must be available in the NFV infrastructure layer (NFVI), which can emulate the virtual environment by the software installed on the physical hardware. The building blocks of this layer are physical (hardware) resources, a virtualization layer, and virtual resources, as shown in Fig. 2.6.

In the ETSI NFV program framework, hardware resources are divided into computers (client computers, servers, processors, and memories that can be combined into clusters), data storage resources organized using Storage Area Network (SAN) [32] or Network-Attached Storage (NAS) technologies for data storage [33]) and network resources consisting of sets of network cards. Developing specialized hardware resources for implementing virtual network functions is unnecessary because we can apply virtualization technology to physical hardware available on-site (COTS hardware) and build the requested environment. Therefore, virtual environments (virtual resources) are created by virtualizing the available hardware, which can be connected even when located on different physical hardware and even in different locations. To enable this connection and provide the NFV infrastructure needed to implement virtual network functions, network devices (switches, routers, and so on) are used. These devices are installed physically and are not part of the resources allocated to a virtual network function.

The part of the NFV infrastructure that is responsible for creating a suitable virtual environment (virtual machine with computer, network, and storage resources) in which the VNF software application will be executed is the virtualization layer (hypervisor), i.e., through direct interaction with the physical hardware. Its role is twofold: (i) it must decouple the software application from the hardware, and (ii) allow the VNF software applications to function independently.

Figure 2.6 shows that the structure of this layer, in addition to the previously mentioned NFV infrastructure, also consists of a virtualized infrastructure manager

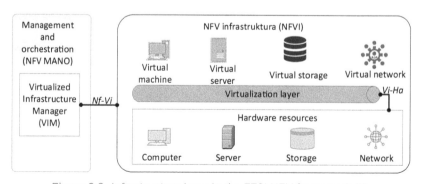

Figure 2.6. Infrastructure layer in the ETSI NFV framework [1].

(VIM) responsible for managing its resources [1]. The management process implies that this manager, having full information about hardware resources and their operational attributes (power supply and status), directly implements management functions over the virtualized infrastructure. In other words, the virtual infrastructure manager also manages the virtualization layer, thus controlling the hardware resources. It is important to note that one virtual infrastructure manager can control multiple devices, and even multiple virtual infrastructure managers can simultaneously control various hardware devices from one or more locations. The VIM can allocate resources under traffic engineering rules to support defining operational rules, define hub-to-facility mapping, and provide information for provisioning virtual infrastructure orchestration (VIO).

2.4.2 Virtual Network Function Layer

The layer of virtual network functions (VNF) layer is a part of the programming framework, which is responsible for their implementation. The structure of this layer is shown in Fig. 2.7. This layer is composed of two basic building elements: a Block of virtual network functions (VNF block) and a control block (VNF Manager – VNFM) [1].

In general, the idea of virtualization of network functions (regardless of which network function it is – router, firewall, load balancer, nodes in mobile networks, and other devices) emphasizes software development:

- which can be implemented on any hardware with the necessary resources and
- with identical characteristics and external interfaces, as in traditional computer networks.

Certain specificities must be considered when realizing network services via NFV infrastructure. In a real environment, we can implement network services by using only one VNF software or by combining several VNF software applications

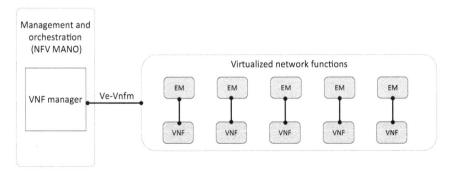

Figure 2.7. Virtual network function layer in ETSI NFV framework [1].

(between VNFs, a particular dependency can exist). If there is a dependency between VNF software applications, then such network services are implemented per a specific procedure. That procedure implies that the data must be processed according to some predefined sequence to ensure connectivity between VNF instances (software applications). This kind of implementation is called service chaining and is executed following the graph for forwarding VNF instances (VNF Forwarding Graph – VNF-FG). If there is a dependency between VNF software applications, then such network services are implemented per a specific procedure. That procedure implies the data must be processed according to a predefined sequence to ensure connectivity between VNF instances (software applications). This kind of implementation is called service chaining and is executed following the VNF-FG instances.

Implementing network services using the NFV concept can be nicely explained using the example of vEPC (virtual Evolved Packet Core) implementation in 4G, 5G, and 6G [34] mobile networks. It is a standard framework for processing and routing voice and other packets through the IP backbone, the key virtual components of which are:

- Mobility Management Entity (MME) – responsible for authentication and monitoring of users on the network, as well as session state management.
- Serving Gateway (SG) entity – enables the routing of packets through the network.
- Packet Data Network Gateway (PDN GW) entity – manages the quality of the provided service and enables deep packet analysis.
- Policy and Charging Rules Function (PCRF) entity – helps implement the charging policy and enables disclosure of services-related data.

Some VNF instances, such as the MME and SG, operate in parallel to enable some vEPC functionality but perform their functions independently. The MME entity manages the mobile devices, authenticates the user, and selects the appropriate SGV, while the SGV forwards the user's packets independently of the MME function. However, implementing the VNF instance for the PDN GW implies data processing after implementing the VNF instance for the SG, indicating a dependency. Figure 2.8 shows the interconnection of the mentioned VNF instances, carried out under a certain procedure or sequence, and represents the so-called VNF-FG.

To properly understand the activities in the core of the mobile network, we should focus on two types of traffic: control and user traffic. Therefore, it is necessary to introduce the Network Forwarding Path (NFP) concept to identify the

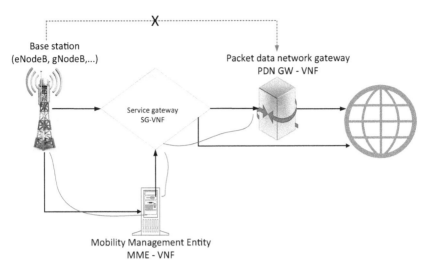

Figure 2.8. A vEPC implementation in mobile networks using the NFV concept.

actual traffic flows on virtual links. Figure 2.8 clearly shows that the control traffic has two paths, and the user traffic has only one. Therefore, the network service is implemented by combining the activities of the component functional blocks, including individual VNF instances and the VNF graph for packet forwarding. Forwarding Graph [1].

The VNF instance manager (VNFM) is responsible for configuring and managing VNF instances and their resources. Its role is to communicate with the VIM, and before starting the instantiation of a new virtual network function or modifying the resources assigned to one of the existing VNF instances, to check whether additional hardware is available. Essentially, this manager manages the configuration of VNF instances, i.e., parameters that directly depend on their performance, security, errors, and resource distribution (Fault, Configuration, Accounting, Performance, and Security – FCAPS).

The element manager (EM) is responsible for the implementation of management functions, which can be applied to one or more VNF instances [1]. This entity ensures reliable communication, i.e., interaction by proxy model, with the VNF instance manager (VNFM) and the VNF instances themselves. For this purpose, it uses proprietary methods to communicate with VNF instances. In contrast, it uses open standards for communication with the VNF instance manager, as shown in Fig. 2.9 (the VNF instance manager can have a centralized or distributed architecture).

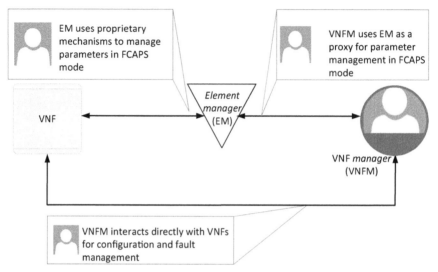

Figure 2.9. Management of VNF instances by the VNF manager.

2.4.3 Operational and Business Support Layer

This layer consists of two functional components, as shown in Fig. 2.10 [35]. The first component is the Operation Support Subsystem (OSS), which manages the network, errors, configuration, and service operations. The long component is the mobile operator's Business Support System (BSS) from user management, services, and user requests. In the NFV architecture, the mobile operator's BSS/OSS systems most often integrate with NFV management and orchestration through standard interfaces.

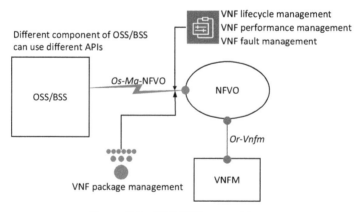

Figure 2.10. OSS/BSS support layer.

After moving to a virtual infrastructure, many operators do not make changes regarding the tools used for management and do not implement new OSS/BSS applications. They prefer to rely on systems that are built within organizations. This approach limits the ability to take full advantage of the NFV programming framework, as it is not designed to communicate with functional management blocks such as VNFM and VIM. Therefore, one of the solutions can be the gradual evolution of existing tools and systems to create conditions for connection with functional blocks for management and to take advantage of the advantages of the NFV program framework, such as elasticity, agility, and flexibility.

2.4.4 NFV Management and Orchestration

By virtualizing network functions, we introduce a much higher level of programmability into computer networks, which entails applying a new method of managing the network infrastructure and orchestrating resources and services. Unlike traditional networks, where network functions are tied to specific hardware, in modern computer networks, we use virtualization technology to decouple the software implementation of network functions from computer storage and network resources. In this way, building new virtual entities (VNF instances) and establishing connections within the NFV infrastructure (NFVI) is possible. In most cases, network services are provided by interconnecting these virtual entities. On the other hand, in practice, there are also examples of a certain network service being implemented by connecting virtual entities with network functions implemented traditionally, i.e., using dedicated hardware.

Therefore, network services can be fully or partially realized by connecting virtualized and non-virtualized resources. Virtualized resources are generally associated with virtual machines, which can be viewed as containers that run programs and execute applications on software computing resources (rather than a physical computer). Such an environment is created on physical hardware. It functions as a virtual computer system with its central processing unit (CPU), memory, network interfaces, and data storage (with storage organized on block or file access).

For the implementation of virtual network functions, the orchestration of virtual resources on virtual machines is of particular importance, which implies allocating the virtual resources necessary to release those that are no longer needed. Orchestration is a complex task, especially considering different requirements and constraints (e.g., some VNF instances require low latency, while others require high-bandwidth links to communication participants). It should be noted here that allocating the necessary resources has a dynamic character, especially considering that the needs of VNF instances for resources change and that it is required to respond to them almost in real time. In other words, the NFV concept relies on the service orchestration process as on a service definition model using VNF instances and applying different topologies of their connection.

NFV Management and Orchestration (MANO) systems were primarily developed to manage virtual network functions in 5G/6G networks in an agile and flexible manner. In this sense, the ETSI ISG has adopted appropriate instructions, which describe the requirements and standards that the software and hardware of the NFV MANO system should satisfy from the realization of virtual network functions [18]. However, mobile operators offer different solutions. They should choose the best solution: the MANO system that suits their needs. For mobile operators to make a quality choice, it is necessary to define the MANO system's key performance indicators (KPI), based on which the performance analysis and comparison could be performed.

Defining key performance indicators, which would be used to quantify the performance of the NFV MANO system, is a big challenge, especially when considering the dynamics and flexibility of services provided by VNF instances [36]. In addition to performing traditional infrastructure management, providing life cycle management of VNF instances and network services is necessary. All key performance indicators of the MANO system can be classified as functional and operational. Functional performance indicators define the so-called non-runtime features of the MANO system, such as:

- Number of committed resources (resource footprint).
- List of different VIM platforms (virtual infrastructure manager solutions) that the MANO system can manage.
- The number of virtual infrastructure managers that one MANO system can effectively manage.
- The maximum number of VNF instances that the MANO system can monitor and manage within the NFV infrastructure.
- Support for DevOps (procedures and tools that increase delivery applications and services compared to the traditional software development process), management of VNF images, and integrated monitoring.

Operational performance indicators define the so-called run-time operations, and their quantification is done through the measurement of delay and efficiency determination of the control procedure/task. One of these indicators is the time required to launch the virtualized network function image (so-called onboarding process delay), i.e., a virtual machine with all its resources. This image is a package which contains the following:

- VNF descriptor file (VNFD) – a file with information about the configuration, network requirements to be met, resources to be provided, routing and security policies, available IP ranges, and interfaces.

- Network Service Descriptor (NSD) – a template that describes the network service requirements in terms of function, operation, security, characteristics of virtual links, quality of service, quality of experience, and reliability. It includes VNF-FG (identifies the types of VNF instances, the sequence of their chaining, and the characteristics of the virtual links connecting them).

The next important indicator is the time required to start one VNF instance inside a virtual machine, and the network service becomes operational [37]. That is a critical parameter when it comes to complex network services (composed of multiple VNF instances), where the role of the MANO system is precisely to provide the necessary resources for instantiating VNFs and connecting them via appropriate virtual links and then configuring each VNF -a following the information contained in NSD templates and VNFD files.

A further important indicator is the delay in orchestrating various management procedures. Namely, with each management action, the delay can be quantified by measuring the time interval from the moment when the action was started to the moment when the action initiated by that action was completed. The use value of this indicator largely depends on the monitoring system that continuously monitors the state of VNF instances during their life cycle.

Also, an important indicator is the quality-of-decision, which represents a metric that can be used to quantify the performance of the MANO system in terms of managing the life cycle of VNF instances (VNF Life Cycle Management), their scaling, and migrations. In other words, this indicator indicates the effectiveness of management decisions from the point of view of committed resources (e.g., whether long-term and short-term resource requirements for a specific VNF instance are provided in the selected computing node or how the instantiation action affects other VNF instances in the same computing node).

2.4.5   NFV Referent Points

By virtualizing network functions, a much higher level of programmability is introduced into computer networks. One of the basic requirements implemented within the ETSI program framework is providing open and consistent communication between its functional blocks. Reference points are defined to identify and effectively monitor this communication precisely. They represent a specific working environment for VNFs by applying the NFV concept and building the NFV infrastructure (without defining a special control protocol, a hardware-independent life cycle, performance, and portability requirement of VNFs are guaranteed). In this sense, the ETSI NFV framework defines the following reference points:

- *Os-Ma* is a reference point between the OSS/BSS system and the MANO control block, which defines the communication between OSS/BSS and NFVO as follows:
  - Activates network service and VNF instances lifecycle management by generating and sending adequate requests.
  - Exchanges information about the status of functional blocks defined by the NFV framework.
  - Creates different policies and forwards management instructions, which is necessary for NFVO operations.
  - Exchanges data obtained using analytical methods.
  - Forwards record that refers to the use of NFV resources and calculate billing accordingly.
  - Exchanges information about the capacity of the NFV infrastructure and its availability.
- *Ve-Vnfm* is a reference point that defines the communication between the manager of virtual network functions on the one hand and EMs and VNF instances on the other through:
  - Requirements for managing the lifecycle of VNF instances.
  - Exchange of configuration information
  - Exchange of information necessary for managing the life cycle of network services.
- *Nf-Vi* represents a reference point where virtual infrastructure managers exchange information with functional blocks of NFV infrastructure (e.g., information on configuration and state of hardware resources, availability of virtual resources, and their allocation according to current requirements).
- *Or-Vnfm* is the point of reference through which the NFV orchestrator communicates with the virtual function manager related to the instantiation of VNF software applications (e.g., authorization, validation, reservation and allocation of virtual resources by the VNF instance manager, forwarding the appropriate information to enable the VNF instances to adequately configured within VNF-FG) and forwarding collected information about the state of VNF instances that is necessary for managing their life cycle.
- *Or-Vi* is a reference point through which the NFV orchestrator directly communicates with the virtual infrastructure manager and forwards potential requests for reservation and resource allocation based on previously exchanged information about the configuration and state of virtualized hardware resources.
- *Vi-Vnfm* is the reference point through which communication occurs between the VNF instance manager and the virtual infrastructure manager (e.g., they send requests to the VNF instance manager to allocate resources

based on information about the configuration and state of the virtualized hardware resources).

- *Vn-Nf* is a reference point through which performance information is transmitted to the infrastructure block, indicating the need to migrate VNF instances to another.
- *Wi-Ha* is the reference point through which the virtualization of hardware resources takes place.

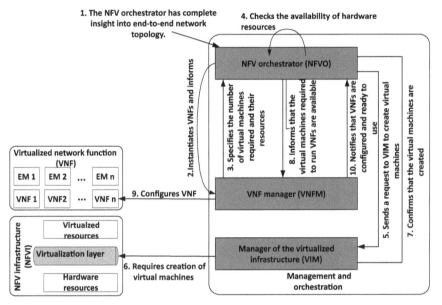

Figure 2.11. End-to-end (E2E) communication flow in the ETSI NFV framework.

Figure 2.11 shows a generic scheme that describes end-to-end (E2E) communication in a general way, which takes place between different functional blocks defined by the ETSI NFV program framework, intending to implement some network service.

2.5   Advantages of Applying the NFV Concept

The NFV concept application aims to eliminate numerous problems that hamper the application of new and increasingly demanding services in computer networks. The virtualization of network functions changes the network's design, infrastructure configuration, individual network units, and the way of managing the network, fundamentally affecting the introduction of a new work model in the network environment. Figure 2.12 shows the main advantages of implementing this technology.

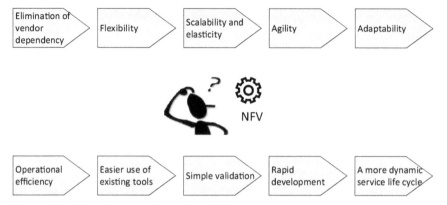

Those advantages primarily refer to the following:

- Elimination of vendor dependency (no vendor lock-in) – allows the creation of the conditions to replace the existing equipment or expand the infrastructure faster and at a lower cost (it is possible to choose equipment based on the availability of functions, software licensing prices, and support models after implementation).
- Flexibility – free hardware choice (the NFV concept enables the use of COTS hardware), the possibility of building a network environment that best suits service requirements, and running VNFs across different servers or moving them around as needed.
- Scalability and elasticity – introducing into the network a higher level of programmability, which will enable the creation of a network environment in a flexible and scalable manner and resource allocation and release dynamically (when there is a need for it, and it is the so-called fast elasticity, which is primarily characteristic for the cloud environment).
- Agility – enables fast deployment and creation of new network services, reducing time-to-market and improving competitiveness.
- Adaptability – enables adaptation to changing customer requests and other conditions (NFV components possess flexible and customizable character).
- Operational efficiency – fast implementation of network services and functions on request and, as needed, allows the application of a virtual network function or services in different places in the network without changes or with minimal changes in the configuration. Also, hosting VNF instances on standard hardware reduces operational costs because there is no longer a need to host them on special, purpose-built hardware.
- Easier use of existing tools – provide easy implementation of the existing tools from traditional computer networks, which even more easily can be used in modern computer networks (on the same physical infrastructure)

- Simple validation – simpler implementation of a test environment enables the check of new solutions and validation of various service capabilities when necessary.
- Rapid development – The open-source components of NFV prioritize code development and represent the base for quickly delivering proof of concepts (PoC) for use case implementation specified by the standards (the simplification led to the development and deployment of sustainable solutions easily).
- A more dynamic service life cycle – implies ease and fast usage of VNFs, maintenance over their lifetime, and deployment when needed (the NFV facilitates such an approach and provides benefits from VNFs by performing adequate tasks).

2.6   Conclusion

NFV allows for the separation of network services from dedicated hardware, meaning that network operations provide new services dynamically and without installing new hardware. This way, we can deploy network functions more easily and quickly than in traditional networks. Besides that, virtualized functions run on generic hardware, which is less expensive. The application of the NFV concept includes additional reasons, such as pay-as-you-go models that allow us to pay only for what we use, fewer appliances that lead to lower operational costs, and faster and easier scalability, which do not require the procurement of additional hardware. The application of the NFV concept has certain risks that we must consider. These risks refer to security in NFV-based networks. Virtualizing network components increases their vulnerability to new attacks compared to the physical devices. Traditional tools for traffic monitoring need to be more efficient to identify malicious traffic between virtual machines within a network infrastructure. The complex layered architecture can cause numerous issues. For this reason, we must implement more comprehensive security policies.

At each layer of the NFV infrastructure, we have solutions representing an example of applying different virtualization techniques. This application aims to enable the rapid development of network services with elastic scale and automation. In the next section, we will provide many more details, which can give a closer look at each virtualization technique, the subject matter, goals, and their ranges. Accurately understanding virtualization technology's essence, benefits, and limitations is crucial to properly comprehending the NFV concept and the principles of modern computing environments.

DOI: 10.1561/9781638283591.ch3

Chapter 3

Virtualization Technology

3.1 The Historical Development

In daily life, we can meet different types of virtualizations that support the creation of virtual (software) representations of servers, storage, networks, and other physical machines. Virtualization indicates that its application provides a high level of abstraction of computer hardware on which different software applications can be executed [5]. The beginnings of this technology are related to the 1960's and the application of mainframe computers. These computers were used to process demanding and complex data, and multiple virtual servers were created on them. This technology allows the software installation and update on one virtual server without affecting the operation of other virtual servers. During that period, the professional community continued with activities on virtualization and other resources. Virtualization (sharing) of hard disks into separate logical partitions was also implemented [38]. IBM introduced System/370™, the first of its architectures to use virtual storage and address spaces. Whether a batch job or a timesharing user, each user may have his virtual storage. A segment table maps each virtual storage with page tables for all allocated segments.

Time-sharing enabled users to share computer resources, aiming to increase users' efficiency and the efficiency of expensive computer resources they share. It represented a significant breakthrough in computer technology, which caused the prices of computing capacity to drop considerably. Moreover, it became possible to use a computer without even owning one. Despite the time-sharing advantages, in the 1990s, proprietary solutions and the "one server – one application" management model were still dominant. Such solutions did not allow software applications to run on third-party hardware. Irrational use of server resources was a reality. The emergence of hypervisor technology and the ability to run multiple virtual machines with different operating systems on one computer simultaneously greatly reduced the dependence on hardware manufacturers. The hypervisor allowed the optimal use of physical IT infrastructure by allocating underlying physical computing resources such as CPU and memory to individual virtual machines as required.

Virtualization technology is important in building modern computing environments and is a part of our daily lives. Its capabilities significantly impact the development of the ICT sector, primarily through significant savings in resources and money. By applying some of the virtualization techniques, it is possible, for example, to reduce hardware procurement costs, the cost of rental space for computer infrastructure, and electrical consumption. All of these indicate that technology virtualization exponentially increases resource utilization. The application of virtualization technology has other goals, such as simplified resource administration, greater data security, and resistance to possible hardware failures [9, 39].

Virtualization allows us to abstract applications and their components from the hardware they run on. This technology enables a logical (virtual) view of computer resources, strikingly different from the physical view. The aim is to improve system performance, increase scalability, achieve greater operational reliability, and build a unique domain for security and management. A virtualization application can create a virtual display into:

- Computational resources divided into several separate computing environments are, in essence, several operating systems simultaneously run on one physical machine.
- Several physically separated computer machines aggregate (merge) into a larger computer resource (grid computing), which the operating system sees as one logical set of computer resources.

Users often have different needs depending on what they want to achieve, and they can use other tools to realize goals, such as [9]:

- allowing any device to access any application over the Internet, even if that application is not compatible with the device,
- isolation of applications from each other to enable safe operation and greater environmental manageability,
- isolation of applications from the operating system to enable function on other versions of the operating system,

- launching multiple application instances to run simultaneously on different machines,
- reduction of time required to run an application through segmentation of data or the application itself and by delegating tasks to multiple computer systems,
- system optimization allows it to work smarter and more by reducing the time the processor is idle,
- to ensure the required redundancy to affect the high reliability and availability of applications and data.

Virtualization offers significant benefits for almost any business or development environment. Its implementation has become part of the smart government strategy, which aims to improve the efficiency of various processes in society and even the work of public administration bodies, significantly affecting those processes [40]. Public institutions often implement servers to run certain applications and, in doing so, consume only a small part of the available resources. They were dissatisfied when the applications would not run and the servers were completely inactive. Their network staff can identify active and passive computing resources anytime by looking into the existing infrastructure. Breaking the inefficient use of resources and reducing costs have become important tasks for many public institutions. With the implementation of virtualization, we can allocate the resources required for the correct execution of tasks. The remaining resources become available for other applications, reducing the cost of purchasing and maintaining additional hardware.

3.2   Virtualization and NFV Concept

The organizations' networks usually consist of many server machines. Experience of the Spiceworks community shows that they work in a mode that rarely exceeds 30% of the system load [41]. This state indicates insufficient utilization of the available resources and the need to increase it by applying advanced technologies (such as virtualization). To overcome this problem, we can implement virtualization technology and provide that multiple server applications run on one physical machine. Instead of acquiring and installing a physical server for each application, the organization can install and run various server applications on one physical server. The results of virtualization are savings in electrical consumption and the reduction of financial resources necessary to procure and maintain server equipment, including administration.

Virtualization as a software technology changes the fundamental principles of information technologies and creates conditions for realizing a wider range of possibilities in different environments. When it comes to environments that primarily consist of server infrastructure [9], this technology should enable:

- decreasing the number of physical servers needed to build a suitable environment,
- significantly greater infrastructural savings by reduction of electrical consumption (for server hardware and cooling systems), decreasing the number of active network components, and reduction of space necessary for server infrastructure hosting,
- to implement a centralized administration of computer infrastructure through a single management console,
- installation of server applications independently of the hardware and creation of the possibility that applications run on another functional hardware and
- to perform faster and less expensive data backup.

We must emphasize that the server infrastructure is only a part of the computer network infrastructure and that virtualization technology can be applied to other parts of the computer network, such as data storage, firewalls, load balancers, and others. That is why there must be a software platform with a central administrative function over all virtualized network resources in the computer network. The platform's role is to enable the creation of multiple virtual (logical) network environments (so-called slices) on one (shared) physical computer network infrastructure. In this way, we can achieve the key goal of virtualization (Fig. 3.1), to enable different groups of users on one (shared) physical infrastructure to:

- form their own and mutually isolated virtualized environments where users are not aware of network hardware details,

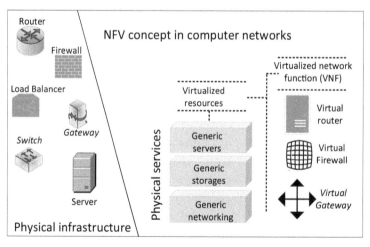

Figure 3.1. Virtualization in modern computer networks.

- use traditional services of equal or even better quality compared to an unvir-tualized environment,
- implement new, smarter, and resource-demanding services,
- make interconnections using virtualized network functions (VNFs).

The virtualization-based model of the network infrastructure organization creates the conditions to realize numerous advantages, the most important of which are [9]:

- free choice of network topology and methods for routing and forwarding packets,
- simple infrastructure management,
- easy and quick expansion of the virtual network with minimal equipment acquisition and maintenance costs,
- a higher level of security in the network,
- a greater level of network elements' programmability and
- an efficient and inexpensive implementation of an environment for testing new technologies and services on the Internet.

The application of virtualization inevitably leads to the development of a new business model, which implies a different distribution of responsibilities in the telecommunications market [42]. The infrastructure provider is in charge of managing the physical and virtual infrastructure. The service provider is any legal entity or individual capable of creating and implementing different services in the virtual network. To fulfill the demands of increasingly sophisticated services and to solve the needs of different groups of users, we can apply different concepts of network infrastructure virtualization [9]:

- building multiple heterogeneous virtual networks on one physical network,
- combination the resources of different physical networks to create one virtual network and
- switching of virtual machines from one network to another.

3.3 Virtualization Software

Virtualization software (hypervisor) plays a key role in creating virtual machines. Its task is to manage hardware resources, create virtual machines (a simulated environment often called a guest machine), and the environment in which they run. Existing hypervisors are divided by type and design (Fig. 3.2) [9].

The task of the hypervisor's software is to provide a certain degree of abstraction of computing resources and create an environment in which the program runs the

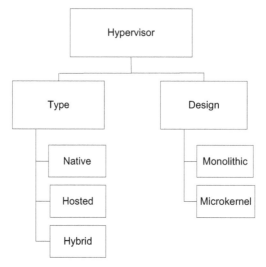

Figure 3.2. Types of hypervisors.

same as if it were on an equivalent physical machine. In other words, the hypervisor has complete control over virtualized resources. At the same time, it must be considered that, statistically, most of the operating system's instructions execute without the intervention of the hypervisor. In practice, there are three types of hypervisors [43]:

- native or bare-metal hypervisor – placed between the hardware and the operating system. It runs directly on the hardware and creates virtual environments with its operating system (e.g., Citrix XenServer, VMware ESX, and Microsoft Hyper-V),
- the hosted hypervisor, located on top of the host operating system, manages hardware resources. It allows virtual machine operating systems to be installed on the host to run in parallel and share resources (KVM and VirtualBox),
- hybrid hypervisor – generally runs directly on the hardware but uses the host operating system for I/O operations (IBM VM/370, VMware Server, and VMware Workstation).

From the aspect of software architecture, we can meet the following hypervisors [9]:

- monolithic hypervisors (Fig. 3.3) – have special modules (hypervisor-aware drivers) that allow the virtual machine's operating system to communicate with host hardware,
- microkernel hypervisors (Fig. 3.4) – use the host's operating system, which acts as the root (parent) partition, to access the hardware and use a wide range of existing drivers not part of the hypervisor.

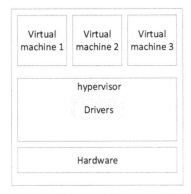

Figure 3.3. Monolithic architecture of hypervisor.

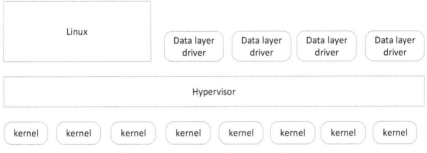

Figure 3.4. Microkernel architecture of hypervisor.

3.4   Overview of Virtualization Techniques

In a real environment, we can meet various virtualization techniques. These techniques can support hardware, software, and even network virtualization. Today, the following virtualization techniques are most often used [41]:

- Full virtualization,
- Hardware-assisted virtualization,
- Paravirtualization,
- Partial virtualization,
- Application virtualization,
- Desktop virtualization,
- Operating system-level virtualization,
- Memory virtualization,
- Storage virtualization,
- Data virtualization,
- Network virtualization.

3.4.1   Full Virtualization

The full virtualization technique enables the complete virtualization of a physical machine (server) and creates a virtual environment necessary to run the operating system of a virtual machine (guest). The guest's operating system is completely isolated from the physical host in such an environment. Between them is a hypervisor, which provides a guest operating system to run in the original design (Fig. 3.5).

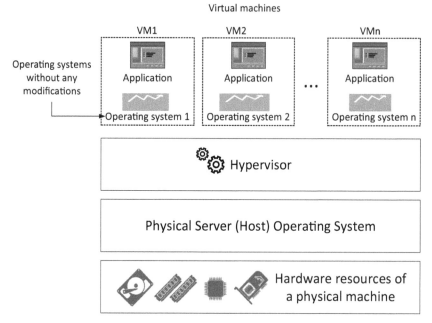

Figure 3.5. Full virtualization technique.

This technique increases the computer system's security and significantly affects its flexibility and scalability (we can create multiple virtual instances on one physical server with its operating systems). As a result, we obtain a global system with new possibilities. With its implementation, some shortcomings that existed on physical servers can be eliminated, such as resource utilization on each server. Full virtualization is, in practice, implemented in solutions such as VMware Workstation, VMware Server, VirtualBox, Parallels Workstation, Oracle VM, Hyper-V, KVM, and others.

Full virtualization has certain constraints, such as the reflection of hardware features in each virtualized machine. We can virtualize servers, data storage, or desktops, but hardware features reflect in virtualized machines to occur full virtualization. In some cases, synchronicity between hardware and software resources must necessitate the purchase of new hardware. Depending on what we need to virtualize, such an expenditure could be significant. Further, configuring an OS as stand-alone, fully virtualized needs expert-level implementation knowledge and causes additional costs.

3.4.2 Hardware-assisted Virtualization

In addition to significant savings, virtualization technology also enables the application of new functionalities. Implementing these functionalities requires hardware manufacturers to focus on developing new devices with more powerful processors and new types of memory to support virtualization (examples are AMD, Intel, and Oracle). Hardware-assisted virtualization is a technique where underlying hardware provides special CPU instructions to aid virtualization. These instructions allow a virtual context to be set up so that the guest executes privileged instructions directly on the processor without affecting the host. This technique makes hypervisor implementation less complex and more maintainable. However, to enable the operation of new devices, it is necessary to apply special drivers (developed for a specific type of device, as shown in Fig. 3.6). Only in this way it is possible to provide support for [44, 45]:

- separate startup of virtual machines' operating systems,
- effective virtualization with the help of hardware, primarily the motherboard,
- the hypervisor to intercept and emulate privileged operations (operations of the highest priority in the operating system) on the virtual machine.

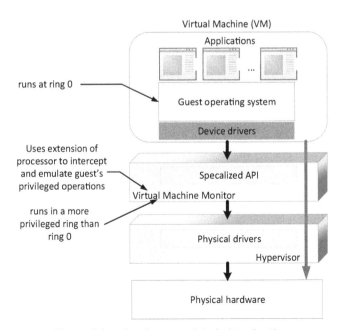

Figure 3.6. A hardware-assisted virtualization.

Examples of hardware-assisted virtualization techniques are VMware Workstation, Xen, Linux KVM, and others. Its limitations are that it creates high processing
capacity costs and reduces server consolidation's scalability and efficiency.

3.4.3 Paravirtualization

In some solutions, virtualization technology allows a virtual machine to run in a
similar, but not the same, hardware environment as a physical machine (it presents
virtual machines with an interface similar to real hardware). That is why it is necessary to port the virtual machine's operating system, i.e., modify and adapt to work
in a virtual environment [1, 41]. Modification is done by recompiling the operating system's kernel or installing a specially developed Application Programming
Interface (API), i.e., paravirtualized drivers (para-drivers), as shown in Fig. 3.7.

The task of paravirtualized drivers is to enable real-time access to the hypervisor and ensure communication between the virtual machine's operating system
and the physical machine's operating system (native operating system). The virtual
machine's operating system receives the hardware data directly from the physical
machine's operating system. Therefore, simulation of the complete hardware is not
required, and the performance of the virtual system is significantly better (the allocation of the necessary resources is performed by the hypervisor, which results in an

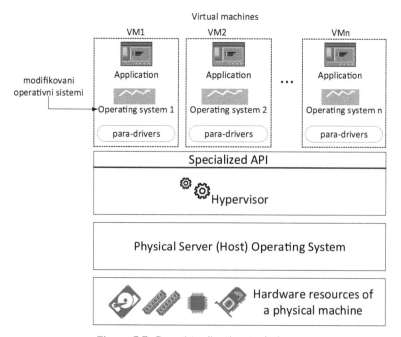

Figure 3.7. Paravirtualization technique.

almost natural execution of operations. It should emphasize that in solutions with the applied paravirtualization technique (systems based on UNIX, some variants of BSD, or Open Solaris), the speed of the guest's operating system is less than the speed of the physical host's operating system by a maximum of 10%, which is precisely the consequence of the modification operating system of the virtual machine.

3.4.4   Partial Virtualization

In a real environment, we can meet examples with partially applied virtualization (only a part of the environment is simulated [44]). Such an approach imposes the need to modify the virtual machine's operating system. It is a prerequisite that an operating system can run in such an environment. This partially virtualized environment supports resource sharing and process isolation but does not instantiate virtual machines' operating systems (Fig. 3.8).

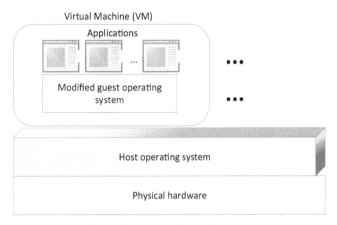

Figure 3.8. Partial virtualization.

3.4.5   Virtualization of Applications

The running of certain applications is often related to the need to emulate an adequate runtime environment. This virtualization technique implies that the emulator (in addition to creating the environment) can manage the lower layers of the operating system. In doing so, the applications are unaware that they are not communicating with the host's operating system but with the emulated environment [46]. This technique enables the virtualization of applications, and it implements a software interface between the applications and the operating system, which takes over part of the work of the operating system and presents the necessary resources to each application (e.g., locations on the file system). In this way, we can avoid problems between applications on the one hand and operating systems and the environment in which they are running on the other. These problems are mainly due to software incompatibilities, software bugs, and various types of mismatches with the environment (Fig. 3.9).

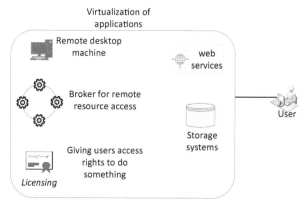

Figure 3.9. Virtualization of applications.

In practice, we can implement this technique of virtualization through [47]:

- Portable Applications – software runs from portable memory media (flash drives or optical media) and does not require installation in the operating system.
- Cross-platform virtualization – the application compiles in a "non-platform" specific format and then runs by platform-adapted middleware on any operating system or processor.
- Virtual Appliance – installation of image files that contain a virtual machine for a specific virtualization platform.
- Simulation – a complete software implementation of a processor or computer system.

3.4.6   Desktop Virtualization

The virtualization technique of the user's desktop environment aims to build an environment independent of the device that the client uses to access remotely. It is similar to virtualization of applications and can be done on the client and the server side. This technique is executed through a client-server communication model (Fig. 3.10).

Remote desktop virtualization implies that users can access the virtual machine from any location and run in a desktop environment created according to their request. Access to a server with virtualized resources does not depend on the local environment. It is enough for the user to have an Internet connection and to be

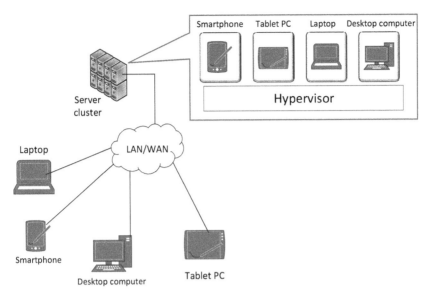

Figure 3.10. Desktop virtualization technique.

able to configure a session via Remote Desktop Protocol (RDP) or Virtual Network Computing (VNC) protocol [48]. In cloud gaming, we can meet this virtualization technique due to the possibility of sharing Graphics Processing Unit (GPU) resources. This approach enables greater utilization of this still-expensive resource, which can be upgraded or replaced with more modern and faster chips without affecting the cost of using services.

This technique uses strong server machines or even server clusters in business environments at a central location. The Virtual Desktop Infrastructure (VDI) created by its application enables [49, 50]:

- Centralized and efficient administration,
- Quick recovery of the virtual machine in unwanted situations using snapshots (a snapshot of the current state of the virtual machine),
- Lower costs – users work on a shared server infrastructure, whose resources are allocated to users as needed,
- Secure access and work on virtual infrastructure for users,
- Work in multitasking mode (multiple virtual desktops run on the same physical machine and move backward through operating systems and applications),
- Effective backup of data.

This technique is characterized by the fact that hypervisors are often not used in virtualization. We can perform this virtualization by using a large number of computers, implemented in the form of modules (board with processor, memory, and hard disk) and placed in appropriate housings at a central location (blade solutions) [51]. In doing so, customers retain their physical devices, which are moved from the customer's location to a central location. This technique enables simplified management and administration. It also provides greater security, and what is particularly important is that the price of such a solution is of little importance for organizations that want to implement it.

3.4.7   OS-level Virtualization

This virtualization technique is executed at the host's operating system level. Its application notes down rapid growth in recent years. The base of a solution is its kernel's usage for creating multiple and mutually isolated user-space instances (Fig. 3.11) [9].

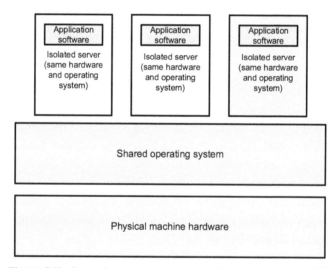

Figure 3.11. Operating system level virtualization technique [9].

In this case, we use the term containers for the virtual instances, which often run as private virtual servers. These virtual instances share the host operating system kernel and have separate root file systems [52]. The advantages of this virtualization technique are the secure operation of virtual instances (each instance isolated from the other) and centralized administration and configuration performed on the host operating system. This solution is often encountered in Linux-Vserver, FreeBSD Jails, OpenVZ, Solaris Containers, Virtuozzo, and other classic Linux systems.

3.4.8   Memory Virtualization

For the normal operation of any software, providing the appropriate amount of random-access memory (RAM) is necessary. However, the available amount of

RAM is not enough in some situations, so there is often a request for its expansion in a fast and efficient way to avoid "bottlenecks" and stoppages in the operation of applications. In this case, the memory virtualization technique appears as a natural solution. This technique allows a part of the hard disk to be joined to the RAM through the operating system quickly and efficiently. That part of the disk represents additional (virtual) RAM. We can use it to avoid interrupting processes (Fig. 3.12) [53].

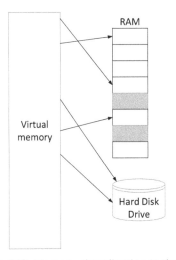

Figure 3.12. Memory virtualization technique.

Switching to and working on such virtualized memory is accompanied by a drop in performance (software running on a slower medium). Despite this, the memory virtualization technique is often applied in server virtualization because it is possible to identify the current memory state and forward the obtained information to a remote host in the network [54]. Although a larger capacity of RAM on server machines reduces the need for memory virtualization, the need to preserve the integrity of the process. Moreover, it can harm system stability, which we must consider as a possibility because there is always the chance of an immediate overload of the available memory.

3.4.9 Storage Virtualization

Data storage technology is an area of computing that is continuously evolving. The reason for this is the implementation of advanced networking solutions that provide high-performance communications between servers and storage devices. These solutions create the conditions to improve the work of companies, state administrations, and other societal structures, whose functioning depends on information stored in data storage. Implementing new technologies ensuring data protection, facilitating access, and simplifying management has long been a reality in the IT environment.

In some organizations, there are still non-consolidated data storage systems. The inefficient use of existing capacities characterizes these storage systems, such as the inability to quickly and easily add new hardware, the constant replacement of storage space due to the short life of devices, the high costs of complex administration, and manual data backup. For storage consolidation and cost reduction, it is necessary to implement new solutions that would increase the flexibility and reliability of the system [9]. A solution is storage device virtualization. It implies the creation of a virtual layer of storage by combining several physically separate storage systems into one virtual storage network, which is managed centrally and is completely transparent with file systems, hypervisors, and applications (Fig. 3.13).

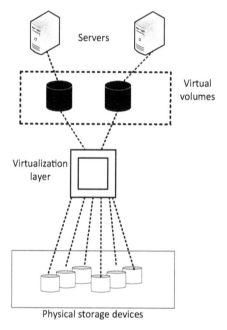

Figure 3.13. Storage virtualization technique [9].

It is clear that virtual storage performs better and uses less space than physical devices. Its application directly reduces the need for new device procurement and costs. The first solutions in the field of storage virtualization appeared in the 1950's by physical disk partitioning and creating more logical (virtual) disks. A new solution to storage virtualization technique appeared based on Redundant Array of Inexpensive Disks (RAID) technology. These arrays are formed by aggregating several physical disks into one logical disk. We can divide this virtual disk into smaller logical units according to needs, and implemented solutions have a much higher level of abstraction. In this manner, it is possible to enable the aggregation of multiple physical storages into one virtual data storage via different systems and interfaces, i.e., protocols (e.g., SCSI, iSCSI, or Fiber Channel, including FCoE – Fiber Channel over Ethernet) [9]. The administrator on the centralized console assigns virtual storage to an application server, and this server treats it as a real data storage device (virtual storage appears in the list of devices connected to the server).

Storage virtualization enables users to access data regardless of location (by abstracting the logic from the physical storage space). It is a shield for application servers because it defends them from the influence of heterogeneous storage, protocols, mixed disk arrays, storage controllers, and network cards. By ensuring the necessary level of interoperability, we can create different virtual environments in which the server treats them in the same way (regardless of the configuration behind the virtual one). This approach eliminates the user's dependence on equipment suppliers and other specific technology, reducing initial and exploitation costs. Administrators can independently choose the best solutions and more efficiently adapt the storage to the user's needs.

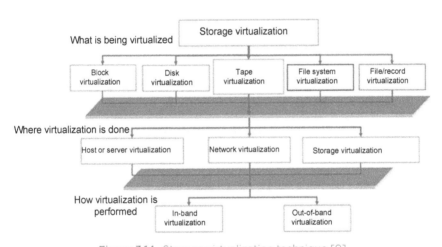

Figure 3.14. Storage virtualization technique [9].

There are three levels of storage virtualization in the network, as shown in Fig. 3.14.

These virtualization levels indicate the subject(s) of virtualization, the location of virtualization, and its implementation. The first level of storage virtualization defines the object of virtualization, whether it may be blocks, disks, or file systems. The second level of storage virtualization indicates where implementation occurs (server, network, or storage) and how it changes the environment and its functions. The third level of virtualization defines the methodology of virtualization, which can be [55]:

- In-band virtualization – abstraction occurs on the datapath, that is, on the same path where both data and metadata pass (information about how the domain manager performed the mapping).
- Out-of-band virtualization – physical separation of the datapath from the metadata flow (metadata control), and the mappings indicate execution of storage aggregation.

3.4.10   Data Virtualization

Modern users work with different types of data, which can be structured, unstructured, semi-structured, or even written in other formats. Each aims to extract a certain context from the data, more specifically, to obtain as much useful information as possible by applying the appropriate data processing method. One must consider data locations in several logical and physical locations (ERP systems, websites, applications, and file repositories) that provide users with a unique presentation interface for necessary data access. That interface should abstract the complete structure of the data storage and transfer system. This way, users believe data exists in one logical location [42].

The primary task of the data virtualization technique is to enable user utilization of applications to use resources without location details, interface with access and implementation mechanisms, platform used, and the amount of available resources. This virtualization technique is closely related to the following concepts [9]:

- Encapsulation – represents the separation of external aspects which the object made available to other objects from internal details of its implementation,
- Abstraction – identification process of important aspects of virtualization, while details are not a subject of consideration,
- Data federations – data stored in a heterogeneous set of autonomous data storage locations is made available to users as a single integrated storage using on-demand data integration,
- Data integration – implies the process of combining data from a heterogeneous set of storage to create a unique view of all data,
- Enterprise Information Integration (EII).

Virtualization software plays a key role in data virtualization (Fig. 3.15), which should provide an abstraction of technical aspects relating to stored data (location, structure and storage technology, API, and Access language). It depends on what the virtual data access will look like (access to different data sources from one common, logical access point) and how the data transformation will be performed (reformatting and adaptation to user needs.) Integration must also be enabled by the application of data virtualization software [11]. It involves combining different data sets

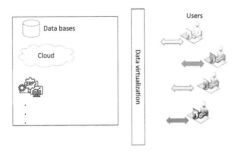

Figure 3.15. Data virtualization technique.

from multiple sources and delivering them through various transactions executed by client applications.

To ensure the accuracy and relevance of the delivered data, i.e., the quality of the virtualized data, the following procedures are applied [12]:

- Data transformation – implies the process of converting data from a source format to a destination format.
- Data mapping – represents connecting a data field from one source to a data field in another source). Data transformation is a part of data mapping because as data moves, the data mapping uses the transformation formulas to get the data in the correct format for analysis.
- Data validation – brings many benefits, such as improving data quality and usability, reducing data errors and risks, and enhancing data security and compliance. It ensures that data is accurate, complete, consistent, and relevant to the use case.
- Data parsing and standardization – typically provides data standardization capabilities, enabling users to standardize and validate their data. It usually includes an interface to design, build, and manage data quality efforts.
- Data cleaning – recognizing and correcting errors, inconsistencies, outliers, and missing values in data collection. Sometimes, it involves transforming, aggregating, filtering, or merging data to suit analysis and visualization goals.
- Data enrichment – refers to appending or enhancing collected data with relevant context obtained from additional sources.

3.4.11 Network Virtualization

Most computer networks still have a traditional, hierarchically organized network infrastructure, which is quite heterogeneous and mostly built from devices from different manufacturers. This fact indicates the complexity of network infrastructure management, especially due to the lack of a single management interface. One of the reasons is that most manufacturers supply equipment/devices that use their own (proprietary) protocols for connection [1]. That complicates and sometimes makes it impossible to interact with devices from other manufacturers. A special challenge for administrators of traditional networks is the implementation of user requests, which relate to implementing new and increasingly resource-demanding services (a direct result of developing and applying new, more advanced information and communication technologies). Given that a large number of functionalities depend on the hardware, there needs to be more flexibility to adequately respond to the users' needs, which impacts the cost of implementation of those services and the maintenance of the existing computer infrastructure. In other words, modern trends in computing intensify the problems associated with changes in the amount and types of network traffic, demands for greater availability, and the need for parallel processing of large amounts of data.

Other computer network virtualization concepts are also applied in addition to the existing virtualization techniques in the network (VLAN, VXLAN, and VPN) to meet different user demands [9]. These concepts imply the existence of a single software platform with centralized administration over virtualized network resources. Its task is to enable the creation of multiple virtual networks on one physical network or to create a combination of virtualized resources from different physical networks to build one – virtual network (Fig. 3.16).

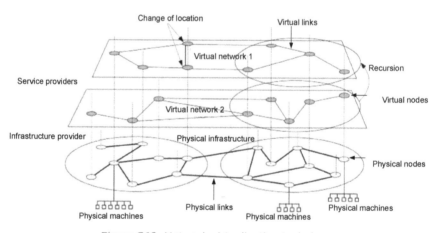

Figure 3.16. Network virtualization technique.

Network virtualization aims to introduce a layer of abstraction between physical infrastructure and the applications and services that use it. As a result, network functions, hardware, and software resources can be delivered independently of hardware. Service providers can optimize server resources (i.e., fewer idle servers), allow them to use standard servers for functions that once required expensive proprietary hardware, and generally improve their networks' speed, flexibility, and reliability [56].

Network virtualization brings two key innovations. It allows the creation of multiple virtual networks on one infrastructure and the resources of different networks to be combined to build a new virtual network.

3.4.12 Advantages and Shortcomings – Summary Review

Virtualization brings many benefits. It keeps the budget by reducing hardware costs and helps organizations to automate and outsource routine tasks and centralize resource management. Also, virtualizations provide users access to their data anytime, anywhere, from any device type. However, before implementing any kind of virtualization in computer infrastructure, we must possess the right picture of the advantages and shortcomings of each of them. In Table 3.1, we give a summarized review of the benefits and weaknesses.

Table 3.1. Advantages and shortcomings – summary review

Type of virtualization	Outcome of virtualization	Advantages	Shortcomings
Full virtualization	Provides complete simulation of the underlying hardware.	Provides full simulation of each VM and the VMM.	Requires the right combination of hardware and software elements
Hardware-assisted virtualization	Enables a computer to run multiple operating systems or applications simultaneously by creating VMs that use the hardware resources of the host system.	Improves performance, security, and flexibility for various scenarios, such as cloud computing, server consolidation, and software development.	Causes some challenges, such as compatibility, complexity, and cost.
Paravirtualization	Provides partial simulation of the underlying hardware.	Highest performing VMs for network and disk I/O.	VMs suffer from a lack of backward compatibility and are not very portable
Partial virtualizaton	Only certain components or resources of a system are virtualized, while others remain in their physical form.	Offers a more targeted approach to virtualization. Enables optimization of infrastructure and improvement of resource utilization.	It represents a historic milestone on the way to full virtualization.

(Continued)

Table 3.1. Continued

Type of virtualization	Outcome of virtualization	Advantages	Shortcomings
OS-level virtualization	Provides OS single instance.	It tends to be efficient as it is single OS installation management and updates.	Does not support mixed families, such as Windows and Linux. VMs are not as isolated and secure as other virtualization forms.
Virtualization of applications	It provides the ability to run server applications on user's desktop	Creates pre-packaged applications for user's instant access.	Not all types of software can be virtualized.
Storage virtualization	Assembles multiple physical disks into a single entity.	Offers high-performance storage solutions.	Introduces a high degree of complexity, interoperability, and scalability issues.
Desktop virtualization	Provides users with an operating environment that is separate from their local physical system.	Access from anywhere. Centralized OS & application updates and security Faster, reliable, and easier backup/ recovery of data Allows to allocate/ limit server resources that can be used per user,	Capex intensive. No reduction in the number of end-user client machines. The network infrastructure needs to handle all that extra bandwidth that Desktop Virtualization is going to introduce.
Memory virtualization	Computers use secondary memory to compensate for the scarcity of physical memory.	Provides benefits in terms of costs, physical space, multitasking capabilities, and data security.	Holds vital storage space. Slower speed than physical memory Stability problems Context switch requires extra time.

(Continued)

Table 3.1. Continued

Type of virtualization	Outcome of virtualization	Advantages	Shortcomings
Data virtualization	Data handling involves adding a layer of extraction on the logical level.	Access in real-time. Cost-effective. It improved data governance and security. Reduced complexity.	Time spent locating test results. High network traffic costs. There is no batch data support.
Network virtualization	Combines network hardware and software resources into a single virtual network	Easy network use and customized access to critical network services.	Introduces a high degree of complexity and performance overhead.

3.5   Difference Between Virtualization and Emulation

Conceptually, virtualization is a set of techniques that organize available computing resources into separate work environments. It is possible to build such an environment using hardware or software partitioning, hardware emulation, software process simulation, or resource abstraction and merging multiple physically separate entities into a single logical entity. From this, we sometimes use emulation during resource virtualization. Strictly speaking, there are significant differences between these two technologies [1].

In emulation, special software (emulator) allows programs or processes to run on platforms other than the ones for which they were designed. Most emulators have the task of simulating some hardware environment architecture, but there are cases when certain software (e.g., operating system) must adapted to work in a particular environment [1]. We can see an emulator as an application translator running on the available hardware. The hardware needed for emulation (CPU, memory, disk, I/O processes) must not be limited to the underlying operating system. Moreover, an application made for one operating system or processor can also run on another. Essentially, the emulator runs as an application on the underlying operating system, which relies on the resource-sharing and allocation capabilities of that operating system on another platform.

The goal of virtualization is different because it should enable the sharing of hardware resources between other applications or operating systems. As basic building blocks, virtualization uses the process of resource separation and their mutual isolation. Fig. 3.17 shows both technologies schematically and tabulates their essential differences, which point to the fact that emulation represents the

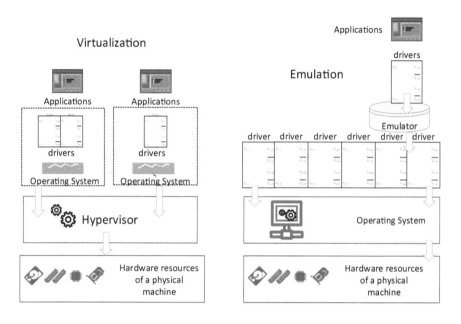

Figure 3.17. Virtualization and emulation – schematic view and features.

Virtualization	Emulation
Hardware can be directly accessed	Hardware cannot be accessed without special software
The virtual machine can run code directly	A compiler is required for the source code
Virtual machines are relatively faster in executing various functions	Emulators are comparatively slower
Creating virtual instantiations is more expensive than emulation	Emulation is a cheaper process
Virtualization provides better solutions for backup	Backup and recovery after a failure is not possible without virtualization

ability of software in a computer device to simulate the behavior of another program or device. At the same time, virtualization is a technique used to create virtual instances (environments).

3.6   Virtual Machines

In practice, different definitions describe virtualization technology but mostly explain virtualization as a procedure for abstracting physical resources and building mutually isolated virtual environments. Each environment has its layer of hardware, software, data, network, and memory. The layers are isolated, so their processes are easily controlled and can be directly accessed to make changes and allocate resources according to the user's needs. This way, virtualization deployment enables the building of environments called virtual machines or virtual containers (Fig. 3.18). Strictly speaking, there are differences between virtual machines and virtual containers. They mainly refer to building virtual environments, their isolation level, and the results of applying different virtualization techniques.

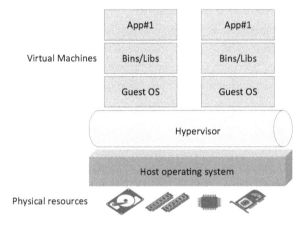

Figure 3.18. Virtual machines.

The basic components of each virtual machine are [38]:

- The physical machine's operating system – runs directly on the hardware and supports virtualization and an appropriate set of applications installed,
- Virtual Machine Manager (VMM) or hypervisor – creates a virtual machine, assigns resources to that virtual machine, changes its parameters, and deletes it on request,
- Virtual machine operating system – represents a guest operating system that runs on a virtual machine and is compatible with the offered resources (the hypervisor provides needed resources).

The virtualization techniques allow the running of different program codes on physical machines. The question that accompanied the appearance of the first virtual machines was: Is the host processor capable of serving other operating systems on virtual machines in addition to native operating systems? This question is very important because different applications run on virtual machines. Their functionality depends on the operating system and its ability to engage the necessary hardware resources (the operating system, through its kernel, communicates with drivers and engages hardware resources) [55].

Each virtual machine is characterized [38] by:

- Isolation from other virtual machines on the host, even though they share resources (this allows an error on one virtual machine not to affect other virtual machines on the host),
- The ability to copy and transfer a file to another physical machine (a virtual machine is a software container that encapsulates virtual hardware resources, an operating system, and an application),
- Partial hardware dependency because there is no knowledge about most of the hardware features it is running on,
- Simpler configuration than physical machines (necessary resources we can allocate easily),
- Absence of the need for additional hardware procurement,
- Performance dependence on the available hardware resources (memory, hard disk speed, and number of processors).

3.6.1   Resource Allocation for a Virtual Machine

Virtualization should enable efficient usage of hardware resources on physical machines (such as memory, CPU, interfaces, and disk space). In this sense, resource allocation is a very important process that needs an answer to how to divide resources between the VMs in physical machines. Effective resource allocation is a prerequisite to ensure all VMs complete jobs successfully without consuming excessive resources. A hypervisor is key in running virtual machines and allocating needed resources. Its task is to provide adequate mechanisms, which should enable optimal resource allocation, has a hypervisor [1]. The operating system of a virtual machine treats the allocated resources as physical. In the case of the CPU, the allocated resources depend on the host CPU infrastructure and the type of virtual machine operating system. For example, we can take a physical map using Intel's Xeon E5-2680v2 CPU with ten cores/sockets with dual threads. In this case, the hypervisor can offer 20 virtual CPUs to the virtual machine. It is similar to allocating memory to a virtual machine, which its operating system treats as its physical memory.

The hypervisor is important in defining the necessary disk space to run the virtual machine's operating system. There are two methods of allocating disk space: thick and thin provisioning [1]. In the first case, the wide provisioning method implies that the disk necessary for the virtual machine is pre-allocated and reserved on the host's operating system. The advantage of this method is that the virtual machine receives the data required storage space in advance. At the same time, the shortcoming is the need for more possibility to use this space for other purposes. Unlike this method, the thin provisioning method saves disk space and prevents it from being wasted. This method aims to simulate the full capacity needed for the normal functioning of the virtual machine's operating system by creating and reserving a smaller file on the host operating system. In parallel with occupying the pre-allocated space, the hypervisor increases the reserved space and lets it grow to the required size.

It is important to note that virtual machines are unaware of disk virtualization. They treat virtual disks as physical disks, which should provide storage space for virtual machine data. We can create files that represent virtual disks in one of the following formats [1]:

- Virtual Machine Disk (VMDK) – is an open-source virtual disk-drive format that allows cloning of a physical hard disk and backup of VMs off-site. VMDK files can be dynamic or fixed. Dynamic disks start with one size and expand with the size of the files in the OS of virtual machines. Fixed disks are static and do not change in size.
- Virtual Disk Image (VDI) – a regular file that represents a replica of a portion of the actual hard disk and contains the contents and structure of a physical hard disk.
- Virtual Hard Disk (VHD) – is a disk image file format that enables replication of an existing hard drive, including all data and structural elements.

Sometimes, it is possible to use these files to package a virtual machine for transport across hosts (these files contain the virtual machine operating system, application, and data). Numerous tools can convert files representing virtual disks from one format to another. For example, when the new host uses a different hypervisor, it is possible to convert the file from the base format to a format supported by the new hypervisor. As an alternative to the distribution of virtual machines mentioned above, we can apply the packaging method, which converts the image file of the virtual machine into the International Organization for Standardization (ISO) file format. We can transfer and install this file as a virtual disk of another instance on another physical machine. The existence of different types of hypervisors is the reason for the increasing usage of the Open Virtualization Format (OVF), which is compatible with other formats.

Virtual machines represent isolated environments, and it is necessary to implement a mechanism for connecting and exchanging data with the outside world and other virtual machines. For this purpose, it is required to implement a technique that enables virtual machines to share the network interface card (NIC) of a physical machine [9]. In practice, we can meet different techniques. One of them is creating a virtual card (virtual Network Interface Card – vNIC) by the hypervisor. This card, the hypervisor, presents to the virtual machine's operating system as its physical network card. The task of the hypervisor is to perform appropriate mappings on the physical card for this purpose. Connecting virtual machines, i.e., their virtual network cards with the network card of the physical machine, can only be done via a virtual switch (vSwitch).

3.7   Virtual Containers

Container-based virtualization focuses on creating isolated user spaces (containers) whose processes run on the host operating system's kernel with limited access to resources (Fig. 3.19). Unlike virtual machines, containers do not have their own virtualized hardware but use the hardware of a physical machine [57]. The container's software runs on the native operating system and communicates directly with the kernel. Virtual instances created in this way can run in a few milliseconds and be more efficient than classic virtual machines because, among other things, their image files are smaller than for virtual machines. Moreover, they do not contain a complete chain of tools for running the operating system (e.g., device drivers, kernel, or daemon process for initialization).

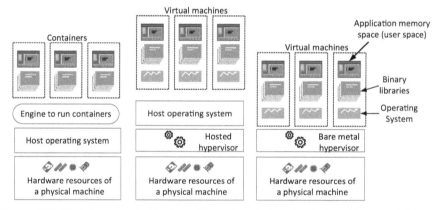

Figure 3.19. Containers and virtual machines (created by hosted and bare metal hypervisors).

The application of the containerization technique directly corresponds to the development of the Linux kernel. Therefore, we often come in contact with the term Linux Containers (LXC), although all containers are not Linux. The goal of the container's creation is to ensure appropriate isolation between applications at the kernel level and build isolated environments. To achieve this goal, we use numerous features already built into the Linux kernel, such as the chroot function, namespace isolation, and control groups [58]. Taking into consideration the increasing interest in containerization, more details about containerization will be provided in the next section.

3.8   Conclusion

In traditional networks, servers only run on dedicated hardware with specific applications. It leads to lower capacity utilization and higher operating costs. To solve this problem, we can use software that provides a layer of abstraction over the physical hardware. On a single physical server, it is possible to create numerous virtual computers, operating systems, and applications and make more efficient use of hardware resources. The key virtualization component is a hypervisor, which assigns each virtual machine needed resources, such as underlying computing power, memory, and storage. Consolidating the applications into the virtual environment and running several different operating systems on the same physical machine is a solution that brings numerous cost savings to users.

Virtualization brings additional benefits, such as downtime reduction, lower energy consumption, enhanced resiliency in disaster recovery cases, and maintenance efficiency. Nowadays, our attention focuses on a new technique of virtualization – containerization. The fundament of this technology is the creation of isolated user spaces (containers) whose processes run on the host operating system's kernel with limited access to resources.

In this section, we presented an overview of the existing techniques for various types of virtualizations. Virtualization offers many advantages, but certain shortcomings still exist. We cannot apply virtualization on every server and application currently in existence. Therefore, many users must implement a hybrid approach. Some solutions need exorbitant costs of implementation. Virtualization takes less time to implement, but there are additional procedures that we need to complete to achieve the expected result.

DOI: 10.1561/9781638283591.ch4

Chapter 4

Containerization

Sometimes, developers have issues deploying their code to remote machines. They traditionally develop codes in controlled computing environments, such as code writing that runs efficiently on a local machine. Problems occur when they try to run code on a remote computer, and possible reasons are inappropriate operating systems running on the remote device or using incompatible software installed to launch the application, e.g., using different versions of interpreters. It indicates a lack of portability caused by OS-specific dependencies, and solving these problems is time-consuming for software developers.

The containerization technique is a viable solution for a multitude of issues. This technique ensures that software code is shipped with the corresponding configuration files, libraries, and dependencies required to run the code on any infrastructure. Containers are virtual entities that are more efficient than virtual machines regarding portability and resource consumption. Many use the term "lightweight" for them. Each application can be associated with the operating system without processes requiring overhead because applications share the same kernel. Containers possess other advantages over virtual machines, such as smaller capacity requirements and shorter start-up times. Other benefits include the possibility of reducing server and licensing costs.

4.1   Containerization Fundamentals

The development of Linux kernels triggered the widespread use of containerization, intending to create isolated environments at the kernel level. For this purpose, we can use features built into the Linux kernel, such as the chroot function, namespace isolation, and control groups [58]. The chroot mechanism is one feature that ensures changes to the root directory follow a certain process (this implies changes to all its subprocesses). Thus, we can restrict access to the file system to one folder, which the observed process and its subprocesses treat as the root directory (/). We can also use the chroot mechanism to test software in isolated environments to install or repair systems. It provides only the displacement processes of the root directory to another directory somewhere within the file system.

It is important to note that the chroot mechanism is not a security feature on Linux. Some software may bypass it and directly access parts of the file system. Despite implementing the *chroot* mechanism, some processes may be able to see other processes and information, such as user and group IDs, access the hostname, and communicate with them. The namespace functionality prevents this and isolates processes, groups of processes, and their mutual communication. This functionality implies applying a flexible separation mechanism by creating a namespace for each process, thereby defining the kernel resources the process can access. An application started under Linux uses processes and their IDs defined by its namespace. These processes are not visible to other applications.

Furthermore, an application can be assigned a separate network namespace, allowing it to have its own routing plan and network stack organization. An interface or route created in an application that uses a particular network namespace will only be visible to other applications on the same host if they have a shared namespace.

In practice, we can meet one of the following six types of isolation based on using *namespaces* at the kernel level typically [1]:

- Isolation of *user namespace* – enables creating a separate set of user and group IDs for processes.
- Isolation of *Unix time-sharing* (UTS) *namespace* – allows creating a separate view for the hostname and domain name for the application.
- Isolation of system identifiers – using *Inter-process communications* (IPC) *namespace* structures communication between processes in the form of message queues.
- Isolation of processes – *mount namespace* provides a file system view for each process.
- Isolation of process ID number space – *Process ID (PID) namespace* isolates process ID from other applications on the host. For example, an application

that uses a special PID namespace can start some of its child processes with a PID. This PID can be the same as an existing one on the host but without creating conflict due to implemented namespace isolation.

- Isolation of network interfaces – *Network namespace* provides isolated access to each application's network interfaces and routing tables.

Namespace functionality enables an individual view of system resources for each process. This isolation method gives access to unlimited usage of resources (e.g., *mount namespace* cannot limit the disk space that the process consumes). The Linux kernel possesses control group (*Cgroup*) functionality, which provides a resource allocation mechanism for each process or set of processes, such as CPU time, memory, and disk I/O. This mechanism enables resource utilization measurement, defines different usage priorities, and even limits resource usage. *Namespace* and *Cgroup* functionalities support the creation of isolated environments and cooperative management of physical resources.

At first glance, virtual containers and virtual machines appear to be similar. These similarities are minimal because virtual machines run in a hypervisor environment, where each virtual machine has its operating system with associated binary files, libraries, and applications. The key difference indicates higher consumption of system resources, especially when several virtual machines run on the same physical server. Containers are smaller than virtual machines. They share the same operating system and kernel, taking only seconds to run. There are important differences compared to hypervisor virtualization that affect the application of containers [1]:

- Sharing the physical machine's operating system kernel instead of hypervisor software allows virtualization implementation at the process level (namespace and Cgroup functionality enable access through APIs such as LXC *runtime with API*).
- Containers use the native operating system to run applications directly, saving resources using the same kernel, binaries, and libraries.
- Compared to virtual machines that use a hypervisor and consume much more resources, containers offer higher throughput for memory read/write operations and better CPU utilization while providing performance similar to a physical host.
- Some applications cannot run from the native operating system.
- Less security than virtual machines is the consequence of kernel and library sharing, e.g., if a container application causes a kernel crash, it will affect all containers running on that physical machine.

Containerization significantly differs from other virtualization techniques based on the creation of virtual machines. Instead of virtualizing the entire hardware, we create isolated environments with limited access to system resources at the operating system level. This limited access to system resources represents the fundamental characteristic differentiating containers from virtual machines.

Today, in computer environments, virtual containers are often used for [59]:

- migration of existing applications to more modern network environments such as the cloud – existing applications can be transferred to a container with minimal modifications, creating prerequisites for high portability of applications,
- efficient support for distributed applications in a way that microservices can be more easily isolated, deployed, and scaled,
- easier construction, testing, and implementation of virtual environments using the same container image files, and
- easier scheduling of repetitive jobs and tasks applies to background processes, such as ETL (Extracts, Transforms, and Loads data) functions or batch jobs.

4.2 Types of Virtual Containers

Typically, users install and run various applications in virtual containers. Some applications run independently as a standalone container, while others are operating systems. It is possible to group containers into two categories: application containers (App container) and operating system containers (OS container). Figure 4.1 shows the structure of the application container [60].

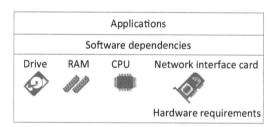

Figure 4.1. The structure of the application container.

As seen in Fig. 4.1, the application container runs independently. It contains packaged application binaries, software dependencies, and hardware requirements. After installation, we can directly start the application container using local hardware, the binaries, and the libraries of the host operating system and its kernel. Such a container has its namespace functionality for networking purposes and disk mount points, running only one service.

In practice, it is possible to use these containers and isolate different services running on the native operating system. Thus, we can create a group of application containers where each application provides some service. Such an approach in software architecture is called microservice architecture, which has an ideal application where scalability, minimality, and cohesiveness are required [61]. In this architecture, each service possesses the resources necessary and runs independently. Each service grows and scales independently, changing and upgrading without affecting other services. This service communicates with other services using the appropriate API. A modular approach in the software architecture provides solid isolation, scalability, and fast recovery and allows the merging of application containers (microservices) into one software (Fig. 4.2) [62].

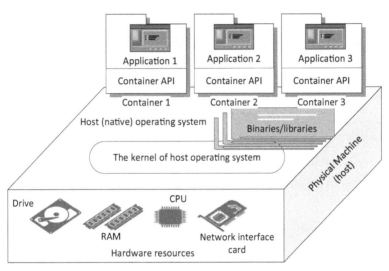

Figure 4.2. A virtualized environment with containerized applications.

Users can sometimes install an operating system in the container (OS container). This container runs the operating system in the virtualized environment. Like in a virtual machine, the guest operating system runs applications inside the container (Fig. 4.3) [1, 52].

Why is the guest's operating system started before starting the application directly? The answer is that the applications in the container use the kernel, libraries, and binary files of the native operating system. Applications may require a greater degree of independence. We must grant access to libraries or system binaries that are different from the native operating system. For this reason, we must install a guest operating system containing the libraries and system binaries necessary to run a specific application. It eliminates the dependency on the host operating system, with the host and guest operating systems still sharing the kernel. Implementing OS containers provides better isolation, security, and independence for the containerized application. The only limitation is that the container and native operating system must be fully compatible because they share a kernel.

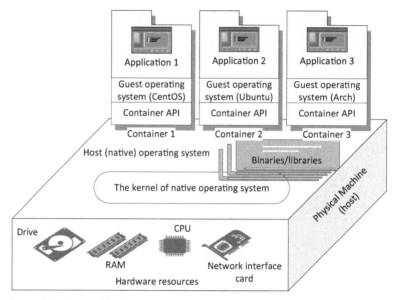

Figure 4.3. A virtualized environment with containers for operating systems.

4.3   Basic Terminology

Each virtual container can be in one of two states – rest or running state [63]. In the rest or idle state, the container behaves like a *Container image* file or a set of files on disk, which is the *Container Repository*. Before the user starts a container from the rest state, he must run the container's engine. The *container engine* has a task to unpack files and send metadata to the operating system's kernel. For this purpose, the engine transmits an API call to the kernel and initiates additional isolation and mounting file copies representing the *Container Image*. It is important to note that the containers behave like a normal Linux process after starting. We can meet various container engines based on *Open Container Initiative* (OCI) standards, such as LXD, CRI-O, or *Docker*. Most of them do not run containers but use tools such as *Runc*, which should provide [1, 64]:

- Responses to requests that users sent through the API,
- Unpacking and expanding the container's image file on the disk using the graph driver,
- Preparing the mount point for the container, and
- Processing of metadata for passing to the appropriate *Container Runtime* environment.

We consider containers as execution environments for virtual applications that run on top of an operating system's kernel. Containers emulate the operating system rather than the underlying hardware. Their application provides an isolated environment and file sharing with the native operating system. A particular challenge is the replication and transfer of containers from one host to another. To understand these processes, we must possess knowledge about the building blocks of a virtual container, such as:

- Configuration files defining its environment,
- A set of files on disk that represent its mountable namespace,
- Executable files and libraries belonging to the application.

Each container contains libraries of the native operating system and binary files. Moving the container to another location in the network is a complex task. Some container engines like LXC cannot pack the container files and the environment as a group. Before the OCI standard and *Runc* tool emerged, users utilized LXC as a container runtime [65]. There are many purposes for LXC runtime utilization:

- Communication with the kernel at the moment of container process initiation,
- Adjusting to the *Cgroup function*,
- Update *SELinux policy* (uses labels to enforce access control for applications, processes, and files on the system) and *AppArmor policy* (by creating profiles, affects the access of individual processes to the kernel),
- Access to attachment points, as defined by the container engine, and
- Access to container engine metadata.

4.4   Docker

User needs quickly exceeded the technical capabilities of LXC runtime. In 2014, the professional community developed the *libcontainer* tool as an integral part of the new *Docker engine*. This engine appeared under the name *dotCloud*, intending to provide a new method for container packaging. This new method ensures greater portability, required replication level, and more efficient container version control [65]. The idea was to run Docker as a single process, i.e., *Docker engine*, which would work with *Docker image* files. Figure 4.4 shows the method of packing applications, binaries, and dependencies into one *Docker image* file, ready for transfer or replication. We must note that Docker services are backed by containers and defined by a Docker image and set of runtime arguments.

Docker is a platform that we can use to deploy, run, and modify containers. This platform manages containers as standardized, executable components by combining application source code with operating system libraries and dependencies. That is important if we need to run that code in any environment. Container-based

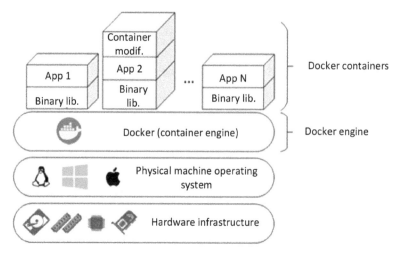

Figure 4.4. Docker architecture and image file.

virtualization has proven to be an effective solution for developing and deploying distributed applications, especially when organizations move their applications to the cloud or hybrid multi-cloud environments. It is possible to create containers without Docker, using capabilities already existing in Linux and other operating systems. With Docker, users can perform containerization easily, quickly, and safely. The reason is that the Docker platform possesses the following advantages:

- Portability – allows users to create or install a complex application on any machine,
- Automation – using *Cron jobs* and Docker containers, users can easily automate their work and save time by avoiding certain repetitive tasks.
- Large community – has a *Slack channel* for many developers in different locations on the web.

The Docker platform also has the following shortcomings:

- Running an application from a Docker container is faster than running on a virtual machine but slower than running applications on a physical server,
- It is impossible to run applications requiring a *Graphical User Interface* (GUI). Users should possess the knowledge to work from the command line, and
- Docker runs on the native operating system, which means any malware hidden in containers can find their way to a physical machine.

The Docker platform consists of four key components (Fig. 4.5) [66]:

- *Docker client* – this component is responsible for creating, managing, and running containerized applications and communication with one or more servers.

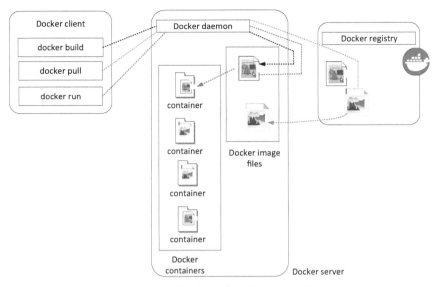

Figure 4.5. Docker – functioning model.

- *Docker server* or *Docker daemon* – waits for REST API requests from *Docker clients* and manages images, containers, networks, and volumes while communicating with other *Docker daemons* to manage *Docker services*.
- *Docker image* – represents a read-only template with instructions to the Docker server related to creating a container. It is possible to download from the *Docker Hub* website or any *Docker image repository*.
- *Docker image registry* is an open-source server-side application that stores and distributes images. In practice, we can use the *Docker hub* for public image distribution.

The Docker platform uses a client-server architecture for communication. The client communicates with the daemon, which performs the tasks of building, running, and distributing Docker containers. In doing so, the client and daemon can run on the same physical machine, or the client can connect to a remote daemon. Communication between these components of the Docker platform takes place using a REST API via a UNIX socket or a network interface. The Docker compose tool is also often used to define instructions for creating multi-container applications.

4.4.1 Docker Alternatives

Reasons such as the complexity of an architecture that relies on daemons and the desire to avoid vendor lock-in and conform to specific development requirements necessitate the search for an alternative to the docker engine. Today, several options for the Docker engine exist. One is *Rocket* (*Rkt*), but we can use other solutions, such as Rkt, for packing and transferring containers, except for a Docker platform. Rkt has a mechanism for running applications in Linux. This solution uses the open App Container specification, which defines the image format for packaging containers. Today, we can utilize the Open Container Initiative (OCI) format, which all container tools can use and adapt to best fit needs [67].

Another alternative is *Podman*, a daemonless, open-source Linux native tool designed to make it easy to find, run, build, share, and deploy applications using OCI. *Podman*, like other engines, relies on compliant OCI *Container Runtime* to interface with the operating system and create running containers. *Podman* can run containers on Windows and Mac systems with a Podman-managed virtual machine. The next alternative is *Containerd*, a Cloud Native Computing Foundation (CNCF) container runtime project that handles all aspects of container lifecycle management for its host system. It can create, run, and delete containers as needed. It also handles image transfers and storage, container supervision, low-level storage, and network attachments. Besides the mentioned solutions, other solutions, which are used less often, can be found in practice, such as Vagrant, Buildah, ZeroVM, and others.

4.5   Container Orchestration

The term orchestration comes from the word orchestra, a musical ensemble consisting of a conductor and musicians. The musicians' task is to perform a specific piece of music on their instrument, while the conductor or orchestrator's role guides the performance. The conductors define the tempo, part of the composition, and timing and make real-time adjustments.

We can apply this analogy to applications and services in the network. The goal is to create a clear picture of each service in the system whose conductor is also an orchestrator. To achieve this goal, the orchestrator utilizes a set of tools configured to ensure optimal execution of applications and management of their state. One of the orchestrators' key roles is to provide the coordination between applications. Each application must run in a precisely defined space and time to improve the system's performance [68].

Often, the question arises about where to expect the greatest benefit from orchestration. As a logical answer, it imposes a network with many interconnected services, such as Google. This network uses over a million servers. The number of services (containers) that run weekly is billions [69]. In such an environment, orchestrators are the mainstay of the architecture because manual monitoring, individual setup, and software installation are not practical. The orchestrator is the main manager of the entire system. Its role is reflected in the system and application startup process and maintaining the state and high system availability.

From the orchestration aspect, we must point to the containers' light and short-lived nature. Starting them in production requires a massive effort, especially if done manually. A good example is microservices, usually isolated in special containers. Their running requires managing hundreds or thousands of containers. With container orchestration, organizations can automate many operations and significantly reduce management complexity.

Orchestration implies automating many operational activities and running containerized workloads and services. These activities encompass the whole container's lifecycle management, including provisioning, deployment, scaling, networking, and load balancing. By working in a containerized environment, organizations gain the following benefits:

- Simplification of operations – the most important benefit because containers are highly complex, which can quickly and easily get out of control without proper container orchestration,
- Resiliency – container orchestration tools can automatically restart or scale, increasing resiliency,
- Additional security – container orchestration protects applications and reduces or eliminates human error during instantiation.

Large companies have recognized the role and importance of container orchestration. Above all, it refers to Google's internal Borg project and Microsoft's Service Fabric project [70]. The Borg project laid the foundations of the Kubernetes platform. There are also Docker Swarm, Apache Mesos Marathon, Nomad, and other similar projects.

4.6   The Kubernetes Platform

Kubernetes is an extensible open-source platform that enables the management of different types of containers, automatic deployment, scaling, and application management. Their characteristics are the portability of applications and consistency in operation on other infrastructures. Since containers are a good solution for connecting and running applications, managing them effectively in a production environment is very important. We must pay special attention to the automatic container management system, ensuring their operation without downtime. If a container goes down, another container must be started [71].

The Kubernetes platform makes it possible to entirely define an application's elements packed in containers in the program code and the infrastructure required for its functioning. The platform provides numerous functionalities, such as [72]:

- Service detection and traffic balancing, i.e., communication between all services in the system, is transparent via DNS (Domain Name System) records. We direct all traffic to a service that we can schedule using the round-robin method,
- Orchestration of abstracted systems for data storage with independent applications regardless of the storage type,
- Update the current version of any application and automatically return to the previous version in case of errors (rollout and rollback),
- Optimal usage of available system resources – balancing of containers depending on processor time and system memory requirements,
- Automated system recovery – in case of errors, provides and executes containerized applications automatically.
- Management of application configurations with the possibility of encryption – the configurations can be easily and quickly replicated to many different applications, e.g., parameters for accessing a database server.

The main components of Kubernetes are:

- Cluster – a control plane that consists of one or more computing machines or nodes.
- Control plane – processes that control Kubernetes nodes, where all task assignments originate.
- *Kubelet* – primary node agent runs on nodes, reads the container manifests, and ensures the defined containers are running.
- The pod is the smallest deployable computing unit that is possible to create and manage in Kubernetes. It represents one or a group of containers that share an IP address, IPC, hostname, and other resources.

The Kubernetes platform possesses many functionalities, distributed architecture, and the possibility to replace one component without affecting the rest of the system. These capabilities significantly influence the application of Kubernetes, the development of various software distributions, and the building of numerous platforms. Kubernetes distribution represents a set of applications and services connected to a single unit. It is possible to optimize the components of the Kubernetes platform to meet the users' needs of a particular distribution. Some distributions aim to be close to the standard Kubernetes version. They incorporate additional functionalities on top of the source Kubernetes platform, such as drivers for network services and disks. Other distributions adapt the Kubernetes system to requirements like speed, ease of use, and integration with external services. There are sixty-nine certified Kubernetes distributions, the most famous of which are Amazon Elastic

Kubernetes Distro, Cisco Container Platform, IBM Cloud Private, k3s, Rancher Kubernetes, Red Hat OpenShift, Oracle Cloud Native Environment, and VMware Tanzu Kubernetes.

The Kubernetes platforms are services that companies offer by abstracting the physical installation, management, and maintenance processes of Kubernetes clusters. They present services concerning users' business needs, such as container installation, privilege instruction setting, and network. There are currently 48 certified vendor platforms. Some of them are Microsoft Azure Kubernetes Service (AKS), Alibaba Cloud Container Service, Amazon Elastic Kubernetes Service (EKS), Google Kubernetes Engine (GKE), Huawei Cloud Container Engine (CCE), IBM Cloud, Oracle Container Engine, Red Hat OpenShift Dedicated and Tencent Kubernetes Engine (TKE) [73].

The popularity of the Kubernetes platform continues to increase due to its close association with Docker technology. We use Kubernetes for container orchestration in a multi-cloud environment. This type of container orchestration refers to using container management orchestration tools in multiple infrastructure cloud environments. Along with numerous other reasons, optimizing infrastructure costs, flexibility, portability, and scalability play a key role. An example is dynamic expansion of the cloud from the local environment when necessary. We must note the increasing usage of multi-cloud environments and containers due to portability and the ability to run in any environment.

4.6.1   Architecture of Kubernetes Platform

The Kubernetes platform appeared due to the requirement to create complex applications that are highly available, scalable, portable, and deployable in small independent modules. The platform's fundament represents a client-server communication model and a cluster of several nodes [74]. The architecture of Kubernetes is complex, and at the highest level of abstraction, there are two main components (Fig. 4.6):

- The Master node's role is to manage the Kubernetes cluster,
- Several worker nodes for running specific user applications.

Its design supports horizontal scaling, which means adding and removing resources as needed is possible, according to the current load in computer infrastructure and requirements of various applications. We can run the Kubernetes cluster in a cloud environment, on local infrastructure, and in a hybrid environment, e.g., on-premises, cloud, and VM. For the Kubernetes cluster to run, it is necessary to provide infrastructure such as bare-metal servers, virtual machines, and cloud resources, install Kubernetes software, and set various configurations and settings.

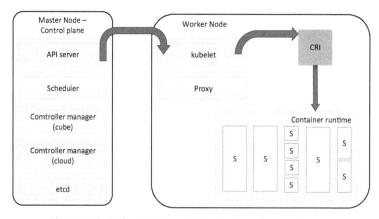

Figure 4.6. Kubernetes – architecture and components.

4.6.2 The Role of Nodes in the Kubernetes Platform

In the basic architecture of the Kubernetes cluster, the Worker nodes represent the computer environment where containers are running, while the control plane role is a Master node (Fig. 4.7). It takes care of the cluster's state and the running of containers, which implies [75]:

- Pods scheduling and monitoring of Worker Nodes,
- Resource provisioning for each container and Pod,
- Starting Pods, monitoring the state of containers and Pods, and restarting them as needed,
- Adjusting the number of containers on the Pod depending on the load and
- Configure the network so containers can communicate with each other and the outside world.

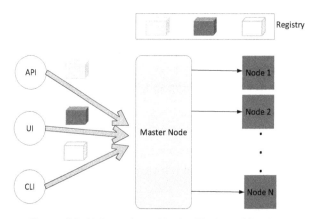

Figure 4.7. Kubernetes – Master Node architecture.

The control plane's functionalities are possible to implement using the following services:

- The *kube-apiserver* is a central control plane component. It allows sending requests to the API server and creating, updating, or deleting Kubernetes resources through REST API calls. We must emphasize that the API server stores its states in the *Etcd* database and represents a stateless service [76],

- *Etcd* is a distributed database that is the backbone of the Kubernetes cluster. The features of this database represent a simple interface (interaction is possible via the HTTP protocol), hierarchical organization of data in a key-value format, and the ability to monitor data changes [72],

- The *kube-scheduler* is a control plane service that monitors the newly created Pod and assigns it to a certain Worker Node. It must check all Worker Nodes and define an optimal node according to constraints and available resources, such as percentage of processor time and minimum RAM. After selection, it must inform the API server. If there is no suitable node, deploying the Pod is impossible, and the Pod's state remains pending [77],

- *Kube-controller-manager* constantly monitors the cluster and responds to events. It consists of several closely specialized controllers with a precisely defined scope and method of operation. Each controller uses a watch mechanism to receive notifications about any resource changes. The main task is to track that the current state converges into the new desired state [78],

- *Cloud-controller-manager* is an optional system component that enables the cluster's connection with cloud API. During this process, isolating the elements that interact with the cloud from other components within the cluster is possible.

The Worker node also possesses installed services, which represent key components that enable the implementation of certain functionalities (Fig. 4.8):

- *Kubelet* – tracks changes on the API server and performs the tasks that the API server publishes for it. It must send a status report back to the API server whether the result is successful,

- *Kube-proxy* – is responsible for network communication between applications running on nodes and their communication with external users.

- *Container Runtime* (CR) is a software component that runs containers on a host operating system. It is responsible for the whole container lifecycle, including image loading from the repository, resource monitoring, and resource isolation required for containers. Sometimes, users need to incorporate multiple runtimes into Kubernetes. They would use the *Container Runtime Interface* (CRI) that a container runtime requires to place on behalf of Kubernetes. Kubernetes supports numerous CRs, such as *containerd* and CRI-O (the CRI implementation for OCI-compatible runtimes), and many manufacturers also build their solutions [79].

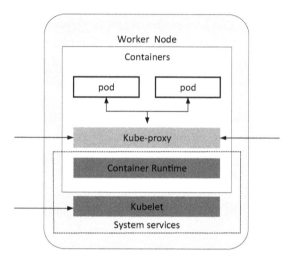

Figure 4.8. Kubernetes – key components of worker node.

4.7   Kubernetes Objects

Kubernetes objects describe the cluster's desired state [80]. They provide important information for the API server, such as a list of containerized applications running on which nodes, the availability of needed resources, and different policies that shape the behavior of applications. Users can treat Kubernetes objects as records of intent because they define the desired cluster's workload when they create an object. The management of Kubernetes objects is possible only through client-server interaction, where the client sends a request to the API server in YAML (Yet Another Markup Language) or JSON format. We can create, modify, and delete objects using the API server.

A special type of Kubernetes object is a *namespace*. We use this object to create virtual units within the cluster. Users employ the namespace to shape parts of a cluster by applying different policies, such as limiting resource consumption. They provide access control by using a namespace in particular locations in a cluster. Users define a role object type and assign it using role binding. This way, namespaces allow flexible resource allocation into clusters, such as granular organization, managing, and securing resources. Namespaces enable users to create virtual spaces to isolate the resources from one another. Work with objects sometimes requires the use of different namespaces. In this case, we must isolate objects from other domains and make them independent. For example, namespace A can create object X while supporting the creation of object X in namespace B. This object is fundamentally different from the object in namespace A.

Mandatory fields in each object are:

- *ApiVersion* – indicates the version of Kubernetes,
- *Kind* – indicates the type of object,
- *Metadata* – users enter values related to a specific object, such as object name, namespace, labels, and annotations. They can use tags to find and filter Kubernetes objects, while annotations are descriptions and are not filterable.
- *Spec* – describe the desired state.

In Fig. 4.9, we show the program code for one Kubernetes object:

```
apiVersion: batch/v1
kind: Job
metadata:
  name: job-serverinfo
spec:
  template:
    spec:
      containers:
      - name: job-serverinfo
        image: php:cli
        command: ["php", "-i"]
      restartPolicy: Never
  backoffLimit: 1
```

Figure 4.9. The code for a single Kubernetes object.

The Kubernetes objects consist of resources such as CPU, memory, disk size, I/O, and network bandwidth. Managing these resources is essential because it allows for controlling each resource and application's needs at any time. For example, the application makes a lot of HTTP requests and needs to limit its available memory so that it does not consume all the RAM and crash the cluster. We must treat any resource in Kubernetes as a lightweight object representing a single cluster entity. Each object in the cluster has a unique name for that type of resource and a unique UID string that generates Kubernetes to uniquely identify objects across the whole cluster. There are several types of Kubernetes objects: Pod, ReplicaSet, Deployment, StatefulSet, Job, CronJob, Service, ConfigMap, Secret, Volume, and others.

4.7.1   Pod

Pod represents the simplest deployable object in the Kubernetes system. It manages/runs one or more containers on the Worker node. The containers share resources like network interfaces, memory, and dependencies. They also communicate with each other and coordinate activities for their termination. The containers run from Container runtime, and their mutual communication occurs as they run on the local system. They can use different communication methods, such as socket and HTTP. Each Pod possesses a unique IP address and network ports for communication with other objects in the system. It also has persistent or non-persistent (temporary) data storage. The continuous data storage data can be recovered if the Pod shuts down. If the Pod possesses temporary storage, data disappears after the Pod shuts down.

Like individual application containers, we should consider Pod as a temporary entity. If the Worker node is not operational, the Pod running on the Worker node will be scheduled for deletion after a timeout period if it is not in function.

During its lifetime, the Pod goes through different phases:

- Pending – the Pod has not fully started because one or more of the containers are not ready to run,
- Running – we created all the containers, bound the Pod to the node, and it is ready for execution,
- Succeeded – the Pod and all its containers started successfully,
- Failed – the Pod failed to start because the containers terminated; at least one is in error.
- Unknown – typically occurs due to a communication error. The node where the Pod is running and the Pod is in an unknown state.

4.7.2   ReplicaSet

Running the Pod as an independent resource is possible, but this is not good because it loses all the benefits Kubernetes offers. Instead of running an individual Pod, it is preferable to use the *ReplicaSet* concept [81]. We should replicate Pods for several reasons, such as:

- Redundancy – by having multiple copies of the Pod on different physical servers, the other copies continue to work in case of a server failure,
- Scaling – with multiple copies of Pod, the system can accept and process more requests and
- Traffic balancing – by having multiple copies of the Pod on different servers, traffic can be balanced and thus achieve an even load on the server.

Users can define many Pod replicas using a *ReplicaSet* object, which represents a process that runs multiple copies of the same Pod. We can group Pods within a ReplicaSet into a single unit that we can reference easily. ReplicaSet ensures that there are always a certain number of copies on the Pod. In the event of an error, the system is not in the desired state. Pod switches to the failed state, and the number of defined copies decreases. The *ReplicaSet* will start a new pod, and the system will return to the designated (original) state. The same applies if the configuration of the *ReplicaSet* object has changed and the defined number of pod copies is less than the number of currently running copies. It is necessary to satisfy the defined condition and stop a certain number of Pods.

We can select the pods with the appropriate labels and manage them using the label selector inside the spec section of the *ReplicaSet* object. This way, it is possible to isolate certain pods at runtime and remove them from the *ReplicaSet*. Moreover, we can define and add Pods outside of the existing *ReplicaSet*. The Pod's isolation we can use to examine the Pod's state if it has a problem without affecting the operation of other Pods. The advantage of adding existing Pods to a *ReplicaSet* is the ability to make additional copies without stopping the Pod's running.

The task of the *ReplicaSet* is to ensure that the number of replica pods under its command is always in the desired state. Although very useful, there are better solutions than *ReplicaSet*. Sometimes, the *ReplicaSet* cannot be an ideal solution to locate applications because it is impossible to provide its update properly. *ReplicaSet* links to a specific image and its version, and after the update, the object deletes, and a new one is created, so the state of the pods is lost [81].

4.7.3   Deployment

Manual update of containerized applications is time-consuming and requires significant effort. It consists of multiple actions. An example is stopping the current version of the Pod, starting the new one, and updating the latest version of the application. We must check if the new version of the application launched successfully due to the possibility of human errors. Kubernetes aims to automate these actions, eliminate potential bottlenecks, and make the process more efficient.

Deployment is the Kubernetes platform's top-level application management object [82]. Its role is to describe the application's life cycle and to define the desired cluster's workload, such as selecting the type of image, the number of pods, and the method for updating applications. The Kubernetes deployment provides additional possibilities:

- Automatic scaling, debugging, and updating of applications according to the latest version,
- Specification of the desired state of the application and its maintenance,

- The presence of the required number of application replicas,
- The application updates without interruptions.

Deployment manages *ReplicaSets* in the background on the server side without client interaction. It means that through the Deployment object, *ReplicaSet* gets the functionality of Pod replicas and works directly with Pods. Figure 4.10 shows the relationship between *Deployment*, *ReplicaSet*, and the *Pod*. We must emphasize that the task of *ReplicaSet* is to raise a new Pod in case of a Pod's failure during deployment.

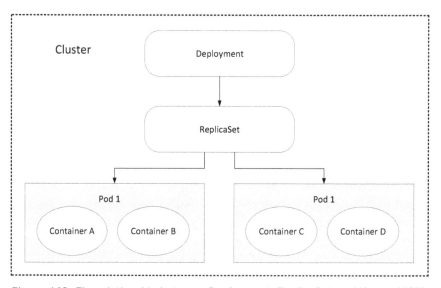

Figure 4.10. The relationship between Deployment, ReplicaSet, and the pod [83].

The main task of Kubernetes *deployment* is to provide a simple transition from one application version to another. This transition is a two-way process. It is possible to update the application to a new version, but we can also revert to previous versions. For example, if an error occurs in the latest version of the application, it is possible to do a rollback, i.e., return to the previous version. The transition from one version to another represents strategy, which depends on user requirements. In practice, several strategies exist, and each possesses certain advantages and constraints. In most cases, we can meet the following strategies [84]:

- The *recreate strategy* represents the simplest strategy, which implies terminating all instances (containers) from the current version and then starting all new containers,
- The *ramped* or *rolling update strategy* provides a controlled, phased replacement of the application's Pods and ensures that a minimum number of Pods is always available. In practice, we can start with a Deployment update and

then launch a new ReplicaSet (with a new application version). The controlled number of replicas will increase and decrease in the old one. After the number of replicas in the old ReplicaSet drops to zero and the new one reaches the desired number, the old ReplicaSet disappears, leaving only the new one.

- The *Blue/green* or *red/black strategy* simultaneously supports creating two environments, blue and green. After testing the new environment (blue), the load balancer routes traffic from the old (green) environment to the new environment.
- The *canary strategy* aims to redirect some users to the new version of the environment while the remaining users access the old version. It is important to note that the share of the latest and old environments is variable.

In Table 4.1, we summarize the advantages and shortcomings of the mentioned strategies.

Table 4.1. Advantages and shortcomings of the strategies used.

Strategy	Advantages	Shortcomings
Recreate	The user must run the application from the beginning because the state between versions is not saved.	For applications that consist of resource-demanding services, the system takes time to stop and restart.
Ramped (rolling update)	A controlled transition to a new application version (without downtime) allows services to adapt to changes. Easy implementation and the possibility to deploy on any application are the main advantages.	Sometimes, it is slow, especially in the case of a large number of pods. Perform troubleshooting is difficult if the new version of the application possesses an error.
Blue/green	If an error occurs in a new computer environment, it is easy to roll back to a safe, old environment in real time. This way reduces the risks of experimentation in a production environment. It provides a great mechanism to push software into production quickly.	Setting up can be complex and risky, and sometimes, it is necessary to repeat it several times to work properly. This deployment requires doubling the production environment and causes costs (e.g., users on-premises purchase more equipment, while in the cloud, they pay double for the infrastructure). During the transition, it does not support changes in a database schema, and the database stays read-only.

(Continued)

Table 4.1. Continued

Strategy	Advantages	Shortcomings
Canary	It enables a granular transition of users to a new environment. A certain number of them can have negative operational issues, but this number is kept low by performing the rollback to the old version quickly. It provides a rapid update, high development velocity, and a reduction of cycle length. It improves users' trust because they know that the software vendor continuously tracks and takes care of problems as they occur.	It introduces additional complexity because it is necessary to manage multiple API versions and database schemas. Remote software deployment on customer devices or sites is difficult for management and requires time to ensure customers have updated and evaluated the software. This deployment requires a certain level of visibility, which refers to user behavior and system and application issues, but in many environments, this level of visibility has yet to be available.

We must note that providing the required number of replicas in the Kubernetes system is always necessary. The deployment object utilizes the Deployment controller. One of the many tasks of this controller is to track the number of active replicas. If one of the replicas is not functional due to hardware, software, or other reasons, the controller will automatically replace it and create a new one. The controller represents the entity that allows users to manage the update, downgrade, and service scaling (Pods) without downtime. The controller enables the containerized applications to run in the cluster without interruption.

4.7.4 Horizontal Pod Autoscaler and Vertical Pod Autoscaler

In a real environment, there is a need to continuously control the number of replicas for each Pod and their scaling. In some cases, it is necessary to deploy more Pods as a response to increase the load. To provide this horizontal scaling, we can use a *Horizontal Pod Autoscaler* (HPA) [85]. Its main task is to analyze the current state and automatically update the workload according to current demands. The term horizontal scaling implies increasing the number of replicas and decreasing the number of Pods following the system's current state. HPA provides information about the system's current state by using a service that downloads data about processor occupancy, system memory, and other downloadable metrics. HPA ensures that applications have enough optimized resources to run, avoiding excessive resource consumption and performance degradation (Fig. 4.11).

In practice, it is important to identify the proper size of resource requests associated with the application Pod. In the initial phase, the Pod creates schedules according to the initial request. These requirements change over time, and re-evaluation is

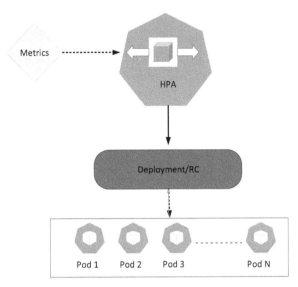

Figure 4.11. Horizontal Pod Autoscaler [86].

necessary to prevent problems with over-allocated resources or the absence of essential resources. Kubernetes utilizes the *Vertical Pod Autoscaler* (VPA) for this purpose.
Its main task is to adjust the Pod's configuration based on the results of the Pod's
resource load measurement [87]. Instead of just scaling the number of replicas, VPA
can adjust CPU and RAM limits and requirements for a particular pod. This way,
we reduce excessive and inefficient resource usage, application downtime, and large
cloud storage costs. This Kubernetes object uses the Custom Metrics API to gain
insight into current resource usage. We must note that VPA only works on particular Pods in a certain namespace. It is possible to configure VPA to use different
scaling algorithms, such as those based on predictive modeling.

4.7.5   Job

The *Job* is responsible for task execution on the Kubernetes platform. It is different
from other Kubernetes controllers. Its role is to construct transient Pods to perform
assigned duties. The *Job's* tasks can be very different, such as starting an application
that enters initial data into the system or launching the integration script to connect
system components. Its core task is Pod instantiation. The main function of this
process is that the Job stops itself after successful completion.

Kubernetes uses the *Job* to execute one-time tasks in a cluster reliably and
deterministically without manual control. Depending on the user's needs, the Job
controller can work differently. For example, the *Parallel Job* can run multiple tasks
simultaneously. The next one, the so-called *Parallel Job* with a fixed number of
completions mode, can run concurrent tasks a few times before they are considered

complete. In a *Non-parallel Job*, it runs one Pod at a time. Completions set the required number of successful starts attributes until it finally switches to the completed state. The value of the parallelism attribute indicates the number of Pods that need to run in parallel (Fig. 4.12) [88].

```
apiVersion: apps/v1
kind: Deployment
metadata:
  name: sajt01-deployment
spec:
  selector:
    matchLabels:
        app   aplikacija01
    replicas: 5
    template:
      . . .
```

Figure 4.12. Running a job object.

4.7.6   CronJob

More and more applications require periodic execution of scheduled tasks, such as data backup or periodic input of fresh data into cache server [89]. To execute these tasks on the server, Kubernetes uses a *CronJob* mechanism. *Cron* is a background service that executes jobs according to schedules defined in the *Crontab* file. For example, *CronJob* can run in the background to instantiate the *Job* while running multiple Pods in parallel and achieving the desired number of successful runs. It is necessary to optimize tasks so they may be repeated (Fig. 4.13).

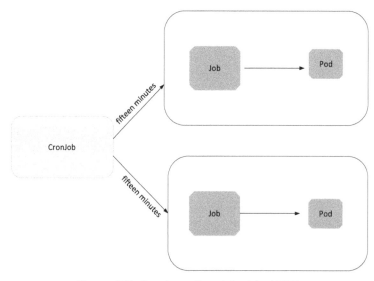

Figure 4.13. Running a CronJob object [89].

CronJob represents a standard mechanism that runs scheduled jobs in regular, predefined intervals. Its application in computer infrastructure implies:

- Data processing, periodic storage cleaning, and automatic report generation,
- *Job* specification, which defines the Docker container and its commands,
- Task scheduling by configuration using a YAML *Crontab* file.

4.7.7   Service Object

Traffic routing of logical pools of Pods or external resources is an important functionality on the Kubernetes platform. We use the *Service object* as a logical abstraction for a deployed group of pods in a cluster that performs the same function. The *Service* originated from needing each Pod to have an IP address. Since a Pod represents a temporary object, a *Service* enables a group of Pods that provide specific functions of web services to obtain a name and unique IP address. This IP address will stay the same as the *Service* running it. The role of the *Service* is to connect a set of pods to an abstracted service name and IP address to provide discovery and routing between pods.

The *Service* object should provide a persistent IP address and DNS service name for an application and its replicas. *Service* is not a node-specific object. It points to pods regardless of location and running time in the cluster. By knowing a service IP address and a DNS service name, we can access the application as long as the *Service* exists. We must note that clients use DNS as a standard mechanism for *Service* discovery on the cluster. Its task is to monitor the Kubernetes API and make its name available for resolution after creating a new service. Further, Service works in a way that:

- Allows other applications on the cluster to communicate with the replica group as a single entity regardless of the number of replicas currently running,
- Performs load balancing, which means that application access requests will be distributed across replicas to ensure optimal performance and
- Ensure communication security by using encryption and identity verification.

4.8   Kubernetes Labels

Labels are metadata in Kubernetes that represent a *key-value* pair linked to objects (Pods and *Services*). They are used to identify a Kubernetes object and cannot change any functionality directly. They help users to map data structures onto objects. Users can add labels to resources in a few different ways. The first implies that users enter labels in configuration files to set labels when the resource is created or modified. The *Kubectl* CLI (Command-Line Interface) tool is the second choice, which is used for small resource modifications and does not have automatic reflection in configuration files. Finally, it is possible to add and remove labels and other details using the CLI editor [90].

Within the *Service* object, we can use attributes, such as selector and port, to create a logical set of Pods, to choose the protocol for traffic forwarding, such as TCP, UDP, SCTP, HTTP, and PROXY, or to define the communication endpoints. One endpoint will be available to other services within the system, while the second represents a target for traffic forwarding (Fig. 4.14).

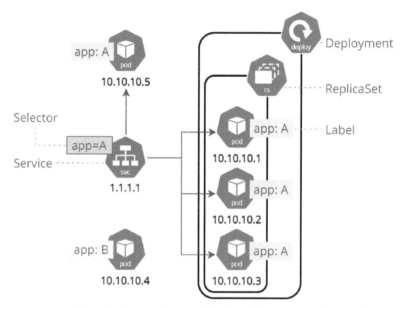

Figure 4.14. Application of Service object on Kubernetes platform [90].

4.8.1   Kubernetes Selector

Label selectors allow the identification of the objects tagged with particular labels. In practice, equality-based and set-based selectors exist. An equality-based label selector specifies the exact value for a possible comparison. A set-based selector is similar, but this selector allows the user to select several values in the selector. Only one value should match the object to qualify. Selectors are typically used in clusters with many resources running, where they can help to discriminate and quickly identify the required resources.

Specifying the selector attribute in the *Service* object is necessary to define a logical set of Pods. We must use the ports attribute and the Endpoint objects created manually for traffic routing. The instantiated *Service* object receives a virtual IP address, whose value depends on the attribute type field. This attribute can have one of the following values [91]:

- *ClusterIP* – default value if the type of attribute is not defined. The *Service* object obtains an internal IP address from the cluster range. Only resources from the internal cluster can access the *Service* instance,
- *NodePort* – this value allows the Service instance to receive the address of the Kubernetes node and a communication endpoint. The *Service* instance is visible on the network and outside the Kubernetes system and advertises to all system nodes. It is unnecessary to know the Pod's location.
- The *kube-proxy Service* will forward the traffic to the appropriate node and the communication endpoint.
- *LoadBalancer* – The *Service* is allocated an IP address outside the Kubernetes system. Network communication to the logical set of Pods occurs outside the Kubernetes system. *Service* uses a public IP address over the Internet.
- *ExternalName* is a special case where DNS records can be used instead of selectors. They often refer to services outside the Kubernetes system.

External access to cluster applications represents a common request. For this purpose, the Kubernetes platform exposes the Ingress object, which should enable communication between applications on the cluster. Users can define routing rules on Ingrees and forward application requests based on URL, hostname, or another attribute (Fig. 4.15) [89, 92].

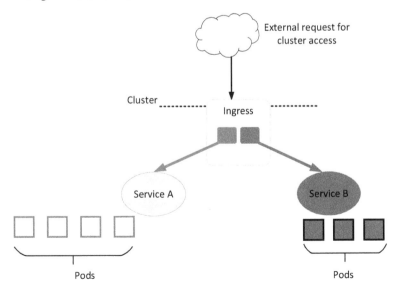

Figure 4.15. Deploying the Ingress object on the Kubernetes platform platform [92].

4.8.2 ConfigMap

Data storage and exchange have great importance for Kubernetes. Kubernetes utilizes the *ConfigMap* object to store and present various data types, which can present data as a file or in a key-value format. The Pods use *ConfigMap* as a configuration file or environment variable. Its implementation aims to isolate environment-specific configurations from container images and make applications portable. The application of *ConfigMap* possesses some limitations. These limitations refer to the confidentiality of stored data and the lack of possibility to hold large chunks of data. *ConfigMap* does not provide encryption services, and anyone can access it. For configurations greater than 1 MiB, mounting a new disk or other database is necessary.

In practice, there are different methods of accessing *ConfigMap*. The first method is remote access by Pods in the same namespace. The second is to define a a *ConfigMap* separately from Pods and use them for other components of the Kubernetes cluster. The third access is to mount *ConfigMap* as a data storage. We can use the values defined in the *ConfigMap* object for Pods and other objects. We use them to configure containers running in a pod in the same namespace. The *ConfigMap* object must exist before we reference it in the Pod specification, and it is a prerequisite for the Pod to run.

Many applications depend on configuration data used during either initialization or runtime. Often, we must adjust values assigned to configuration parameters on *ConfigMap* to update applications with configuration data. Another reason to utilize *ConfigMap* is to provide a solution that keeps configuration data separate from application code [93]. It is possible to facilitate application management and reduce the code volume required to change the configuration. It represents the twelve-factor methodology. The goal is to provide the preconditions for simple modification, depending on the environment. This way, dynamic changes are introduced at runtime. Finally, the *ConfigMap* object is a text YAML file, which can be created or updated only in the Kubernetes cluster (Fig. 4.16).

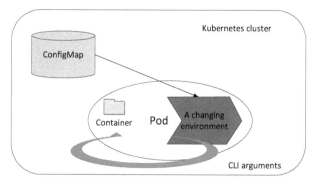

Figure 4.16. Application of ConfigMap object on the Kubernetes platform.

There are three ways to use *ConfigMap* on Kubernetes. The first is through environment variables, as shown in Fig. 4.16. The second refers to configuring the application through command-line arguments. The third concerns the presentation of the *ConfigMap* value through the file system added to Pod [79]. It means propagating changes automatically to each Pod in an update, and containers' restart is unnecessary. Each of these three ways of using *ConfigMap* has its advantages. The choice comes down to preferences and how to implement the application inside the container.

4.8.3   Secret

The *Secret* is similar to the *ConfigMap* object and usually contains sensitive information, such as passwords, OAuth tokens, and SSH keys. A *Secret* object eliminates the need to store sensitive information inside the container application code. It provides greater control over the use of sensitive information and reduces the risks of accidents. There are several types of *Secret* objects: *opaque*, *basic-auth*, *ssh-auth*, *tls*, and others. They all have origins from the *opaque* type. Each type adds its attributes over the *opaque* type in order. In the case of the *ssh-auth* type, the *Secret* object facilitates communication between the SSH server and the client [91]. There are three ways of using the *ConfigMap* object: through environment variables, command line arguments, and the file system presented to a Pod. If *Secret* is present through the file system, the changes automatically propagate to the file system after the update. The container can see those changes without restarting the container itself. We must emphasize that the *Secret* object is separate from the application and enables storing sensitive information in a central place [94]. Unlike *ConfigMap*, it stores encrypted data protected from unauthorized access. It can provide information for Kubernetes resources, such as *deployments*, Pods, or Services. Most importantly, an application can create it manually or generate it using the Kubernetes API.

We note that the local disk inside the Pod is short-lived. All information placed on the file system is lost after the Pod is deactivated; a new Pod will start. Kubernetes solves this problem by introducing logical disks. It supports many types of logical disks (*Volume*) by the *Container Storage Interface* (CSI) abstraction [78]. Any logical disk whose implementation satisfies this interface represents an object within the system. After presenting the logical disks to the system, a Pod can simultaneously use the disks presented to it. The object *PersistentVolume* (PV) represents a part of the space on the logical disk created by the administrator. It is available for claim by user request, i.e., object *PersistentVolumeClaim* (PVC). *PersistentVolume* can be static or dynamic. The dynamic method uses *StorageClass* abstraction, where the disk space (PVC) request uses its attributes for mapping. At the same time, the static *PersistentVolume* is created manually by the administrator.

Some PV types are *azureDisk*, *azureFile*, *csi*, *fc*, *glusterfs*, *hostPath*, *iscsi*, *local*, and nfs. *PersistentVolumeClaim* is an object through which disk access is claimed. The request specifies the amount of disk and the type of access. Types of access are [90]:

- *ReadWriteOnce* – the disk is presented for reading and writing on a single node,
- *ReadWriteMany* – the disk is presented for reading and writing on multiple nodes,
- *ReadOnlyMany* – the disk is presented as read-only on multiple nodes,
- *ReadWriteOncePod* – the disk is presented for reading and writing on only one pod.

4.9   Methods of Saving Application State

In Kubernetes, various applications save their states differently. We grouped them into Stateless and Stateful applications. At the beginning of containerization, the designed applications do not save the states inside the containers. Their primary goal is to be flexible and portable to different architectures. With the popularization of this technology, stateful applications appeared. They store states on a persistent medium in the same location where the application is running. The most famous Stateful applications are databases, such as MySQL, PostgreSQL, and MongoDB. Unlike stateless applications with a transient data flow, the stateful application must keep states and take into consideration the temporary nature of storage. It can be problematic during cluster setup because they need persistent storage to survive a service restart [95].

To clarify the previous remarks, we will begin with the assumption that three Pods represent the members of the MySQL database cluster. Cluster members can communicate and exchange data if the addresses of the members exist on each Pod in the configuration. In case we configure the cluster using Deployment or *ReplicaSet*, after the Pod's failure, a new Pod runs with a new address and without the data of the previous Pod. This state leads to errors in the cluster configuration and can cause inoperability. We must change the cluster configuration of cluster members so that they point to the new Pod. This process is impossible to automate, and we must find another solution.

The deployment and scaling of Pods with *Stateful* applications is challenging. Providing guarantees that the Pod is in the correct order and the Pod's uniqueness is another challenge. To remedy these challenges, we can use the *StatefulSet* object, whose Pod identity is static. If the existing Pod fails, a new one starts. It obtains the identity (IP address) from the old Pod. When implementing a *StatefulSet*, if

Pods possess multiple replicas, they must instantiate sequentially. It means the new Pod runs if the running of the previous Pod was completed. The containerized applications in Pods must have unique names, stable network identities, and persistent data storage. This way, it is possible to ensure that each instantiated Pod is maintained in a unique order and with a unique name. It permanently maintains the application's identity and creates an assumption for scaling it and increasing its capacity (Fig. 4.17) [96].

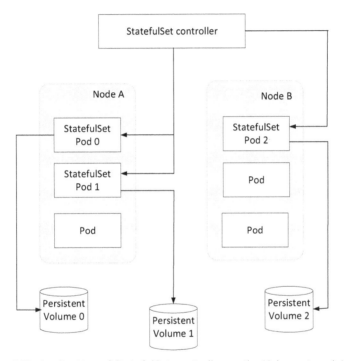

Figure 4.17. Application of StatefulSet controller on the Kubernetes platform.

4.10   Alternatives for Kubernetes

If we consider an alternative to Kubernetes, it is important to define specific requirements, such as simple usage, scalability, community support, possibility of integration with existing tools, and control of applications. In practice, we meet several alternatives with their features and intentions, such as Apache Mesos, Docker Swarm, and Amazon ECS.

Apache Mesos is an open-source manager that provides resource isolation and sharing across distributed clusters or applications. It uses the same principles as the Linux Kernel, and key features are greater scalability, multi-resource scheduling, web user interface for cluster state monitoring, and others. It consists of a master process and frameworks with a master process managing slave daemons running on each cluster node and frameworks that handle tasks on these slaves. Apache Mesos can move resources from one framework to another as required, and many processes in the deployment of applications are automated. Its location is between the application layer and the operating system, allowing it to deploy and manage applications in large-scale clusters efficiently [97].

Docker Swarm is a container orchestrator that can manage multiple physical or virtual nodes whose roles are different. The nodes are classified as manager and worker nodes. The manager node contains the Swarm Manager process (manages the commands in the Swarm mode and reconciles the desired with the real cluster state), while worker nodes contain the workloads. Docker Swarm provides benefits, such as high-availability environments with reliable communication and fault tolerance between nodes (nodes coordinate with each other to ensure reliable operations), load balancing (manager node distributes requests evenly across the worker nodes), and simplicity for easily managing applications and containers in swarm and non-swarm mode. Docker Swarm is suitable for deployment of small to medium configurations and for deployment where it is necessary to prioritize high service availability and automatic load balancing over automation and fault tolerance.

Amazon ECS is a container orchestrator developed to simplify the deployment and management of large-scale containers. It allows to run, scale, and control applications. Its advantages are task definitions for container configurations, seamless integration with different services, automatic scaling based on request, and efficient resource allocation. It can simplify deploying and managing applications, delivering a flexible and robust platform for container orchestration within the AWS ecosystem.

4.11 Software Architectures with One or More Users

Virtualization technology offers a wide range of possibilities. From the aspect of shared (virtual) infrastructure, we recognize two software architectures – architecture with one and architecture with multiple users or tenants (Fig. 4.18). In non-virtualization scenarios, only one user owns and controls the entire server. The user can modify the server's hardware and software independently, without any changes affecting users of other servers. A single instance of a software application and supporting infrastructure serves one customer. This model of resource usage is a single lease. A user who utilizes resources independently for a certain time is a tenant, and this approach is a single tenant [98]. In a virtual environment, it is

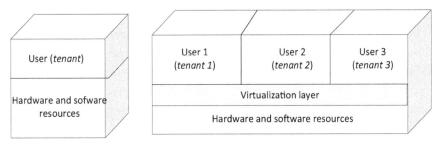

Figure 4.18. Single-tenant and multitenant architecture.

possible to implement a single-tenant architecture in which a user uses one virtual instance for a certain time. However, virtualization technology allows the sharing of a virtual instance and its resources between multiple users. Any change in the shared infrastructure affects other users. The user is only free to modify the system with the support of other users. This software environment represents multitenant architecture [98].

As depicted in Fig. 4.18, multitenant software architecture brings some advantages but also reduces the isolation level between users, affecting security and increasing vulnerability compared to single-tenant architecture. Although this architecture is commonplace in the industry, its shortcomings sometimes become a critical factor (often due to regulatory requirements) influencing the choice of software architecture.

4.12 Conclusion

The NFV concept's development occurred due to the desire to include server virtualization more widely in computer networking. For this reason, the virtualization techniques represent the NFV concept's fundamentals. If we return to the design of the ETSI architecture, we recognize that the NFVI block represents a result of activity at the virtualization layer. These activities can be infrastructure virtualization using a hypervisor or containerization using an LXC or Docker virtual container. They are an integral part of the virtualization layer of each NFVI block [1].

Today, containerization focuses on deploying and managing applications, while NFV's goals are virtualization and optimization of network services and functions. The goals of these technologies are different because containerization primarily deals with packaging and deploying applications to provide them with regular running across different environments. Unlike containerization, the NFV focus is virtualization and network services running on standard hardware. The overlap between Network Functions Virtualization (NFV) and containerization is possible, especially due to further network softwarization, which requires more flexibility, scalability, and efficiency in deploying network services and applications. In practice, overlaps occur in service chaining, where we use containerization to implement and manage specific applications or microservices that complement or enhance the NFV services.

Further, containerization technologies, such as Kubernetes, can manage containers and VMs in the same infrastructure. It is the reason for the fast development of NFV orchestration, which aims to integrate the management of virtual machines and containers within the same infrastructure. Containerization's lightweight nature and rapid development can increase agility, faster service deployment, and efficient resource utilization in NFV-based networks. By using container orchestration platforms, such as Kubernetes or Docker Swarm, it is possible to achieve greater agility, scalability, and operational efficiency in NFV-based networks. These platforms have capabilities to enable the abstraction of the VNFs management complexity, providing a flexible and scalable infrastructure for numerous network services.

The advantages of containerization bring a dominant trend for micro-services with containers, significantly influencing NFV efficiency. There are many benefits, such as the short time needed to create, reload, and delete containers. In the long term, we see that containers' usage in NFV is increasing more than virtual machines. In practice, users utilize the same tools to connect different VNFs, i.e., virtual machines or containers. This approach encourages the development of new, more efficient virtual switches based on solutions that imply advanced packet processing techniques at the kernel and network card level (e.g., Intel's Data Plane Development Kit – DPDK) [99]. More details will be provided in the next section.

DOI: 10.1561/9781638283591.ch5

Chapter 5

NFV-based Network Design

Today, the traditional concept of network service implementation is still dominant in most computer networks. We have specialized functions implemented on dedicated hardware, such as packet switching (L2 switching), traffic routing (L3 routing), network address translation (NAT), firewall, deep packet inspection, intrusion detection system (IDS), load balancing, WAN optimizing and stateful proxy [100]. However, the rapid increase in user requirements, great heterogeneity, and resource-demanding services [98] require the engagement of additional financial resources for equipment procurement and staff training. It increases capital expenditures (CapEx) and operational expenditures (OpEx) and indicates the need to change the current concept of network function application to be more efficient.

The practice shows that adding new functionalities to traditional networks is long and challenging. To implement a new network function, staff often must visit different locations and install devices in a predefined order to form service function chains (SFCs). Service instantiation can take days; worse, service maintenance usually involves repeating the same process. This fact significantly limits innovative approaches and increases the time it takes to bring a new network function to the market [101].

Academic and professional communities know that new technological solutions are necessary to increase the utilization of resources and encourage an innovative approach in the network. They define greater network management flexibility, efficient service provision, and achieving more significant financial effects as key goals. Technologies such as software-defined networking [102] and the NFV [103] support the achievement of these goals. Environments based on SDN decouple the control plane from the data plane and use a logically centralized controller to configure programmable switches based on a global view of the network infrastructure. At the same time, the NFV concept allows the replacement of network functions on dedicated hardware with software-based virtual network functions (VNF) on COTS hardware. The key to the success of the new network management concept lies in reducing service implementation time and providing a diversity of network services.

5.1 NFV Concept in Modern Network Design

The NFV concept brings numerous opportunities and advantages in designing and building modern network environments. The core of the NFV concept is implementing network functions independent of hardware and equipment vendors. It means a free choice of virtual network functions and their running mode regardless of the physical infrastructure design. Figure 5.1 shows the three dimensions of implementing the NFV concept in networks.

As with any complex system, the constitution of an NFV network usually includes numerous software and hardware components that are in close interaction.

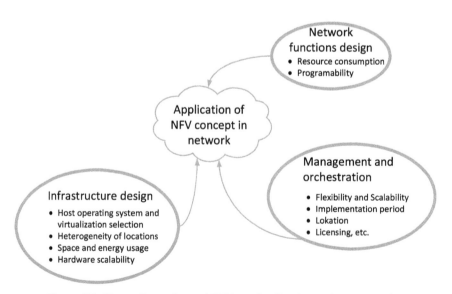

Figure 5.1. Three dimensions of NFV application in modern networks.

Depending on the design's intentions, where to implement VNFs, and in what way, dealing with the life cycle of network functions implies considering different factors. It includes the VNFs execution model, state management methods, other APIs, VNFs interconnection, and various data path acceleration techniques such as batch processing and zero-copy packet transmission. The goal is to describe the design of a typical NFV platform. Although the ETSI program framework defines a reference architecture, most existing NFV platforms do not follow it strictly. Some key ETSI components still need to be implemented in industrial NFV platforms [16], while other implementations have focused only on management aspects.

We can meet different network architecture designs in environments that combine the ETSI reference architecture with existing solutions. An NFV platform generally consists of three primary components: the NFV MANO plane, the service plane, and the NFV infrastructure (NFVI). The MANO plane provides centralized control of service delivery and management. NFVI contains a collection of compute, storage, and network resources distributed across different infrastructure nodes. MANO plane components systematically monitor and schedule resources to build a virtualized environment and adapt various network services. The service layer contains diverse VNFs deployed as service chains to fulfill desired network services [104]. MANO plane components also closely monitor and adapt these service chains to multiplex NFVI resources effectively. Generally, we can enable the service plane through coordinated operations with MANO and NFVI blocks.

5.1.1   NFVI Design

The implementation of NFV aims to create a generic infrastructure characterized by the scalability and elasticity of VNFs. This infrastructure can also be used (shared) for various servers and other data center applications. The basic requirement of such a shared environment is great flexibility in resource allocation for individual software applications. The infrastructure designed this way is quite independent of the network layer. It is impossible to predict all hardware resource requirements that can arise during exploitation.

The telecom operators aim to align resources as much as possible to current needs. They intend to initially provide an infrastructure with significant hardware resources to avoid the need for future changes (expansions). In practice, the installed hardware often cannot meet the growing demands. For this reason, we must upgrade hardware or change the utilization of shared resources per new requirements. The solution is the free choice of scalable hardware that can be replaced without impact on the virtualized applications and hosted VNFs (e.g., servers must be able to scale hardware resources, such as network cards and memory). As an example of a flexible solution, we can take a virtual infrastructure with a system of shared disks, which reduces the possibility of failures compared to servers with embedded disks.

The hardware selection is a complex process related to the telecom operator's intention to reduce costs. Although COTS hardware has emerged as the best solution, the situation is complicated because numerous vendors require more compatibility between their and COTS equipment. This fact directly affects the choice of equipment because reliable operation and vendor support must be guaranteed. Also, we must consider the choice of the host operating system and the hypervisor as the virtualization layer. They must be compatible and easily integrated with the installed hardware to create a stable foundation for the rest of the infrastructure. In the case of COTS hardware, it is necessary to consider the following:

- types of technical support available,
- licensing costs,
- procurement costs,
- possibility of upgrading,
- stability in work, and
- ability to interact with open-source software and commercially available tools.

The optimal network design depends on a balance between all these factors. The preferences of telecom operators are also important because they like the "bundled" software solutions, such as VMware, RedHat, or Canonical packages. In contrast, others insist on open, freely available operating systems (e.g., Ubuntu or CentOS) that run open-source hypervisors like KVM. In the first case, the telecom operator bears the licensing costs but also has results, technical support, and a secure future with a clear upgrade path. There are no licensing costs in the second case, but support will be internal or from the community.

The rational usage of space and energy for the infrastructure is another important requirement regarding operating costs. This requirement is important because data centers are spatially large facilities and consume energy measured in hundreds of MW. Every virtualization-based implementation is significant because of the rational use of the available computer infrastructure and great elasticity. The software footprint can be created on shared hardware and replicated in different locations, making work easier.

The selection of the location for the NFVI infrastructure is also important. It would be ideal to install it in geographically different locations, in areas with a high concentration of users. For the smooth functioning of the infrastructure, there must be geographic redundancy. It implies providing flexibility and VNF running where the greatest need is. The flexibility in providing redundancies is necessary to eliminate numerous problems in traditional networks, especially in the case of network device failure. Traditional networks have redundancy implemented at the device level. In the case of a device failure (e.g., one of the router's hard drives fails), there may also be traffic interruption because the network function is unavailable. It is possible to avoid this problem if we install redundant devices in advance or create a backup path, which can be expensive and sometimes complex.

Within NFVI infrastructure, redundancy is provided at the component level, so the chances of losing network function due to a single component failure are minimal. A network function, such as a router, can be implemented as a VNF on a server using RAID (Redundant Array of Independent Disks) technology. A failure on one of the drives will not affect the network function provided on the other drives. Besides redundancy at the hardware level, the NFV concept also implies redundancy for virtual machines and containers. In this sense, we can implement different virtualization solutions to create a robust network infrastructure design.

5.1.2   Life Cycle of NFV Infrastructure

The hardware infrastructure of traditional networks consists of devices whose life cycle begins with the purchase and ends after a certain period with failures. The devices' life cycle lasts as long as the hardware works without failure and providers possess the support contract and repair components. Their replacement is necessary when they reach the end of their life cycle to reduce the possibility of failure. The devices should return the invested funds within that period, which is sometimes impossible. Similar time estimates and practices can be applied to NFV infrastructure because the host operating systems, hypervisors, and VNFs also have lifetimes. After the lifetime expires, the upgrade is required for enhancements or bug fixes and renewal of the support contract. In the process of NFV infrastructure design, it is necessary to consider factors such as program support, VNFs life cycle, hypervisor software update, and replacement of switches and servers. The coordination between them should enable providers to avoid potential traps and ensure they plan to perform upgrades efficiently.

5.1.3   The Key Principles of NFV Design

Using the NFV concept, we create virtual (logical) networks that look like overlay networks around the physical infrastructure (underlay network). They should overcome the limitations of the physical network under the overlay. Although they share a physical infrastructure, their services are separate and independent of the physical devices and connections between them. The virtual network design is independent, flexible, and without the limitations that come from the physical hardware. With multi-instance technology, virtual networks can provide different services to one or more users (tenant and multitenant access). Figure 5.2 shows that the underlay network is a physical network consisting of many devices, such as switches, routers,

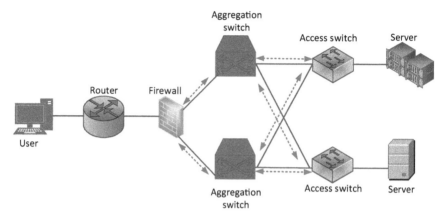

Figure 5.2. Typical underlay network.

load balancers, and firewalls, responsible for transmitting packets over different networks.

Different protocols should be used at different network layers to ensure network connectivity and data transfer between the devices shown in Fig. 5.2. We use the Ethernet and VLANs at layer L2. At the L3 layer, we use Internet protocol (IP) and different protocols for routing traffic within one network, such as Open Shortest Path First (OSPF) or Intermediate System to Intermediate System (IS-IS) or between different networks (Border Gateway Protocol - BGP). With the advancement of technology, Multiprotocol Label Switching (MPLS), which works between the L2 and L3 layers and routes traffic using the shortest path based on labels, has also appeared. Data forwarding in traditional networks is hardware-dependent and burdened with numerous challenges, such as:

- Packet forwarding based on destination IP addresses with a high dependence on transmission paths,
- The long-term process of implementing new and selecting existing services (complex and time-consuming reconfiguration procedure),
- Security problems caused by different types of attacks, and
- Dynamic resource allocation and design change are impossible per user's request.

Virtual (overlay) networks are built using network virtualization technologies to eliminate the limitations of underlay networks, as shown in Fig. 5.3.

Implementing network functionalities in software is a key difference between the NFV and traditional networks. Network functions in NFV-based networks can be added, removed, and transferred exclusively in software. We can achieve such flexibility using open APIs. Their role is to provide third-party software with a documented and publicly available way to access and download data

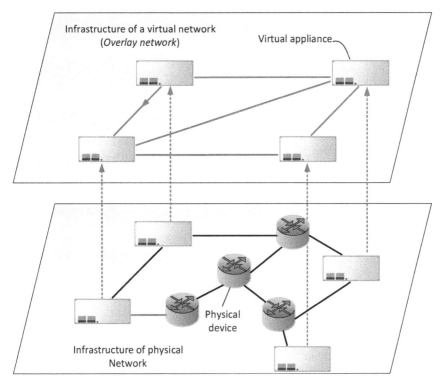

Figure 5.3. An overlay network on top of physical network infrastructure.

from the application or to pass the application parameters necessary for program-ming/configuration. Implementing open APIs enables various orchestration and management tools to control the deployment and lifecycle of VNFs. The virtual-ization layer receives instructions on connecting VNFs in a certain order. Also, the virtualization layer should enable the instantiation of new VNFs and their over-all programmability. Figure 5.4 shows three key principles of designing the NFV networks.

We can notice the underutilization of transport and network resources by ana-lyzing today's network efficiency. The reason is resource over-dimensioning to meet future requirements and to ensure redundancy as a form of protection against hard-ware or network software failures. The new network must have better resource uti-lization during its lifetime and increase the return on investment (in traditional networks, the capital and the operating costs are high).

The NFV concept implies implementing VNFs with only the required resources. The allocation of new or deallocation of existing resources is performed dynam-ically based on traffic requests. This way, it is possible to simplify the network designers' activities. They do not have to dedicate unnecessary power, memory, throughput, and other resources. More importantly, they can flexibly eliminate or

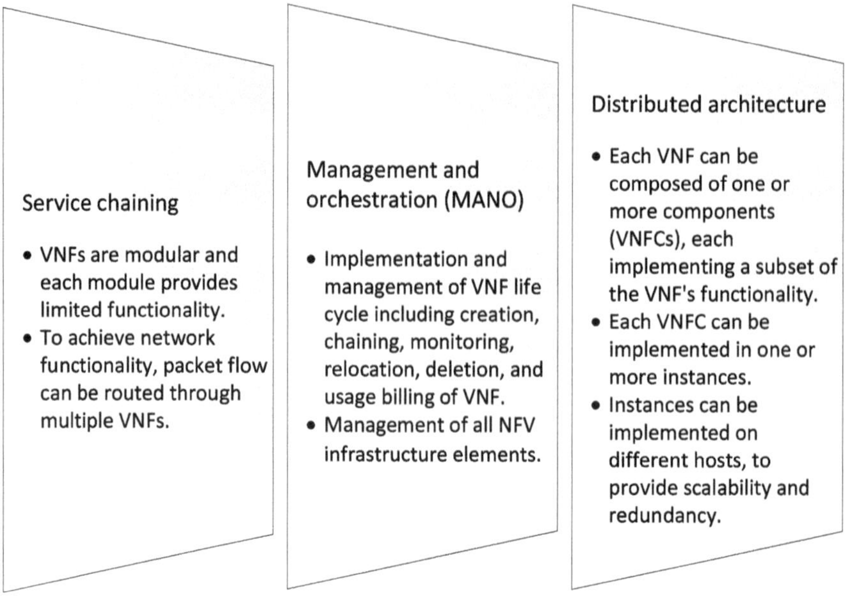

Service chaining

- VNFs are modular and each module provides limited functionality.
- To achieve network functionality, packet flow can be routed through multiple VNFs.

Management and orchestration (MANO)

- Implementation and management of VNF life cycle including creation, chaining, monitoring, relocation, deletion, and usage billing of VNF.
- Management of all NFV infrastructure elements.

Distributed architecture

- Each VNF can be composed of one or more components (VNFCs), each implementing a subset of the VNF's functionality.
- Each VNFC can be implemented in one or more instances.
- Instances can be implemented on different hosts, to provide scalability and redundancy.

Figure 5.4. NFV principles.

provide minimal redundancy of network functions because additional VNFs can be created as needed easily. So, we can expand NFV-based networks dynamically according to resource consumption and demand. What does it mean in practice? Suppose the telecom operator has already implemented the NFV concept in its network and wants to introduce a new type of service. In this case, the operator only introduces new services in network segments that expect business profit. The operator can organize testing of new services quickly and, based on feedback, make changes in the design of virtual devices or VNFs used for new service implementation. It means the operator can incrementally perform any further change and expand the new service offer. Also, the operator can implement this approach for partial or complete service termination.

In NFV-based networks, one important requirement is ensuring network functions' redundancy. The problems caused by a hardware failure are solved at the orchestration layer by reallocating VNFs to new hardware, considering the minimal impact on the network. We can implement most network functions via several VNFs as a service function chain (SFC) on different nodes. Ensuring high VNF reliability represents one of the major and critical challenges for the further expansion of the NFV concept. Distributing VNFs to other nodes has numerous advantages, such as cost reduction and flexible resource management [15]. A problem can also occur due to an error on a VNF, causing the entire SFC to collapse. NFV-based networks have higher reliability requirements than traditional networks, especially at the network's edge, where bandwidth for storage and processing is limited.

We can use two solutions to improve SFC's reliability in NFV-based networks. One solution optimizes the VNF deployment scheme, selecting highly reliable nodes to implement VNFs [105]. The drawback of this solution is that it cannot ensure adequate reliability and avoid hardware failures. Another solution is implementing redundant applications, i.e., making VNF copies [106]. The redundant VNFs effectively provide high reliability of network functions but require additional resources, leading to increased costs. Duplicating each VNF with a fixed number of backup instances can lead to exceeding resource capacity, especially at the network's edge, which causes unnecessary hardware costs. Considering all the above (Fig. 5.5), it is necessary to implement fault protection measures in NFV-based networks at several layers.

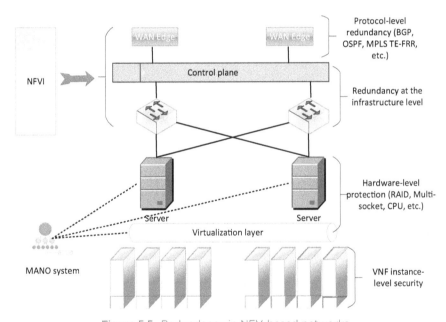

Figure 5.5. Redundancy in NFV-based networks.

Figure 5.5 shows NFV design considerations focused on redefining disaster recovery and failure mitigation at multiple layers. Providing hardware redundancy at the component or device level aims to prevent a failure of a component (CPU or memory module) from propagating to the VNFs, allowing the VNFs to continue operating without any impact. In the case of catastrophic hardware failures, such as a failure of multiple disks, the orchestration layer could instantiate the affected VNFs at new hardware with minimal impact on the network. At the NFI layer, the redundancy mechanisms aim to enable the routing functions available when a device fails, and protocol selection is an important task that depends on many factors. For example, suppose a failure occurs in the part of the network containing end devices (e.g., servers). In that case, choosing a protocol to move the default gateway function to a backup device is necessary. Such a solution is resilient in data center and server virtualization deployments and can enable high availability for network services.

With the NFV concept, we can decouple network functions into separate VNF instances or groups of VNFs, creating a modular network design without incurring costs. Figure 5.6 shows a physical router with multiple functions implemented on one device, such as firewall, Network Address Translation (NAT), and routing simultaneously.

In traditional networks, upgrading previously mentioned functionalities will require changing the complete software or hardware. The NFV design shown in Fig. 5.6 is modular, provides higher flexibility and agility, and allows the easy incorporation of any change into the design. Any change is precise and tightly focused on a concrete function, making it easy to quickly redesign, validate, and deploy the new feature. This way, the network modular design enables the implementation of the VNFs (e.g., NAT, firewall, and routing protocols) from different vendors, selected according to individual function requirements.

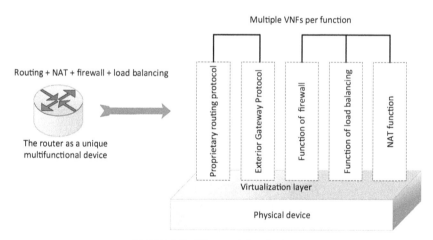

Figure 5.6. The modular design.

The modular design offers a significant advantage in terms of flexibility and agility. We can easily incorporate changes based on feedback from the network into the design because of their narrow focus on a specific function. This way, it is possible to quickly redesign, validate, and implement a new function. Being flexible, the design of NFV-based networks has many choices regarding implementing different network functions. It includes the possibility to mix and match VNFs developed by other vendors.

In the process of NFV-based network design, capacity planning is necessary because the focus is on software and automation support. This process is very elastic and implies the modification of capacity related to VNF resources on the fly without affecting the network. We must consider the business needs and guarantee a certain level of service using the elasticity of VNFs. The orchestrator should be able to analyze the data obtained by monitoring the VNFs and apply the appropriate actions by sending proper instructions to the NFVI and/or VNF layers. The orchestration layer is a network layer where logic and rules determine what changes are needed and when.

5.1.4   The Network Design Validation

Network design validation should provide a high degree of assurance that certain processes, methods, or components within the infrastructure will consistently produce results that conform to predefined criteria [1]. In most cases, this procedure takes a lot of time, creates additional costs, and requires the allocation of significant resources. The process itself is particularly complex when it comes to validating the design of an Internet service provider's network.

The process is much simpler and faster in NFV-based networks. The testing environment is elastic and consists of virtualized network functions, easily deployed by software and linked to a service chain from different network locations. During the flexible testing process, which can even be automated, getting new insights and improving the existing network design is possible. Testing and validation of the proposed network design, especially in the early stages of setup, can indicate potential problems in hardware or applied software solutions.

The ability to instantiate VNFs anytime and anywhere in the network is a significant advance as the network becomes fluid and acquires a more dynamic dimension [107]. That is the reason for performing a high-quality network design validation process and practically checking whether users in a real environment can add, remove, or change new services whenever needed. In practice, a service designed to provide load balancing, greater privacy, or more efficient traffic routing is important, as it can increase QoE (Quality of Experience) for users and revenue for service providers. Before implementation, performing a quality check of the proposed network design offers is necessary. Any design must undergo some level of validation, which is time-consuming and adds significant cost and resources. The test and validation process can take a few months or even a year in a typical service provider deployment where legacy devices and virtual infrastructure are used. Therefore, the design must be checked and perfected as much as possible before its validation, especially since design shortcomings could void the entire effort.

It is crucial to check the offered solutions regarding redundancy and recovery from incident situations and those related to the upgrade and migration of virtual entities. During testing, it is mandatory to check to what extent the upgrade of

VNFs, hypervisors, and hosts affects the occurrence of network interruptions. Only modern hypervisors can update resources like CPU and memory on a running VNF. The validation process has shown that first, we must initiate a new VNF with the necessary capabilities. After the VNF instantiation, it is possible to hand over current tasks in the network. Only then can we upgrade the original VNF with new capabilities.

5.1.5   Location and Time-dependent Implementation

Network optimization refers to using numerous tools and implementing various strategies and best practices for monitoring, managing, and improving network performance. In today's very competitive and dynamic environments, the key requirement is to ensure reliable, fast, and secure data transfer. The existence of outdated or poorly sized hardware and suboptimal software can limit available bandwidth and increase latency. Also, unexpected traffic changes can significantly affect network functions and slow response times, degrading the end-user experience.

The primary goal of network optimization is to provide the best possible network design and performance at the lowest possible cost. Network architecture must enable efficient data exchange. We can manage it only by managing delays, traffic volume, bandwidth, and proper placement of network functions. The NFV concept enables the implementation of VNFs independently of specific hardware. We can move VNFs to other devices and geographical locations; their life cycle is variable.

Proper use of location independence and strategic placement of VNFs can lead to architecture simplification and network optimization. We can demonstrate it in an example of packet switching in the mobile packet core [108]. Regarding the traditional design of these networks, the Packet Data Network Gateway (PGW) provides connectivity between User Equipment (UE) and the packet network. It is installed in centralized locations to minimize costs. It implies that all traffic, including device-to-device traffic, should be forwarded to the PGW, which often leads to congestion, delays, and suboptimal bandwidth consumption (Fig. 5.7).

To eliminate this problem, implementing the NFV concept and multiple virtual PGWs enables the creation of a more efficient mobile network design. We can place virtual PGWs closer to base stations (eNodeB in 4G and gNodeB in 5G networks), which is not feasible in traditional networks due to high costs. So, we achieve the optimal network design by implementing VNFs at the right locations, ensuring efficient bandwidth use, reducing latency and jitter, and avoiding eventual congestion (Fig. 5.8).

With the emergence of IoT technology, the widespread adoption of IoT devices, and high-definition video streaming, creating an optimal network design has

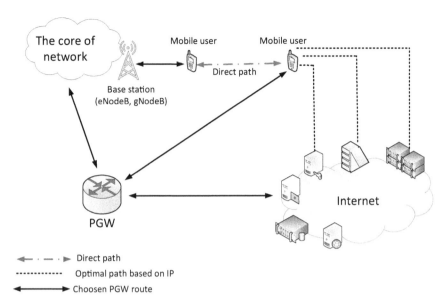

Figure 5.7. Centralized IP management in Traditional Mobile networks.

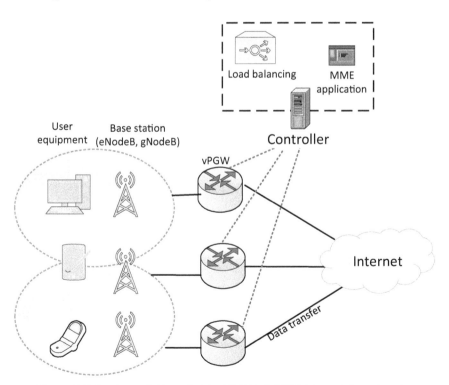

Figure 5.8. Implementation of virtual PGWs (vPGWs) in mobile networks.

become much more significant. The authors in [4] and [103] state that the data from IoT nodes will reach 400 zettabytes. They explain that data analysis from IoT sources has an important role in the modern data-based economy. However, there are more efficient solutions than using cloud resources. The most optimal location for storing, analyzing, and processing this data is the closest to the data sources. It indicates the need to develop fog computing and implement network functions and computing elements near the data source. Today, most data belong to mobile devices as data sources, such as smart devices and smart cars. These devices require network resources to be moved between different fog locations in real-time, based on demand and according to circumstances. All this affects the importance of NFV implementation in cloud and fog infrastructure design.

5.2 Lifecycle Management and Licensing Costs

The life cycle of VNFs must be analyzed from the aspect of each phase individually, including instantiation, monitoring, scaling, updating, and termination [110]. Certain hardware resources are allocated during each phase to create VNFs. If there is no need for a VNF, its resources should be released and allocated to other VNFs needing them. The rational usage of hardware resources is not the only reason to take care of the optimal management of the VNF life cycle. Another important reason is the licensing costs, which arise with the launch of the VNF (Fig. 5.9).

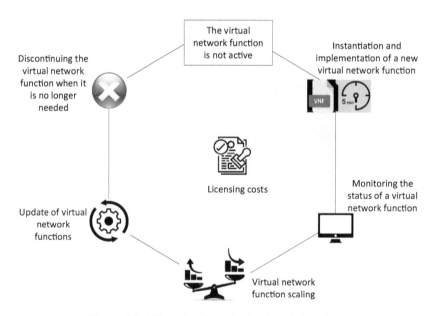

Figure 5.9. Lifecycle of a virtual network functions.

We must emphasize that until the emergence of the NFV concept, network equipment vendors traditionally tied their income to the sale of hardware. With the implementation of NFV, the focus of their business has shifted to software. It means that licensing fees become the base for generating revenue. They usually depend on the characteristics of the virtual function, the number of instances, and capacity. For this reason, during the network design process, we must implement algorithms within the NFV infrastructure orchestrator that consider the optimal number of required virtual instances, capacity, and characteristics [111].

Besides optimal lifecycle management of VNFs, we must consider a multi-tenancy approach. It implies the possibility of grouping users, so-called tenants, who require the same network function on one part of the infrastructure. Applying the NFV to a shared infrastructure makes it possible to implement multiple VNFs simultaneously, meeting different user requirements, such as service level or degree of isolation [112].

5.2.1   Lifecycle Management and Automation

VNFs are software applications representing instances created and modified on demand and near real-time. Each instance has a life cycle, with the ability to dynamically change according to new requirements, e.g., in terms of quality of service, network performance, or at the request of a superior management system. The support for system automation, which manages the lifecycle of VNFs, is the prerequisite for achieving most NFV benefits. Implementing automation mechanisms involves pre-defined workflows and policies that determine our actions based on certain criteria.

To automate changes in the lifecycle of VNFs, the abstraction of life cycle functions such as a lifecycle manager (LM) is necessary. This manager's role is to present management functions as interfaces for application programming. This way, enabling programmatic control via higher-order functions such as NFV orchestrators is possible. Lifecycle APIs represent the base for automating the VNFs' lifecycle management. Their wider application opens the way to a DevOps model for designing, implementing, and managing services based on the NFV [113].

Today, the industry is flooded with numerous NFV orchestration solutions. These solutions differ from each other to a greater or lesser extent, primarily because of the lack of MANO standardization. In modern networks, there are usually two open-source solutions for NFV orchestration: ONAP and OSM. Also, we can meet other commercial solutions, some combining open-source and proprietary components. At the same time, others are completely proprietary software (Huawei Cloud Opera, HPE Network and service director, Cisco NSO, Amdocs NCSO, and Netcracker AVP) [1, 114]. Many non-standard solutions have positive and negative implications for the industry, two of which are particularly important:

- Vendors face loose ETSI specifications for the VNFM northbound interface and interpret them differently, and the path to standardization is very long.
- Many vendors offer complete solutions that include VNF, VIM (e.g., VMware or OpenStack), VNFM, NFVO, and a service orchestrator. These comprehensive solutions are pre-integrated and ready for turnkey implementation. Such solutions need clearer functional demarcations between modules such as VNFM and EM. In practice, problems often occur when components from different manufacturers need to be connected (e.g., duplication of some functionalities and inability to integrate).

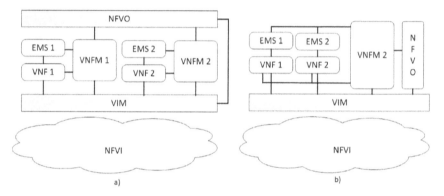

Figure 5.10. Dedicated VNFM approach (a) and generic VNFM approach (b).

Starting from ETSI recommendations and in the context of life cycle management of VNFs, there are two system approaches [1]:

- The vendor delivers VNFM and solutions for VNFs together (Fig. 5.10.a).
- A generic VNFM or a set of generic VNFMs with the ability to manage a set of VNFs can be created (Fig. 5.10.b).

Each of the mentioned approaches has its advantages and shortcomings. In both cases, the VNFM is connected to the NFVO via the northbound interface and to the VIM via the northbound interface. Providers that opt for a dedicated VNFM face the challenge of multiple integrations. Each VNFM must integrate with NFVO and VIM, where individual VNFMs may even have different levels of lifecycle management capabilities. The NFVO must compensate for these differences, and in some cases, it can be a problem. The reason is the complex nature of NFVOs, whose primary responsibility is to manage end-to-end chains of virtual network services rather than managing individual VNFs. In contrast to this approach, a solution based on a generic VNFM is simpler from the architecture perspective. The problem of provider dependency on the vendor can arise here.

5.2.2   Deployment of DevOps in NFV-based Networks

The NFV concept brings significant changes in networking supported in parallel by two main software development trends: DevOps and open software development. DevOps compatibility with open software creates the necessary prerequisites for adapting NFV to any new change and quickly implementing NFV in the design and implementation phases [115]. The role of DevOps is to separate modern software development from the traditional model, where development and operational processes operate in tandem. Instead, DevOps encourages open communication and simultaneous execution of all tasks.

This software development approach represents a challenge. To tackle it, VNF software development teams must know the operating environment in which they must implement their components. It is the only way providers can get systems to deal with frequent VNF software changes. An important aspect of this solution is that the requirements for managing VNFs are defined early during the design phase. We must supplement these requirements with rules for starting management routines automatically.

The mechanism for lifecycle management automation is driven by two key entities: the VNFD and the automation components. A VNFD is a text file containing instructions for deploying and operating a particular VNF and the policies and instructions needed to automate its life cycle. For example, a VNFD describes infrastructure resources, options for configuring certain VNF instances, instructions for autoscaling with parameters to monitor, rules to trigger the scaling function, and which software components to scale. Examples of VNFD modeling languages are OpenStack/Heat Orchestration Template (HOT), Ubuntu Juju, and OASIS TOSCA. Besides VNFD, life cycle management automation requires additional automation components. Their task is to construct automation routines and enable orderly execution, handling exceptions and outages. We introduce VNFD into automation components to automate the life cycle functions. These automation components are responsible for the execution or orchestration of necessary workflows. Guidelines for executing scripts and automation workflows are also encoded in the VNFD. In practice, there are various tools for developing these automation components. Figure 5.11 shows examples of tools, such as Ansible, Puppet, Chef, OpenStack Mistral, SaltStack, and Yang [116, 117]. The variety of integration tools and approaches, shown in Fig. 5.11, represents a challenge that can introduce confusion but lead to market fragmentation. The lack of standardization of modeling languages and tools affects vendors to develop solutions considering most or all options. The vendors model VNFs and define interfaces to accelerate the automation of the industry's VNF lifecycle and make DevOps truly effective.

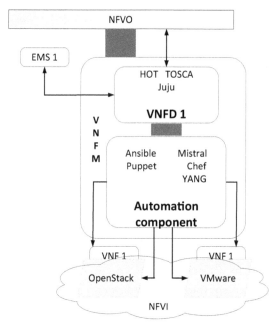

Figure 5.11. Variety of tools to automate the VNF lifecycle [115].

5.3 VNF Performance – Throughput and Delays

From the network aspect, the key requirement related to VNFs is ensuring adequate data throughput and enabling the desired data transfer speeds. With traditional hardware (Fig. 5.12), significant values of data flow can be achieved using Application-Specific Integrated Circuits (ASICs) and fast processors. The goal is to ensure that ASIC code handles most (and even all packets) instead of software. In this way, it is possible to achieve a higher throughput. In exceptional cases, when this is not possible, the software processes the packets at the cost of lower performance.

The NFV focuses on software without deploying specialized hardware to process packets. Data packets are inherently processed in software. The code that processes the packets is part of VNF software that runs on a general-purpose CPU unit on the server hardware. Introducing special software techniques into the VNFs compensates for the lack of specialized hardware. They aim to use more advanced packet processing algorithms to perform better than hardware-based processing techniques. It is important to highlight the importance of delay and jitter on data transmission performance, especially for services that require real-time transmission, such as voice and multimedia. Therefore, providing a virtual CPU unit for each VNF is useful to avoid degradation of packet processing performance.

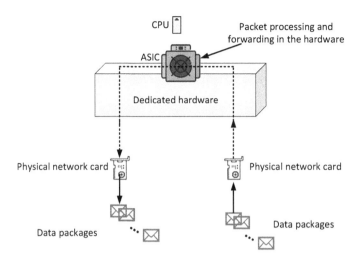

Figure 5.12. Packet processing on traditional network devices.

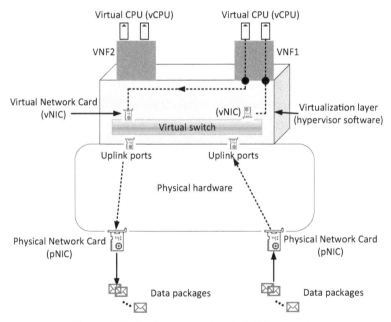

Figure 5.13. Packet processing in NFV networks.

We must emphasize that virtualization introduces additional overhead that can slow down packet processing and affect data flow to a greater or lesser extent. In the shared infrastructure, the virtualization layer acts as an intermediary inter-face between physical and virtual hardware (Fig. 5.13). Communication between VNFs is also important and usually occurs via the hypervisor. Then, virtual inter-face drivers are used instead of drivers for communication with physical network interface cards (pNIC) [1, 118]. This communication affects the performance of data processing speed. As an alternative solution, we can use paravirtualization, which implies that the pNIC drivers are included in the VNF software, reducing performance degradation and affecting the complete solution's flexibility.

5.3.1 VNF Instantiation Time

The time required to run a physical machine, i.e., to load the operating system into the host's main memory or RAM, is higher than the time necessary to run a virtual machine with the VNF or to reboot the system. Considering that VNF is running in a virtual environment, the execution time of the mentioned actions depends on factors such as virtualization technique and the characteristics of virtual machines or virtual containers [119]. Different from these factors, which have a predictable impact on VNFs, there are also factors whose influence could be more challenging to predict, such as the physical machine CPU load, the available memory on the hard disk, and the response time of the orchestrator. We must note that the time required to run, reboot, or remove a running container is shorter than that required to start or reboot virtual machines. Individual factors or combinations can seriously affect the time required to instantiate or remove VNFs. The timely instantiation of VNFs is crucial for NFV to achieve desired characteristics. It primarily refers to the VNFs' availability and deployment at a time when immediate creation or removal of VNFs is required. In such circumstances, just a few extra seconds or milliseconds can produce a serious problem in the network design.

5.3.2 Infrastructure Reliability

To create an effective network environment, the software vendors must demonstrate a certain level of flexibility. The unreliability of the software components can negatively affect the complete infrastructure. For this reason, vendors must be ready to validate software in different environments. NFV prefers COTS hardware, and infrastructure stability is crucial for network design, significantly influencing software selection. In practice, more than reliable software and a robust hardware platform, it is necessary to establish a stable multivendor hardware and software infrastructure. We insist on integration testing and validation of implemented solutions to achieve the required stability.

We can choose a solution that combines scalable hardware, a complete operating system, and a hypervisor. The advantage of such a solution is the successful compatibility test and the suppliers' support contracts. This way, it can enable the path for a faster NFV implementation. Examples of such solutions that offer a fully integrated NFVI system, including a server for virtualization, storage, and networking, are FlexPOD (NetApp) and Vblock (VCE) [1].

5.3.3   High Availability and Stability

High hardware and software availability in traditional networks is generally limited to a single vendor responsible for most network errors. The NFV changes this concept because it allows different vendors to deliver software and hardware. Vendors develop solutions that implement other mechanisms to ensure high availability and create NFV-based designs to provide a reliability level of "five 9" (99.999%). Their task is to assess software resilience, i.e., the software's ability to recover from unexpected events. Vendors must be able to change the architecture when needed to achieve high availability and stability.

We use the term "carrier-class" hardware and services for hardware and software components that are extremely reliable, well-tested, and with proven capabilities [1, 28]. Such solutions offer high availability, fault tolerance, and low impact on failures. It is necessary to implement redundancy in the network to achieve optimal elasticity. For example, resolving a failure within 50 ms is required when traffic loss occurs. Availability represents the percentage of the time when the system is active and fully available. For example, 99.999% means that the system must experience at most 5.256 minutes of unexpected downtime during the year.

NFV-based solutions can be multi-layered, and identifying problems can take time because it is necessary to collect information from different systems, correlate them, and locate errors (e.g., the hypervisor or the host operating system). The NFV network's stability requires examining many components, including the server hardware, hypervisor, host operating system, and VNF software. Also, it is necessary to consider challenges related to ensuring the system's elasticity and moving the VNF to another network location.

5.3.4   Security

A security benefit of applying NFVs is the possibility of improving network security by creating security zones and implementing different protection methods. It primarily refers to IDS implemented as VNFs. It usually implies the implementation of firewalls that detect attacks or Distributed denial of service (DDoS) scrubbers. Usually, we can deploy scrubbers near the source to protect the user's Internet traffic from DDoS attacks. The goal is that users stay online during attacks without service loss. The traffic is the object of real-time analysis, where "traffic scrubbing" filters remove malicious traffic and forward "clean" traffic. The protection concept in NFV-based networks is complex. This complexity is due to network architecture and the potential vulnerabilities, which can occur at different levels. For example, it can be the vulnerability of hardware, hypervisors, containers, and VNFs [116]. A weakness at any layer can lead to security threats at other layers. We must perform security measures at every layer, and access must be granted only to authorized users.

It is necessary to place virtual firewalls at multiple levels to provide protection against intrusions and block the potential attacker's access (Fig. 5.14). As in traditional networks, particular VNF instances can protect other network functions (VNFs) from possible attacks. We must note that virtual machines on physical hosts are also targets. The attackers can exploit open ports through the hypervisor to gain unauthorized access. Therefore, before the hypervisor, the so-called introspective virtual firewall is tasked with protecting the flow of packets to each virtual machine. The physical infrastructure and host operating systems must be protected. In this sense, the firewalls that work independently of introspective and VNF firewalls are implemented.

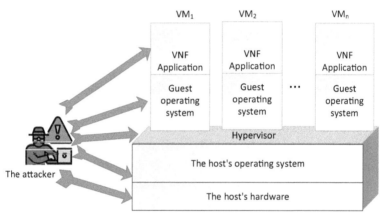

Figure 5.14. Potential vulnerability points in NFV networks.

The previously mentioned protection methods in NFV-based networks represent best practices. They cannot solve every security issue in NFV networks. We must implement other security measures, such as a standard interface in the ETSI NFV architecture, allowing security VNFs to respond to potential attacks in real-time. It is necessary to have a communication channel with orchestration modules and to follow the appropriate instructions. Another issue concerns the secure management and VNFs monitoring and configuration during migration to another virtual entity. Solving this issue is a challenge for the cloud environment, given the dynamism and elasticity of VNF operations. In addition to all the above, trust must exist between hardware and software vendors so that the final product works reliably.

5.4   Migration From Traditional to NFV Infrastructure

The migration from traditional to NFV-based infrastructure represents a natural path of evolution in computing. This path leads to significant changes, which cannot be viewed only from the perspective of technology. It is also necessary to look at the novelties in the management procedures for operating processes and the business model. We must begin with incremental migration and make appropriate changes to traditional network architecture. This approach certainly leads to the parallel coexistence of conventional and NFV-based solutions. The overlap is possible, and from a technical point of view, it represents a serious challenge. It is necessary to enable the existing solutions to continue functioning normally and to build a network environment without obstacles to NFV implementation. The phased migration must be planned, created, managed, and operated according to a comprehensive integration plan to avoid potential overlaps. The plan must consist of precisely defined steps in replacing hardware with software-based network functions, including a timeline and risk management, to achieve maximum benefit from NFV implementation.

A special challenge is the management of a heterogeneous network infrastructure consisting of traditional and NFV-based environments because of their huge differences. Users must know that transformation to a fully NFV-based network is not instant. Management systems must continue to deal with obsolete equipment, and the interoperability problem can become dominant. This issue indicates that managing NFV parts of the network requires significant agility and great dynamics. It is necessary to introduce a higher level of programmability into the network and automate many system processes. Improving the existing or applying new management tools is required to implement an NFV concept effectively. This way, we can achieve the advantages of NFV-based networks, such as elasticity, dynamic resource allocation, network reconfiguration, and service provisioning on demand.

Implementing the NFV concept in the network requires considering orchestration as another important concept strongly related to monitoring and managing network infrastructure. [120] This concept represents a significant novelty in networking because we can consider the management of modern computer environments from different aspects. Orchestration is possible at different levels, such as service orchestration, resource orchestration, technology orchestration, or customer orchestration. In practice, we can explain the orchestration as a server's ongoing selection and resource allocation to satisfy client demands according to optimization criteria. This concept is closely related to applying various artificial intelligence algorithms (Fig. 5.15).

Virtualized networks can span many networks, software elements, and hardware platforms, and NFV orchestration must be powerful and able to work at different layers with many different standards. Figure 5.14 shows that orchestration software must communicate with the data plane resources to instantiate a service, which means it creates the virtual instance of a service on the network. This software makes instructions for VNF interconnection in any desired order, and new VNFs can be

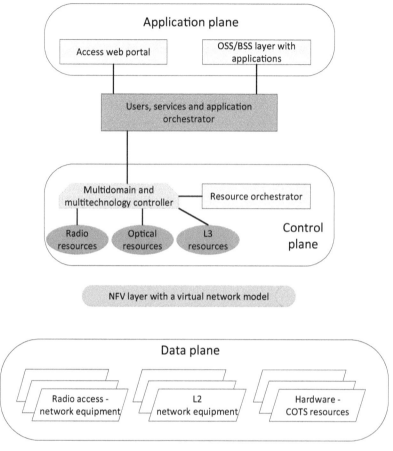

Figure 5.15. Orchestration in NFV-based networks.

instantiated and added to the data or control traffic's path quickly. The emergence of more and more services requires that the orchestration software track the performances and network resources (radio, optical, and L3 resources) to ensure service delivery and must be able to perform multidomain and multi-technology control. Finally, in the application plan, it is necessary to provide service, applications, and user orchestration.

NFV networks grow, change, and evolve incredibly, representing challenges. For this reason, we should provide a systematic approach to network design. It is a prerequisite to achieving all the advantages of efficient NFV implementation. Today's application management still needs adequate responses to all challenges, and most tools should adapt to the vendors' NFV solutions. The customization process is complex and must include more than tools and software. It must consist of training employees in the network operations team. The mentioned complexity comes from the fact that the proper functioning of the NFV system implies effective management and monitoring at multiple levels (i.e., various tools and employees trained to work with hypervisor software, host operating systems, or VNFs). ETSI framework defines several sub-blocks within the MANO system, such as virtualized network functions manager, NFV orchestrator, and virtual infrastructure manager (Fig. 5.16) [121]. Although the control systems in these sub-blocks function independently, they must communicate effectively to manage the entire NFV network infrastructure.

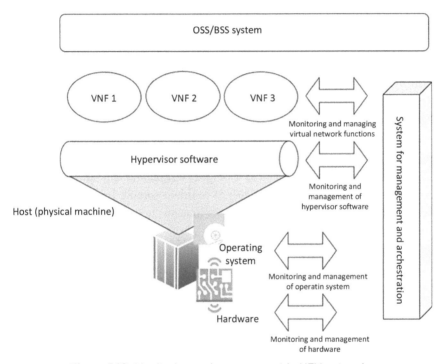

Figure 5.16. Monitoring and management in NFV networks.

5.5 Resource Constraints

Virtualization technology enables resource sharing and isolation between virtual entities. In some cases, the isolation is not full, and failure on one virtual machine can cause a resource loss, affecting all virtual machines created on that host. We call this phenomenon the "noisy neighbor effect," and it represents a specific deficiency concerning the traditional architecture of computer systems [1]. This problem is even more evident with containerization technology. Virtual containers share the kernel of the same operating system, and their isolation is weaker than between virtual machines. The problem must be solved by defining stronger boundaries, sharing resources more efficiently, and applying mechanisms to ensure high availability at the virtualization layer.

A particular challenge in NFV-based networks is fault detection and problem-solving, which requires troubleshooting at multiple levels. Failure that occurs at one architecture level can cause problems at other levels. For example, lower-level shortcomings, such as host CPU overload, noisy neighbor effect, or hypervisor crash, can create higher-level problems and degrade the VNFs' performance. Debugging only on the VNF is insufficient, and it is necessary to identify the root cause of the problem. It is possible only if we examine the functioning of the hypervisor and the host operating system.

VNF problems are software-based, and solving them is very complex, considering the dynamic character of VNFs and the fact that different vendors can develop VNF software. NFV brings independence in implementing VNFs, which is a significant benefit. Implementing VNF software developed by other vendors and defining a common set of APIs and models for managing VNFs is possible. However, besides information obtained using APIs, it may be necessary to provide additional information to solve the problem. As a simple example, we can take the absence of routing in the network. The basic level of problem-solving involves checking the routing table and routing protocol implementation. It is evident that it is insufficient to identify the problem's cause and that it is necessary to analyze the VNF configurations. Independence from VNF vendors can represent a serious challenge in troubleshooting since it is dynamic and developed by different vendors. It implies the usage of operational tools that can interpret messages from other devices and be aware of the device lifecycle state. Most operators rely on alarms, system logs, and employees with the necessary troubleshooting skills. Standard monitoring techniques, such as the Simple Network Monitoring Protocol (SNMP), can be used for troubleshooting to a limited extent.

5.6 Virtualization of Network Infrastructure and Services

Network function virtualization has emerged as a solution, where we implement network services as software-implemented network functions located in data centers, network nodes, or even on virtual machines. Theoretically, the NFV concept can be applied to any network function to simplify the management of heterogeneous hardware platforms [15]. It is particularly important to note the advantages of traffic routing as one of the basic network functions, where IPv4 and IPv6 can work in parallel. NFV concept cannot benefit network devices whose primary function is high-speed packet switching. It brings advantages primarily to network infrastructure for traffic routing, where it is necessary to ensure a rational usage of processing power and memory.

5.6.1   Virtualization of Traffic Routing Infrastructure

Devices like top-of-the-rack (ToR) switches, routers that provide interconnection between provider networks, or NFVI PoPs (Point of Presence) provide packet forwarding and aggregation into the network infrastructure. These devices cannot be candidates for NFV implementation in the initial phase [1]. Other devices, such as BGP route reflectors, routers in operator or LAN networks, and voice and video gateways, are required to ensure location flexibility [122]. Optimization of processing power or dynamic change of available memory capacity is essential for them. We can explain it using the example of a BGP network and the route reflector (RR) as a key control plane functionality. BGP RR is suitable for NFV-based implementation, while CPU and memory usage have significant importance. The RR's main task is to support route management and avoid edge device overload. Virtualizing RRs for each service makes it possible to respond to this task, simplifying implementation without compromising performance and providing high availability.

In networks covering large geographical areas, we implement route reflectors on a regional basis, as close as possible to the edge routers. The increase in network services imposes a new question: Can one route reflector be rationally and efficiently used for all services, and can it save all routes? It cannot; therefore, one reflector per network service is usually implemented as a solution. The provision of redundancies is good practice, leading to an increase in the number of devices and the allocation of significantly higher processing power and memory. Resources such as memory or CPU performance become a bottleneck in traditional networks, and the only choice is to replace the network device [123].

The BGP route reflector represents an excellent example of NFV implementation, which can overcome the problems mentioned. With the virtualization of each BGP route reflector (for each network service) and the creation of the VNFs, we can implement virtual route reflectors (vRRs) redundantly on one or different hosts. It also implies the possibility of permanently shifting vRR to other locations closer to the group of edge devices they serve. Figure 5.17 shows the application of vRR functionality in the NFV-based network without compromising routing performances. The complete independence and high availability of each vRR enable the required level of flexibility and scalability in the network. This way, every time there is a request for a new network service, it is optional (not necessary) to change hardware or the entire platform and install new BGP vRRs. NFV concept will allow time-saving and quick implementation of a new VNF without significantly impacting performance.

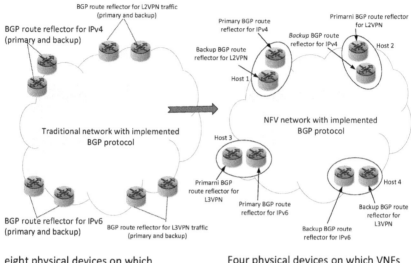

eight physical devices on which   Four physical devices on which VNFs
network services are implemented   (network services) are implemented

Figure 5.17. Transition to NFV networks with virtual BGP route reflectors.

Due to the requirements of many users, the provider edge (PE) equipment is usually configured with different services and provides numerous functions [31]. We install everything on one physical device, multiservice edge, to reduce operational and capital costs. This way, we can eliminate the need for multiple routers per service, but this approach has many limitations. For example, adding a new function and service causes changes that can affect the equipment's performance. From the high-availability aspect, a PE equipment failure can simultaneously affect multiple users and their services, except for a dual-homed device configuration.

NFV can eliminate potential problems by building network environments where users and services do not share PE equipment. By implementing VNFs, we create conditions to apply services in a virtual PE environment (vPE services). In this way, we can perform independent VNF scaling and management and implement it with other services offered for the same user. So, vPE services based on creating VNFs can be individually scaled, improved, tuned, managed, and upgraded. For example, we can consider a vPE router usually located between the access and operator's core network. As shown in Fig. 5.18, this router handles traffic in both directions and depending on the traffic direction, its functionality changes during packet processing. Packets for the core network can be filtered, classified, and used to measure quality parameters. In contrast, traffic for the access network is shaped according to the subscription policy [1].

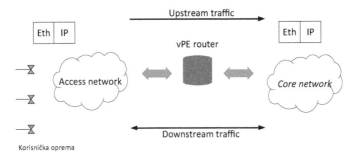

Figure 5.18. Implementation of VNF at the edge of the operator's network.

Unlike vRR, the VNF implemented in PE must take care of control traffic and user packets. Choosing a vPE router is closely related to providing a suitable VNF. Besides guaranteeing the quality of service, routing functions must consider other functions that the operator must support in the multiservice edge. It is important to emphasize that the problem with this device cannot affect all users and services. The creation of VNFs aims to isolate the issues and resolve them faster by adding a new VNF.

In enterprise networks, connections and all communications between branches are mostly performed via the central office equipment (COE). Devices at branch locations, as well as COE, are physical devices, and they provide connectivity functions such as routing, NAT, and QoS provisioning. The network administrators are responsible for any change, such as adding new functionality. In the past, replacement or device upgrades have long been the only solution. It made adding new services expensive and slow, usually resulting in a loss of time and revenue. Virtualization of equipment at user locations enables the improvement of routing functionality. It allows management transfer to the operator's side (Fig. 5.19), and the

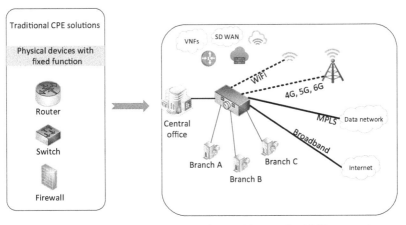

Figure 5.19. The enterprise network transition to the NVF concept.

operator can add new functionality and delete or modify the existing one on user demand. [124]. This way, a double advantage can be achieved: the user gets the desired QoE, and the operator increases revenue.

5.6.2   Virtual Load Balancer

Virtual load balancers (vLB) in NFV-based networks flexibly distribute the work-load on multiple network servers, requiring software installation on the virtualized infrastructure. For example, we can use the existing software running on the phys-ical machine and move it to the virtual machine (Fig. 5.20) [125].

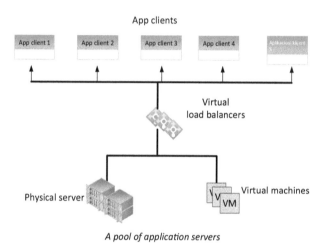

Figure 5.20. Virtual load balancer [125].

vLB that enables load balancing by taking the software of a physical device and running it on a virtual machine is a short-term solution. The reasons are the archi-tectural challenges of traditional hardware devices, such as limitations related to scalability and automation and the need for central management. Centralized man-agement includes separating the control and data planes in data centers. By taking code from legacy hardware and running it on a virtual machine, we still gain a monolithic load balancer for workload distribution with static capacity.

We can implement vLBs as VNFs, which means they can be added and config-ured on demand [1], allowing virtualized servers to achieve full efficiency. VNFs will enable applications on virtual machines to create a replica on any server within its scope and redirect traffic. The vLBs do not have to be located near physical servers (Networks, 2023) to manage packet traffic and distribute user requests (Fig. 5.21).

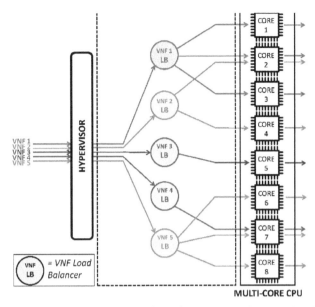

Figure 5.21. Virtual load balancer based on VNF implementation [126].

5.6.3   Network Security Virtualization

Different mechanisms can be implemented in the networks to guarantee network security. Many of them, firewalls, IDS, various methods of protection against DDoS attacks, data scrubbing functions (procedures to modify or remove incomplete, incorrect, incorrectly formatted, or repeated data), and DPI, can have added value if they are virtualized [1, 127]. We can implement VNF applications that provide these mechanisms in different and strategically important locations.

Network infrastructure protection, especially against DDoS, is important to network security and service availability. Sending a huge number of packets (volumetric attacks) or using protocol vulnerabilities (application attacks) can cause enormous damage. These attacks must be detected early, and suspicious traffic must be redirected to locations for filtration. Depending on the type of DDoS attack, the detection and cleaning of malicious packets should occur as close to the network boundary as possible or to the protected network device. Placing network devices to detect and clean malicious packets in many locations generates costs and forces network designers to be selective about their placement. Therefore, virtualizing these functions eliminates limitations and enables positioning DDoS attack protection mechanisms in VNFs implemented on peering network points, transit points, and network devices (including firewalls, routers, and servers). These VNFs can be easily moved and added to other locations along the traffic path as needed without disrupting the existing NFV network design.

We can provide security in traditional networks by implementing a firewall at the network's edge to prevent malicious access [1]. This concept can be a bottleneck in some cases. The firewall's capacity, capability, and positioning are very important when applying the NFV because the virtual firewall can be placed closer to the hosts and not just at the network's edge. In addition to the possibility of increasing and decreasing the capacity of virtual firewalls depending on the traffic, it is also possible to choose the provider that offers this VNF.

IDS and IPS are required to inspect the traffic path. They can block unwanted content or detect suspicious actions that do not comply with the guidelines. The NFV concept is a natural solution for these applications and can help in different ways. It enables a simple solution through elasticity and easy upgrade to new network requirements and thus offers better network infrastructure security (the examples of products are Cisco Next-generation IPS - NGIPSv and IBM Security Network IPS) [128].

5.7   Conclusion

Traditional networks use proprietary networking equipment that is expensive and difficult to scale. It makes these networks costly and unmanageable to deploy new technologies, manage large numbers of endpoints, or migrate to new applications. NFV-based networks aim to change that by implementing network functions independent of hardware and equipment vendors. With VNF implementation, network services become software running on commodity hardware, which we can move from one network location to another. This way creates a generic infrastructure characterized by the scalability and elasticity of VNFs. The basic requirement for such a shared environment is great flexibility in resource allocation for individual software applications because it is impossible to predict all hardware resource requirements that can arise during exploitation.

In NFV-based networks, we can add, remove, and transfer VNFs in software. Such flexibility is possible to achieve using open APIs, which provide third-party software with a documented and publicly available way to access and download data from the application or to pass the application parameters necessary for configuration. Implementing open APIs enables various orchestration and management tools to control the deployment and lifecycle of VNFs. In the next section, we highlight the similarity between NFV and SDN because both technologies abstract networks through virtualization. There are certain differences related to function separation and resource abstraction, which will be explained.

DOI: 10.1561/9781638283591.ch6

Chapter 6

NFV and Software-defined Networking

Most computer networks still have the traditional, three-layer, hierarchically organized architecture. Their extremely heterogeneous infrastructure consists of multi-
vendor devices, and networking is often challenging. Deficiency of interoperability
in most cases burdens their work. The reason is many proprietary protocols and
their slow standardization process. It indicates the complexity of the network management process. We must note that in a traditional network, the management
process takes place within the same physical device as the packet forwarding. It
can cause potential issues such as resource contention (both packet forwarding
and management tasks compete for resources like CPU, memory, and network
interfaces), complexity in maintenance, security risks, scalability challenges, and
isolation of control (separating management from packet forwarding). Numerous
functionalities defined in hardware make responding to increasingly multiple and
complex user requests more difficult. The lack of flexibility in traditional networks
affects the high cost of implementing new services because it is necessary to allocate additional resources, and maintaining the computer infrastructure becomes
more complex. Modern societal trends, such as demographic trends, globaliza-
tion, and lifestyle changes, stimulated by the rapid development of information

and communication technologies (ICT), represent the basic triggers for numerous network design changes. These changes are visible in the emergence of new traffic types, such as M2M (Machine-to-Machine) communication, requirements to build smart environments based on IoT (Internet of Things) technology, and significant traffic volume increases in the network.

It is necessary to introduce a significantly higher level of programmability in network infrastructure to build a more flexible and scalable computing environment. To accomplish these requirements, we introduce SDN functionality in networks [129, 130], which should enable:

- reduction of network complexity and simpler administration by implementing hardware with a unique software interface,
- providing optimal job scheduling between hardware and software and decrease network latency,
- increasing infrastructure reliability and elasticity by enabling dynamic resource allocation as a prerequisite for faster and easier service implementation,
- complete user mobility.

6.1   Software-defined Networking

The traditional computer network architecture characterizes a high degree of non-openness and complex integration of various computer systems. A specific challenge, slower packet forwarding, occurs using specialized hardware with proprietary routing protocols that analyze packets at each network node (Fig. 6.1).

The basic idea of the SDN is to open up computer systems. To achieve this, SDN separates the control from the data plane and centralizes the management process. This way, it isolates the forwarding process from the network management and consolidates control within a software-based controller (Fig. 6.2). By centralizing the control plane in software, the actual network devices can be less complex, essentially becoming forwarding devices that follow instructions from the centralized controller.

The centralization of network intelligence in one place, in the SDN controller [130], is a fundamental part of this networking concept. The aim is to build and maintain a global network picture, significantly simplifying decision-making. So, the SDN controller makes decisions based on the view of the complete network infrastructure and not on its particular elements. From the application's point of view, the network acts as one big logical switch (Fig. 6.3).

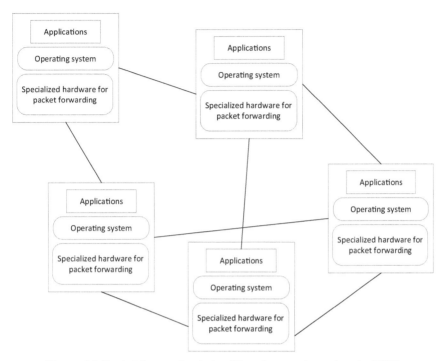

Figure 6.1. Packet forwarding in traditional computer networks [130].

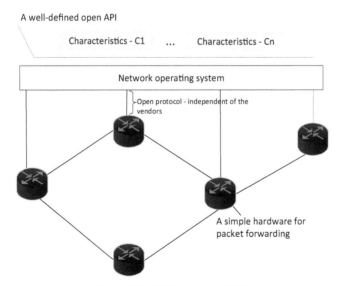

Figure 6.2. SDN concept [130].

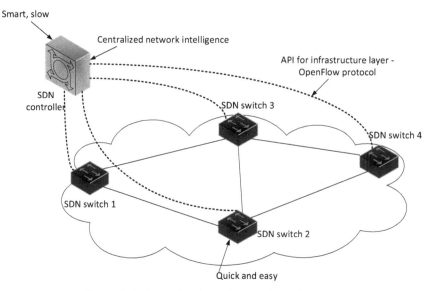

Figure 6.3. Centralization of network intelligence.

The implementation of SDN-based solutions introduces two important features in computer networks:

- Higher programmability – software-based network management and open APIs enable automatic configuration and network resource optimization, regardless of the device vendor.
- Implementation of device-independent network applications – implies the ability to move them from one network location to another.

6.1.1   Architecture of SDN Network

SDN-based computer networks have a three-layer architecture (Fig. 6.4) composed of [131]:

- Application layer – contains user applications and applications for service orchestration,
- Control layer – provides centralized control and monitoring of traffic forwarding using OpenFlow or another protocol for communication with the infrastructure layer and
- Infrastructure layer – consists of virtual and physical elements that forward traffic according to instructions that the SDN controller sends via an open communication protocol.

The SDN controller is responsible for centralized management, aiming to provide optimal network performances programmatically. The additional benefit of

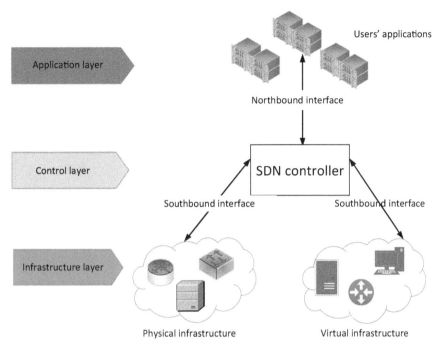

Figure 6.4. Architecture of SDN network.

SDN technology is the possibility to perform some form of software automation. Software automation based on artificial intelligence (AI) allows the implementation of different solutions, including those that occur due to some kind of orchestration in the network (e.g., orchestration of users, services, resources, and technologies). The software control of the network represents the most significant advantage obtained by SDN technology, considering the requirements for modern networks (Fig. 6.5). It is especially related to requirements such as greater agility and scalability, faster implementation of new services, and optimization of operating costs [1]. Maximizing the use of automated tools and applications has made it possible to fulfill the demands of users and their applications. Traditional networks, with many specific devices and operating systems, offer limited support for deploying external devices that could make automated decisions based on network logic.

Traditional networks are a serious obstacle to developing and deploying resource-demanding applications and scripts that automate configuration and management processes. The main prerequisite for removing obstacles is to open a very heterogeneous network infrastructure composed of different vendors' equipment. SDN is a technology that offers solutions based on open standards, and its goal is to eliminate dependence on vendors' equipment. This way, it is possible to break all kinds of monopolies established by using proprietary protocols and the inability

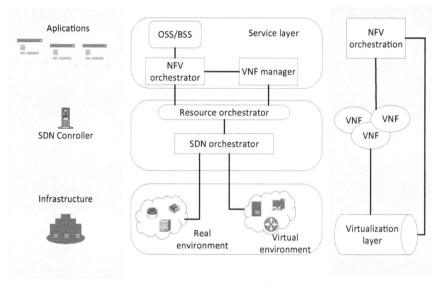

Figure 6.5. Orchestration in SDN/NFV networks.

to program devices easily [132]. The key task of SDN is to dislocate the control function from the network devices, which implicitly solves the interoperability issue caused by vendors' dependency on the control plane. Successful communication between different layers of SDN architecture is possible only using two groups of standards:

- Northbound API – standards for communication between the application and control layer,
- Southbound API – standards for communication between the control and infrastructure layer.

6.2   SDN Deployment Models

Several SDN deployment models exist in computer networks. Some users completely replace the traditional (physical) with a virtual infrastructure. However, the high replacement cost significantly influences most users to opt for other methods. It primarily refers to large computer networks, where users, in addition to implementation costs, generally think about the speed of the implementation as a key criterion for achieving SDN technology goals. To accomplish the SDN benefits, overcome the complexity and limitations of existing infrastructure, and satisfy specific operational needs, providers usually decide to implement a hybrid network infrastructure or overlay networks where traditional networks overlap with SDN functionalities. Implementing SDN functionality via API is also used, but less frequently [133].

6.2.1 Open SDN

The open SDN model represents the classical approach based on control plane separation from the data (packet forwarding) plane. However, in practice, most traditional network devices do not have this possibility, so users decide to replace conventional devices with SDN devices and replace the local control plane with the appropriate SDN control layer [134]. The task of this layer is to establish communication with the data plane via the SDN protocol and to manage its processes directly (Fig. 6.6).

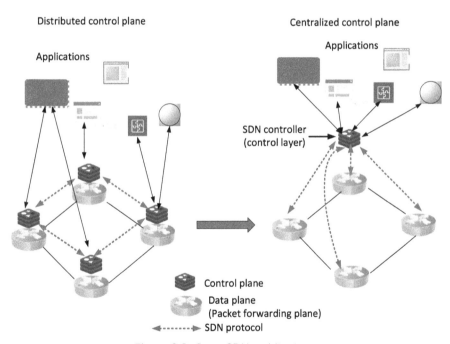

Figure 6.6. Open SDN architecture.

SDN and NFV are technologies backed by the community, which propagates open-source solutions and the deployment of open standards [135]. A better understanding of open-source solutions is closely related to the Open SDN model goals. These goals are the programmability of the control plane and the abstraction of network applications through the control plane separation from the packet forwarding plane. Achieving these goals means communication independence from vendors and establishing interoperability between physical and virtual devices. This way,

we can enable constant visibility of network flows and create a unique and programmable framework for device management, ultimately leading to management
automation.

It is important to note that Open SDN implementation implies the deployment
of everything that determines openness, such as [136]:

- Open standards – generally available specifications for software and hardware
  that are jointly developed and maintained through an open community (e.g.,
  OpenFlow standard),
- Open-source software – applications that are available to everyone so that
  they can be modified and improved (e.g., OpenDaylight software for the
  implementation of control layer functions),
- Open hardware – design specifications of a physical object that are licensed
  so it can be created, modified, and distributed by anyone and
- Open API and software development tools – such as software development
  kits for program development, often define the mutual communication of
  software entities and even significantly facilitate software writing.

6.2.2 Hybrid SDN

Numerous challenges of a technical and financial nature accompany the full implementation of SDN functionality in computer networks. Despite the many advantages of SDN technology, in practice, we usually meet hybrid SDN architectures.
Building such infrastructures requires a strategy defining the incremental implementation of SDN functionality because companies and other organizations need
to provide the necessary financial resources to implement SDN. A hybrid SDN
network represents an intermediate solution because it implies the integration of
legacy and SDN devices that work in parallel and take advantage of both traditional
and SDN networks (Fig. 6.7) [137].

Building a hybrid SDN network implies replacing some parts of the traditional
equipment and gradually expanding the virtual network infrastructure that supports SDN (e.g., OpenFlow) protocols. The base of a hybrid SDN network architecture is the 3C model, which implies [137]:

1. Heterogeneity of the infrastructure in the data plane, control plane, or both
   planes,
2. Interaction between traditional and SDN devices to enable task distribution
   and functionality sharing in the data plane, control plane, or both planes and
3. Combination of different network technologies to minimize the cost, simplify the transition to the SDN environment, and implement the traffic policy, achieving optimal scalability and high-level robustness.

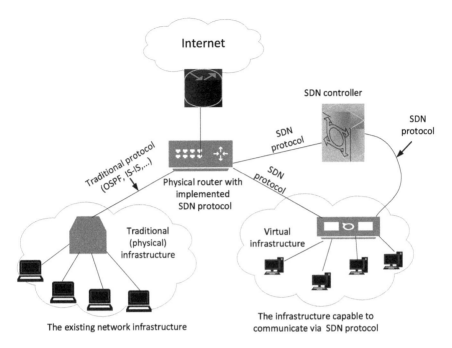

Figure 6.7. Hybrid SDN network [137].

In practice, we can meet four models of a hybrid SDN network (Fig. 6.8) [138]:

1. Topology-based hybrid SDN model – implies network partitioning into zones with several devices, and each device can be a member of only one zone (traditional or SDN zone),
2. Service-based hybrid SDN model – traditional and SDN devices provide different services. The provision of end-to-end services can require that two network paradigms simultaneously control a certain set of devices, while at the same time, only one network paradigm controls other devices (e.g., SDN controller),
3. Class-based hybrid SDN model – implies network partitioning into classes, which can control traditional or SDN paradigms (all network devices usually have both traditional and SDN functions),
4. Integrated hybrid SDN model – SDN is responsible for all network services and uses traditional network protocols as an interface to the Forwarding Information Base, which conventional devices use to forward packets.

A topology-based hybrid SDN model combines the SDN advantages, such as SDN's programmability and centralized control, with the insights gained from the physical network topology. This integration enables optimizing resource utilization, improving traffic engineering, and facilitating granular control over

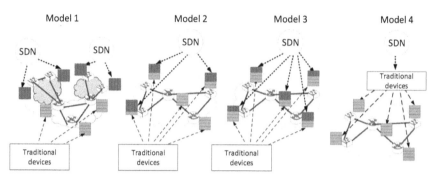

Figure 6.8. The implementation models of hybrid SDN [138, 139].

network elements. Leveraging topology-based insights within SDN allows for greater customization and programmability and brings the possibility to adapt network behaviors according to specific needs or applications based on the knowledge of the network's topology. Besides the mentioned advantages, this hybrid SDN model also has certain drawbacks. The complexity in integration can cause management issues and increase implementation and maintenance costs, create potential security risks due to system integration, dependency on vendor support and standards, operational hurdles in coordinating control and data planes, and limit scalability.

A service-based hybrid SDN model integrates service-oriented architecture with a centralized control plane, which orchestrates network services. By structuring the network into services and enabling dynamic orchestration, it facilitates the seamless delivery of diverse applications, optimizes resource allocation, and allows for incremental SDN adoption, ensuring a balance between stability and the advantages of programmability and centralized management. This model has some drawbacks that refer to integration complexities, including limited agility and scalability, management complexity, potential performance bottlenecks, interoperability challenges, and migration complexities.

A class-based hybrid SDN model optimizes network management by categorizing devices and traffic into classes managed via different SDN policies. SDN controller uses different protocols, with the aim of integrating traditional network devices and SDN components. Further, it implements policies for security and performance based on class distinctions, facilitates dynamic resource allocation and QoS mechanisms, and supports multi-tenancy. So, this model adopts network management to specific needs, balancing flexibility and efficiency across diverse network elements and traffic types. The main drawbacks of a class-based hybrid SDN model refer to the complexity of managing multiple classes with different protocols and potential interoperability issues among network devices. If the network rapidly expands, potential security challenges caused by varying access controls can occur.

The integrated hybrid SDN model uses an SDN controller to manage both SDN-enabled devices and legacy network devices. This approach introduces programmability and automation into existing infrastructure, with the aim of creating an adaptable, scalable, and flexible network architecture capable of dynamic modification and efficient management across the network infrastructure. The complexity of integration can lead to management challenges and operational difficulties. It mainly refers to the usage of different protocols and standards across network infrastructure, which can cause interoperability issues. The integration, where we use different networking technologies, can cause potential security vulnerabilities, significant financial investment, and ongoing resource allocation.

Building a hybrid SDN infrastructure is accompanied by certain limitations, such as the complexity of managing a heterogeneous control plane and problems translating traditional protocols to SDN protocols and vice versa. As a result of these limitations, we have that the reconfiguration process causes inconsistency in packet forwarding, which can lead to loops in packet forwarding and performance degradation in terms of delay and packet processing time [139]. Sometimes, the problem occurs if two or more controllers exist in a hybrid SDN infrastructure. In this case, there can be significant delays, issues with traffic engineering, and difficulty achieving the required level of scalability and even security. Implementing adequate traffic engineering in hybrid SDN is a challenge, especially considering some devices cannot support flow abstraction [140].

In practice, there are different approaches to building hybrid SDN infrastructure, one of which is the Panopticon approach [141]. This approach implies networking of traditional and SDN devices and traffic routing through an SDN switch controlled by an SDN controller. Another approach is building a hybrid SDN infrastructure by adding SDN devices instead of replacing traditional ones [142]. This way, we have networking between SDN and legacy devices; both control planes handle the traffic. The third approach introduces SDN functionality by installing the SDN shim hardware into legacy devices [143] to enable communication between an SDN controller and a modified legacy device.

6.2.3   SDN via API

As part of SDN implementation via API, some vendors have offered a solution that calls functions on remote devices (such as switches) using conventional methods such as SNMP protocol or CLI or through newer techniques such as Rest API. This way, providing control points on the device, the SDN controller can manipulate remote devices using APIs. SDN via API does not require special switches that support it; e.g., the OpenFlow standard already works well with traditional switches [144]. A big advantage of this SDN implementation method is the ability to build orchestration software easily. SDN via API provides increased openness and thus eliminates the need for ownership, enabling various devices to communicate and be controlled through standardized interfaces (Fig. 6.9).

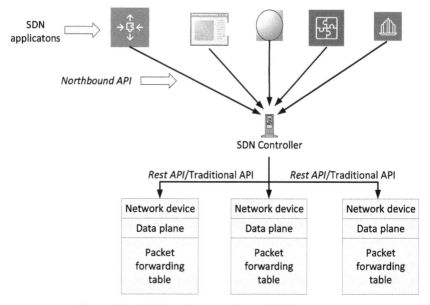

Figure 6.9. SDN implementation model via API [141].

This implementation method represents a step forward in openness and provides opportunities for more comprehensive collaboration instead of using a proprietary CLI. In practice, it need not be open because there is a possibility that APIs originating from different vendors are not compatible, and the proprietary aspect still needs to be eliminated [1]. Applications using an API-based SDN approach must have information about the vendor equipment they should communicate with to use the correct API. The argument in favor of those who propose this method of implementation is the achievement of SDN goals by allowing:

- That applications continue to influence forwarding decisions, and
- API openness, meaning that anyone can create applications and use APIs. This way, it is possible to make the network programmable but not necessarily flexible due to the proprietary nature of the southbound API.

6.2.4   SDN Overlay Network

Today, there is another SDN implementation model, which also implies separating the control from the data plane. The idea is to create a new, independent network implemented on top of the existing network and overlapped with it (overlay network). It does not mean the traditional network infrastructure under the network

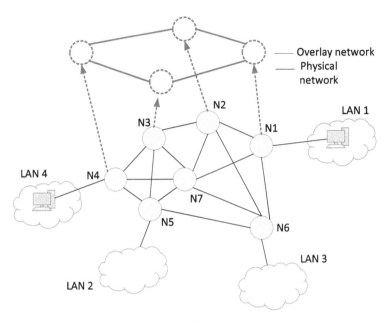

Figure 6.10. SDN implementation via overlay network [145].

created this way remains without a control plane. On the contrary, the devices still have a local control plane where processes traditionally occur. This implementation model runs a virtual network on top of existing hardware infrastructure, creating dynamic tunnels to various local and remote computing environments. A virtual network allocates bandwidth across different channels and assigns devices to each channel, leaving the physical network unchanged. Thus, the virtual network and the underlying infrastructure are connected, and packets are exchanged between them (Fig. 6.10) [145].

Figure 6.10 shows the SDN implementation via an overlay network, which involves the creation of a virtualized networking layer atop the physical infrastructure. The SDN controller has a key role, and it enables the abstraction of the underlying hardware and dynamic control over network functions. It creates policies and configurations, which implies that the overlay network defines how data flows, ensuring efficient routing, QoS, and security measures. The controller communicates with network devices using southbound APIs to send high-level instructions for the physical infrastructure. From the users' perspective, they communicate with the overlay network and use the SDN controller to manage it without requiring support for the underlying physical devices. This SDN implementation meets the basic criteria but has one limitation. The devices under the virtual network must support the protocol used to communicate with that network. Examples of this implementation are VXLAN and network virtualization using generic routing encapsulation (NVGRE) supported by Microsoft [1].

6.3   SDN Interfaces

According to July 2023 [146] statistics, about 5.19 billion users worldwide are connected through different autonomous systems (AS). Managing network infrastructure is complex, considering each network architecture's specificity and the presence of other applications. Using traditional network devices based on ASICs, which require installing a specific operating system, quick reaction and quality response to user requests is a huge challenge. Network management and configuration of network devices become very complex, difficult to perform in some situations, and unable to achieve optimal resource usage. By decoupling the control plane from the data plane, SDN introduces a centralized and software-based logic, which should simplify the management process in modern computer environments and enable the optimal use of resources and their dynamic allocation according to the service requests.

To properly understand communications in the SDN network, it is necessary to create a picture of the three-layered SDN architecture consisting of the data, control, and management plane (Fig. 6.11). The data plane contains physical and virtual infrastructure, which creates the datapath. The SDN controller is the control plane treated as a network operating system (NOS). Its task is to enable the implementation of rules and policies for packet forwarding created on the management plane. Communication between any two planes is performed using four groups of APIs [147]:

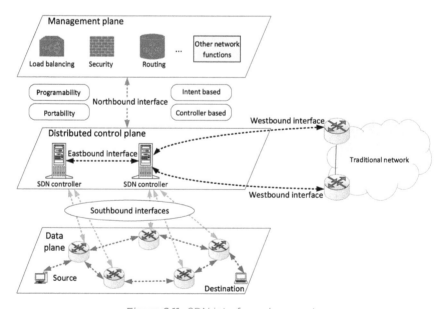

Figure 6.11. SDN interface placement.

- Northbound API – enables high network programmability and transfers rules and policies to the control plane.
- Southbound API – provides communication between the control and data planes; through the control plane, it receives information about devices in the data plane and forwards instructions to traffic forwarding according to the appropriate rules.
- Eastbound API – enables communication between controllers within a distributed control plane.
- Westbound API – provides communication with traditional devices in the data plane.

The NFV concept is complementary to SDN but does not depend on it. It provides a new model of network resources management that enables changes in the implementation of network functionalities, such as firewalls, load balancers, and others. These functions can be implemented as virtual functions and do not depend on hardware. They can be implemented on any device and in the control plane (SDN controller). Such a solution we can apply on the cloud and ensure that in the case of multitenancy access, one virtual controller can manage the resources assigned to different tenants (Fig. 6.12).

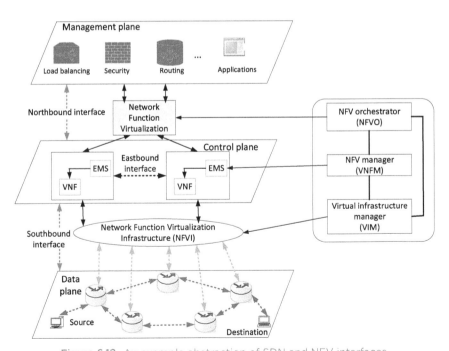

Figure 6.12. An example abstraction of SDN and NFV interfaces.

Figure 6.12 shows an example of NFV implementation in a real environment. The VIM plays the main role in monitoring and managing the virtualized infrastructure. More importantly, it stores information about mapping virtual to physical resources. Further, VNFM manages virtual network functions using an EMS. For each virtual function, it is necessary to enable the full availability of the required resources, such as processor, memory, or data storage, to satisfy service requests. In this sense, the NFVO is a key entity responsible for resource scheduling. It performs scheduling through communication with VNFM or directly with VIM. The NFV concept can also be applied by virtualizing both interfaces (Northbound and Southbound) and creating slices on the available network infrastructure.

6.4 SDN Protocols

We separate the network control from the packet forwarding function by implementing SDN technology. The intermediary role, which should ensure reliable communication between the control plane (SDN controller) and the data plane (infrastructure devices), has the southbound interface. This interface provides the continuity and security of communication, which implies forwarding the controller instructions to devices and delivering information about them to the controller. The southbound interface enables the discovery of network topology, the definition of network flows, and the implementation of management requirements [148]. Otherwise, the forwarding elements would not be able to function.

Communication between the control and data planes occurs through southbound protocols (Fig. 6.13). Some provide direct communication between these two planes, such as OpenFlow protocol, Path Computation Element Communication Protocol (PCEP), and BGP Flow Spec protocol. These protocols are also called SDN control plane protocols. In contrast, another group of protocols indirectly affects the data plane. These protocols use the control plane and modify parameters on these devices; we call them management plane protocols. It is necessary to note that southbound protocols can be open or proprietary. They should provide efficient network control and enable the SDN controller to change dynamically according to real-time demands and needs [149].

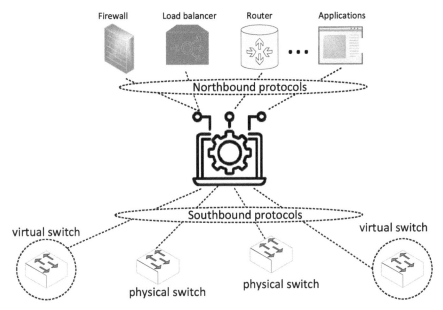

Firewall   Load balancer   Router   Applications

Northbound protocols

Southbound protocols

virtual switch   virtual switch

physical switch

physical switch

Figure 6.13. Southbound protocols.

6.4.1 OpenFlow Protocol

The OpenFlow protocol is SDN networks' first standardized southbound API interface [150]. Its task is to ensure reliable communication between SDN controller and infrastructure devices by implementing the data flow rules. The rules are statically or dynamically defined in the SDN controller software, enabling a high degree of granularity at the application, user, and session levels.

The SDN controller communicates with network devices via the OpenFlow protocol by sending them various instructions. The OpenFlow logical switch usually uses a secure channel to communicate with one controller. It guarantees communication reliability by connecting with other controllers through other channels. Through these channels, SDN controllers send instructions to define rules and modify records in flow tables.

The records and instructions in the flow table represent the fundament for traffic forwarding. For this reason, it is important to provide secure communication via Secure Socket Layer (SSL), which guarantees reliable delivery and processing of messages. OpenFlow cannot automatically provide confirmations or ordered message processing. An OpenFlow logical switch typically contains one or more flow tables, group tables, a metering table, and one or more OpenFlow channels for communicating with external SDN controllers (Fig. 6.14).

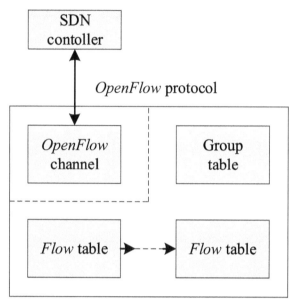

Figure 6.14. Components of an OpenFlow switch.

We must note that the instructions for traffic processing exist in the flow table [150] and that, according to them, traffic forwarding takes place in several steps (Fig. 6.15):

- The first packet arrives at the OpenFlow switch.
- The OpenFlow switch performs a flow table lookup and checks the record matching the field values from the packet header.
- If the match exists, packet forwarding begins according to the action defined in the flow table.
- If the match does not exist, the OpenFlow switch forwards the packet to the SDN controller, which creates an instruction for the new entry in the flow table.

Switches that support the OpenFlow protocol can be OpenFlow-only and OpenFlow-hybrid [150]. OpenFlow-only switches support only the OpenFlow protocol and process traffic according to the above-described method. Unlike them, there are also OpenFlow-hybrid switches, which can process traffic using the Open-Flow protocol or in a standard way using Ethernet traffic processing. In practice, additional management and configuration provisioning protocols exist, such as Open vSwitch Database Management Protocol (OVSDB) and OpenFlow Configuration Protocol, which complements OpenFlow.

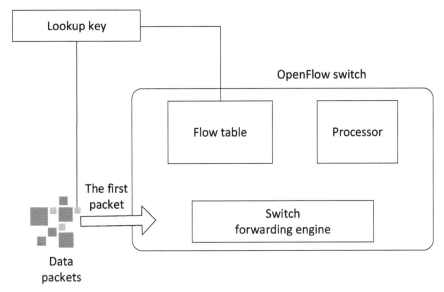

Figure 6.15. OpenFlow packet forwarding.

6.4.2 Open vSwitch Database Management Protocol

Open vSwitch is a software switch created in the hypervisor to enable communication between virtual and physical resources [151]. It is an open-source project supported by various virtualization platforms, such as Xen, KVM (Kernel-based Virtual Machine), and VirtualBox. It can use OVSDB as a protocol for programmable access to network devices, whose traffic forwarding model is similar to the OpenFlow model.

Figure 6.16 shows the architecture of Open vSwitch, which consists of two important components:

- A fast path – located in the kernel and responsible for lookup and traffic forwarding,
- A user's slow path – provide traffic-forwarding logic and interfaces that enable device configuration, such as OpenFlow or NetFlow.

Like the OpenFlow protocol, the OVSDB protocol forwards packets in several steps (Fig. 6.17) [151]:

- The first packet from the data stream arrives at the *ovs-vswitchd* kernel module.
- The *ovs-vswitchd* kernel module forwards the packet to the datapath module, which stores the rules for forwarding subsequent packets.
- The datapath module executes the received instructions and forwards packets to a specific port, where packets can be modified or discarded.

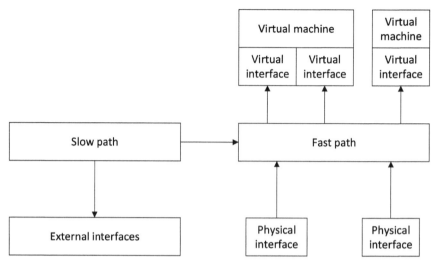

Figure 6.16. OpenFlow switch architecture.

- Suppose the datapath module does not have forwarding instructions; the packet returns the *ovs-vswitchd* kernel module, which decides how to process the packet and sends those instructions together with the packet to the datapath module.

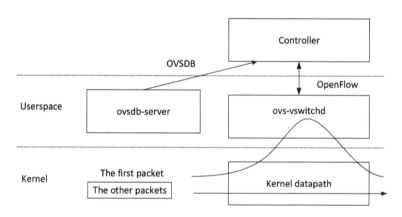

Figure 6.17. OVSDB packet forwarding.

6.4.3   Network Configuration Protocol

Network automation is one of the key requirements of modern networks, including on-demand service provisioning and automatic O&M (Operation and Maintenance). The traditional mechanisms, such as CLI and SNMP, cannot support all requirements for network automation. Their limitations refer to vendor dependencies of CLIs, where any change in structure and syntax causes difficulty in maintaining or parsing scripts automatically. At the same time, SNMP has low configuration efficiency because it cannot support the transaction mechanism [152].

For this reason, academic and professional communities developed Network Configuration Protocol (NETCONF). This protocol is used in the network management system (NMS) for network devices' configurations via standard APIs. As a tool for configuration, NETCONF uses Extensible Markup Language (XML), while for communication between a client (application running on an NMS) and server (network device) uses RPC (remote procedure call). Unlike SNMP, this protocol enables a transaction mechanism that provides many benefits, such as data classification, phase-based submission, configuration isolation, verification, and security mechanisms to ensure message transmission security. Another advantage is that NETCONF defines various operation interfaces and enables the implementation of new protocol operations and specific management functions.

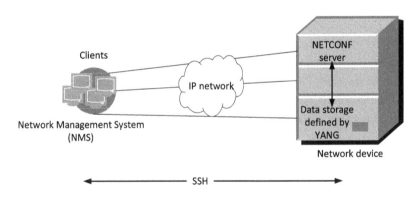

Figure 6.18. The network architecture of NETCONF.

The key components of NETCONF architecture are the client and server, which communicate via SSH (Fig. 6.18). The client manages network devices by sending RPC requests to the NETCONF server to change one or more parameter values and learn from the server's notification (information based on the alarms and events). The server's role is to parse the received client's request and respond. Also, it is responsible for sending notifications to clients in the case of a fault or another event that occurs on a managed device.

NETCONF has a hierarchical, four-layered architecture (Fig. 6.19), where each layer performs specific functions and provides services for the upper layer, with minimal impact on other layers. The secure transport layer establishes a communication path between the client and server, using SSH as a transport protocol to transfer XML information. The messages layer provides a transport-independent framing,

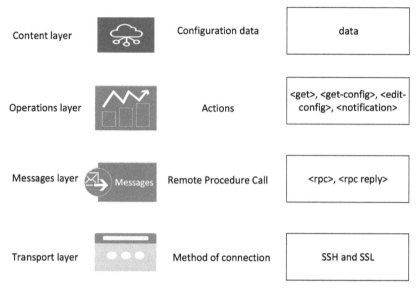

Content layer   Configuration data   data

Operations layer   Actions   <get>, <get-config>, <edit-config>, <notification>

Messages layer   Remote Procedure Call   <rpc>, <rpc reply>

Transport layer   Method of connection   SSH and SSL

Figure 6.19. NETCONF protocol stack.

which must ensure message exchange between client and server. The operations layer defines a set of protocol operations invoked as RPC methods with XML-encoded parameters. The content layer manages data using Schema (a set of rules defined to describe XML files) and YANG (Yet Another Next Generation – a data modeling language designed for NETCONF) data models.

6.4.4   RESTCONF Protocol

RESTCONF is an HTTP-based protocol that uses structured data (XML or JSON) and YANG to provide Representational State Transfer (REST) APIs. It represents a combination of NETCONF and HTTP because it can provide core NETCONF functions using HTTP. In this sense, RESTCONFIG uses secure HTTP to provide operations on data storage (e.g., CREATE, READ, UPDATE, and DELETE) containing YANG-defined data. This way, an alternative to NETCONF for accessing configuration and operational data using YANG models is possible. The REST architecture uses a stateless mechanism for client-server communication between two entities (Fig. 6.20) [153].

We must note that implementing RESTCONFIG brings certain benefits, such as building RESTful programmatic interfaces that support web development. Its standard interfaces are compatible with multi-vendor devices, which ensures reduced costs. Besides the previously mentioned benefits, RESTCONF also provides high extensibility (it allows various vendors to define additional NETCONF operations), and NMS is not required.

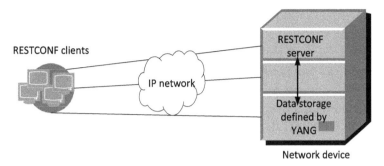

Figure 6.20. The network architecture of RESTCONF.

6.4.5   OpenFlow Configuration and Management Protocol

OpenFlow configuration and management protocol (OF-CONFIG) is a plat-form that supports a vendor-neutral programmatic interface to the OpenFlow switch [154]. The idea for its development appeared at a forum of network opera-tors, such as Google, AT&T, and BT, where operators indicated the need to create a new model capable of remote configuration and monitoring network devices. This way, OF-CONFIG, which defines OpenFlow switches as abstractions called OpenFlow logical switches, enables their remote configuration. In practice, OF-CONFIG enables configuring crucial parameters and provides the OpenFlow con-troller to communicate with the OpenFlow logical switch via the OpenFlow pro-tocol (Fig. 6.21).

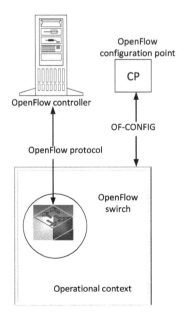

Figure 6.21. An OpenFlow Configuration Point communicates with an operational con-text that can support an OpenFlow Switch using the OF-CONFIG.

OF-CONFIG can introduce an operating context for many OpenFlow datapaths and create a switch equivalent to a physical or virtual switch with many datapaths hosted. We can build such an architecture by partitioning, i.e., resource assignments (e.g., ports and queues) to the hosted OpenFlow datapaths. By using OF-CONFIG, it is possible to provide the dynamic resource association with specific OpenFlow logical switches hosted on the OpenFlow capable switch. We must note that OF-CONFIG does not provide any report about resource partitioning. The resources can be partitioned amongst multiple OpenFlow logical switches so that each has full control of the assigned resources (Fig. 6.22).

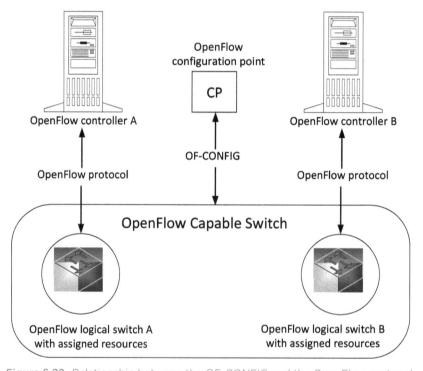

Figure 6.22. Relationship between the OF-CONFIG and the OpenFlow protocol.

6.4.6   Southbound Protocols – Summary

Each of the previously mentioned southbound protocols is used for different purposes and operates within other network management systems from the perspective of configuration, monitoring, management, and programmability of network devices. Their selection often depends on the specific requirements and capabilities desired within a network infrastructure. In Table 6.1, we give a summarized review of the purpose, use, and features of each southbound protocol.

Table 6.1. A summarized review of the SDN southbound protocols.

Protocol	Purpose	Use	Features
OpenFlow protocol	It enables a centralized controller to manage the network devices (e.g., switches and routers).	It enables the control plane separation from the data plane, allowing for centralized management and programmability.	Defines a standardized way for the controller to communicate with network devices, specifying packet handling at the data plane.
Open vSwitch Database Management Protocol.	The protocol is used to manage and configure Open vSwitch instances.	It provides a management interface for Open vSwitches, allowing control of their configuration and monitoring their state.	It provides a schema-based management interface for Open vSwitch instances.
Network Configuration Protocol (NETCONF)	The protocol is used for configuration, monitoring, and device initialization.	It provides mechanisms for remote installation, manipulation, and deletion of the network devices' configuration.	XML-based protocol that uses a secure connection for communication between the client and the server.
RESTCONF protocol	HTTP-based protocol that provides a programmatic interface for accessing YANG-based data models.	It allows for the recovery, manipulation, and configuration of network devices using RESTful web services.	Utilizes HTTP methods like GET, POST, PUT, and DELETE to perform CRUD (Create, Read, Update, Delete) operations on resources exposed by YANG models.
OpenFlow Configuration and Management Protocol	It is used for configuration and management of OpenFlow devices.	It defines mechanisms for the controller to configure and manage OpenFlow devices.	Provides a standardized way to control OpenFlow configuration on network devices.

6.4.7   Northbound Protocols

Northbound APIs are usually SDN RESTful APIs whose task is to ensure that the SDN controller communicates with services and applications running at the application layer. In some cases, these APIs are necessary for efficient orchestration and automation of the network according to requirements from different applications. The applications use them to send a request for resources, such as data, storage, or bandwidth, to the SDN controller. The SDN controller responds by resource delivering or sending messages with appropriate content.

The fact is that northbound APIs support a huge number of applications and represent the most shapeable components in an SDN environment. Via northbound APIs, optimizing load balancers, firewalls, and security applications or implementing applications for any level of orchestration is possible. Generally, many interfaces exist in SDN architecture that can control different applications via an SDN controller. These communications are not different from others between software entities. The protocols commonly used for SDN communication with applications via northbound interface are RESTful APIs or libraries in programming languages like Python, Ruby, Go, Java, or C++. In a real environment, we can meet northbound APIs that integrate the SDN controller with automation stacks, such as Puppet, Chef, SaltStack, Ansible, and CFEngine, as well as orchestration platforms, such as OpenStack, VMware's vCloudDirector or Apache's open source CloudStack. Their goal is to abstract network processes so that software developers can make changes to adapt to the application requirements (Fig. 6.23).

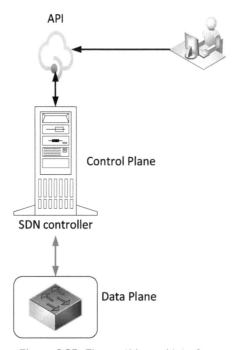

Figure 6.23. The northbound interface.

6.5   SDN Controllers

The idea of separating the control plane from the data plane has gone a development path from 1995 to 2015 through several development phases, such as Active Networking, Network Control Point, ForCES, and Ethane [155]. Active Networking begins the development path that proposes building dynamic networks with devices that perform packet computation and modification. The developers introduced two approaches:

- Programmable switch – maintains the existing packet format and provides a mechanism that supports the programs' download and
- Capsule approach – active small programs replace the passive packets encapsulated in transmission frames and run at each node along their path.

Network Control Point is the next development phase, with a clearer picture of the separation, but it is primarily related to telephone networks. In 2003, the ForCES concept [156, 157] proposed a solution for decoupling the control from the data plane at individual devices and logic's centralization. The proposed solution represents a partial centralization because each control element interacts with the corresponding data plane element. The Ethane architecture [158] connected simple flow-based Ethernet switches with a centralized controller that managed flows. Communication between users was only possible with the controller's permission because it had a global network policy. When the first packet arrived at the controller, it performed route computation for this flow and made instructions that enabled the path establishment along the selected route.

In today's SDN implementations, the controller represents a key component because it manages flows to the infrastructure devices (physical or virtual) and applications at the upper layer. Its brain is a centralized Network Operating System. It provides functionalities like a basic operating system, such as program running, management of I/O operation, security, topology-related functions, shortest path forwarding, and others. Figure 6.24 shows the two types of SDN controllers, centralized and distributed, and the existing controller's platforms that we can meet in SDN networks. Centralized controllers represent control plane (logic) implementation at a single location. The benefit is simplicity of management as they provide a single control point. However, scalability issues are shortcomings because they have limited capacity for data plane devices. Unlike centralized controllers, distributed controllers are more scalable. They provide a better performance, especially if the number of requests to them increases [159].

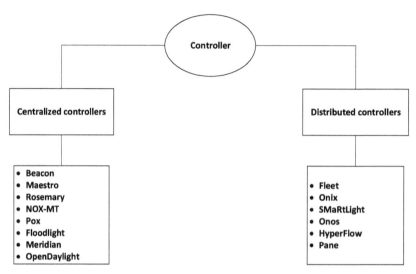

Figure 6.24. Controller's classification.

6.5.1 Beacon

Beacon is a Java-based OpenFlow controller with a multi-threaded architecture, as shown in Fig. 6.25. We can configure a m number of running threads, but the controller can generate $m + 1$ threads. The additional thread listens to the incoming switch connections, partitioning them among the worker threads. Each worker thread is responsible for a fixed number of switches whose requests it will process using static packet batching. The key task of Beacon is to process packets and prepare them for sending using default mode, which implies only one write per I/O select loop. This way, reducing the overhead of socket system calls for each OpenFlow message is possible. Also, we can enable an immediate mode on Beacon, whose task is to write a socket for every outgoing OpenFlow message waiting to be written to the switch to reduce the per-packet latency [160].

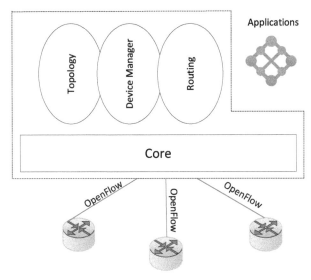

Figure 6.25. Beacon SDN Controller.

6.5.2 Maestro

Today, the OpenFlow protocol represents a systematic choice for SDN southbound interfaces, primarily due to the management flexibility and the direct control possibility of packet flows in various network scenarios. However, the control plane centralization and the OpenFlow controller's performances can be bottlenecks in large networks. In response to potential problems, the Maestro uses parallelism in operation to achieve near-linear performance scalability on multi-core processors [161]. Moreover, it is possible to change some control plane functionalities by implementing simple single-threaded programs. Maestro can implement many designs and techniques to respond to the specific OpenFlow requirements, uses parallelism, and achieves a huge performance improvement in operation, significantly impacting many deployed OpenFlow networks (Fig. 6.26).

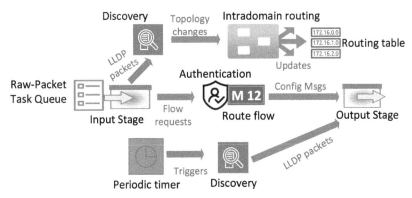

Figure 6.26. Maestro SDN Controller – overall structure.

Figure 6.26 shows the overall structure of Maestro, which sends and receives messages to and from OpenFlow switches via TCP. The Input Stage and Output Stage components manage functionalities such as reading from and writing to socket buffers and translating raw OpenFlow messages to and from high-level data structures. The other functionalities, such as discovery, intradomain routing, authentication, and route flow, can be implemented flexibly as applications and modify their behavior according to defined goals.

6.5.3 Rosemary

The key challenge in designing an SDN controller is defining the optimal concept regarding the requirements for a robust, secure, high-performance solution. The Rosemary controller (Fig. 6.27) implies performing a NOS redesign, including the following criteria:

- the context separation,
- resource utilization monitoring, and
- Micro-NOS permissions structure building to limit the library functionality that enables access for network applications.

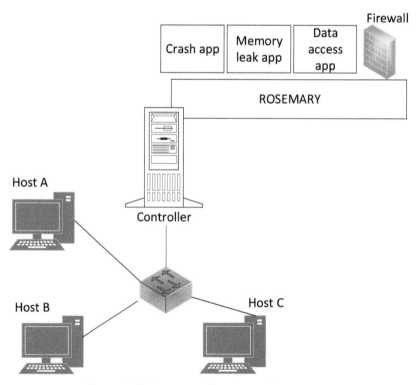

Figure 6.27. Rosemary SDN Controller concept.

Figure 6.27 shows the overall structure of Rosemary, which consists of four components [162]:

1. Data abstraction layer (DAL) – encapsulates underlying hardware devices and forwards their requests to the Rosemary kernel,
2. Rosemary kernel – provides basic network services, such as resource control, security management, and system logging,
3. System libraries – each application chooses the libraries for operations and
4. Resource monitoring – resource utilization tracking for running applications and removing if they do not function properly.

The design principles of Rosemary are as follows:

- Network applications decoupling from the NOS,
- Resource monitoring and control for each network application,
- Resource sharing of NOS modules,
- Capabilities to access NOS resources, and
- Requirements balance regarding robustness, security, and higher performance.

6.5.4 NOX-MT

Controller performance is the main topic of SDN development. The research and professional community tried to discover how fast the controller can process input requests and how many requests it can handle efficiently. The OpenFlow controller NOX provides a high-level programmatic interface for managing and developing network control applications (Fig. 6.28). In the beginning, it worked as a single-threaded open-source control platform to examine the performance characteristics of SDN architecture. In a later phase (NOX-MT), it upgraded to a multithreaded version using I/O batching for optimization [159].

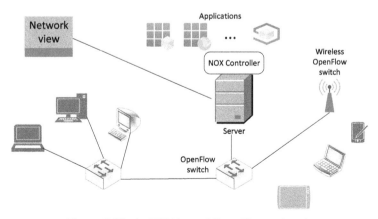

Figure 6.28. An NOX-based OpenFlow network.

Figure 6.28 shows the NOX architecture, which, besides OpenFlow APIs dedicated to communication with OpenFlow switches, also provides network packet processing, threading, event engine, and support for I/O operations. It is important to note that NOX, during the packet forwarding, maps the MAC-switch tuple and port number for each switch and stores maps in the data table. This table has a hash structure, and each new source MAC address must be written in the table. The number of events. i.e., MAC addresses in the hash table are limited by the network's total number of hosts and switches.

6.5.5 POX

Pythonic Network Operating System (POX) is an open-source SDN controller used in SDN for research, experimentation, and development of applications. It provides the SDN framework, where it is possible to create and manage the network, including defining the network architecture, routing protocols, and traffic handling via Python scripts [163]. It appeared as a part of the NOX project and inherited many of its concepts and design principles. This controller communicates with OpenFlow switches, enabling centralized network control and programmability. Due to its simplicity and flexibility, it is useful for educational and research purposes in the SDN domain. We can leverage POX to experiment with different SDN architectures, build custom network applications, and understand SDN principles.

6.5.6 Floodlight

A Floodlight is an open-source, Java-based SDN controller designed to manage network devices and enable communication between them [164]. It provides a platform for developing and deploying SDN applications and centralizing network logic, implying abstracting the underlying devices and centralizing network management and control. Floodlight uses the OpenFlow protocol to communicate with switches and other SDN elements (Fig. 6.29), allowing for programmability and flexibility in network management. Floodlight's APIs and libraries are often used to create custom applications for network monitoring, traffic engineering, and security.

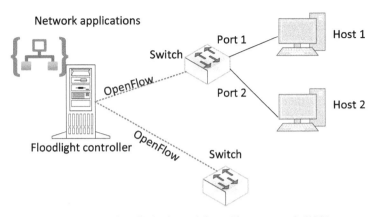

Figure 6.29. Floodlight-based OpenFlow network [165].

The Floodlight controller depicted in Fig. 6.29 consists of core, internal, and utility services that include various modules. For example, it uses topology management based on Dijsktra's algorithm to compute the shortest path. Link Discovery maintains the link state information using Link Layer Discovery Protocol (LLDP) packets while the forwarding module provides flow commute through end-to-end routing.

6.5.7 Meridian

Meridian is a centralized Cisco controller with complete insight into network infrastructure [161]. It can provide better traffic control and the possibility of programmatic configuration, enabling more efficient and flexible network management. Meridian supports multiple protocols and interfaces, allowing the definition of network policies and optimization of network performance through a centralized interface. It abstracts the underlying infrastructure, making deploying and managing networks at scale easier. Meridian can achieve greater agility, automation, and scalability in the network, allowing for easier adaptation to changing business needs and traffic patterns. Meridian can achieve greater agility, automation, and scalability in the network, allowing easy adaptation to business needs and traffic patterns.

6.5.8 OpenDaylight

OpenDaylight (ODL) is a centralized, open-source controller whose basic task is network device orchestration, enabling a dynamic and programmable approach to network management [166]. It has a modular architecture, uses Open Service Gateway Interface (OSGi), and seamlessly integrates new functionalities through plug-ins. The core part is the Model-Driven Service Abstraction Layer (MD-SAL), which represents a data exchange and adaptation mechanism between YANG models (network devices and applications interacting within the SAL). The YANG models provide device or application descriptions about their capabilities without requiring to know the specific implementation details of the other. Within the SAL, models can be a producer that implements an API and provides the API's data, while a consumer uses the API and data (Fig. 6.30).

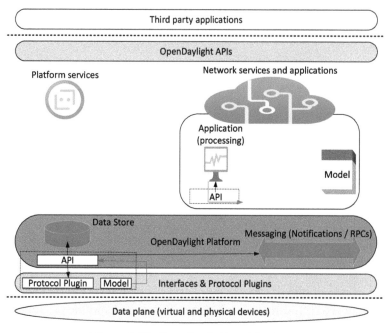

Figure 6.30. OpenDaylight architecture.

Figure 6.30 shows the ODL modular design, which provides a high level of flexibility for users and service providers to build a controller that can fit their needs. ODL supports many protocols, such as OpenFlow, OVSDB, NETCONF, BGP, and others, enabling modern networks to solve different user needs. Southbound protocols and control plane services can be individually selected or combined according to the use case requirements. ODL is the primary place for developing and testing different approaches to policy and purpose, such as ALTO, group-based policy, and network intent composition.

6.5.9   Centralized SDN Controllers-summary

Centralized SDN controllers are central points for managing, routing, and orchestrating network traffic across the whole network. These controllers enable centralized network intelligence, efficient network configuration, and dynamic adaptation to evolving demands. With programmable interfaces, they support the building of flexible and scalable environments by implementing different policies. The usage of open standards and provision of security measures streamline network management and provide interoperability. These controllers allow insights through monitoring and analytics and create the possibility for the automation of network processes. In Table 6.2, we give a summarized review of the type, advantages, and limitations of previously mentioned SDN controllers.

Table 6.2. A summarized review of centralized SDN controllers.

SDN controller	Type	Advantages	Limitations
Beacon	Research-oriented, Java-based controller.	It focuses on extensibility and experimentation, allowing researchers to implement and test new ideas easily.	Limited adoption in production environments, primarily used for academic and experimental purposes.
Maestro	Intent-based, policy-driven SDN controller.	Uses intent-based networking, enabling translation of high-level business policies into network configurations. Simplifies network management and automation.	Potential complexity in defining and implementing business intents.
Rosemary	Controller designed for wireless SDN environments.	Specialized in wireless network management, offering features for wireless networking protocols and optimizations.	Offers features tailored only for wireless networking.
NOX-MT	It is used for flexibility and modularity in the network.	It provides a platform for experimentation and modular development.	Lower adoption in recent years due to advancements in other controllers with better scalability and features.
POX	Python-based controller, based on NOX architecture.	Simplicity and ease of use due to Python language, suitable for educational purposes and small-scale deployments.	Limited scalability and performance for larger networks or production-grade environments.

(Continued)

Table 6.2. Continued

SDN controller	Type	Advantages	Limitations
Floodlight	Java-based, Apache-licensed controller.	Strong community support, well-documented, and used in various computer environments. Provides stability and robustness.	Updates might be less frequent compared to other controllers, potentially slower adoption of new features.
Meridian	Scalable, enterprise-grade SDN controller based on OpenDaylight.	Focuses on scalability, stability, and enterprise-level features, suitable for larger and more complex network environments.	It may require more resources and expertise to deploy compared to simpler controllers.
OpenDaylight	Modular, open-source controller with a huge ecosystem.	Large community support, extensive feature set, modular architecture allowing customization and integration with various plugins.	Complexity due to its wide range of features, potentially requiring more resources for initial setup and management.

6.5.10 Fleet

Fleet is the SDN controller that deals with problems caused by malicious decisions of network administrators and aims to prevent the controller from malfunctioning caused by malicious administrator configuration (Fig. 6.31). Some observations show that human errors are responsible for 50% to 80% of interruptions in the network [167]. Such errors negatively influence the controller's routing, forwarding, and device performance and can easily degrade the system's performance.

Figure 6.31 shows the distributed architecture of this controller, physically located across separate machines. Fleet consists of the administrator layer, which contains a physical machine for each administrator and shared data storage system, and the infrastructure intelligence layer, which manages communication between the infrastructure and the administrator layer [168]. This communication implies creating the flow rules, verifying signed messages, and connecting to a different administrator machine in case of failure on one of them. The administrators upload network configurations on the physically separated machines and use out-of-band

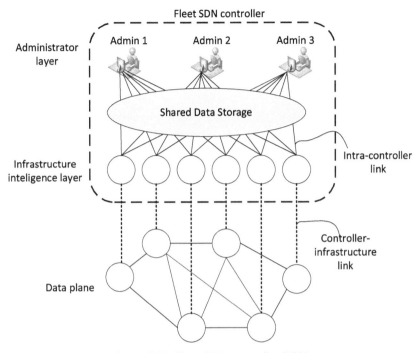

Figure 6.31. Fleet SDN controller [168].

channels to communicate with each other. Shared data storage has the role of providing a consistent network view for all administrators. Fleet does not require one-to-one correspondence between administrators and machines with uploaded configurations and provides separation, which should prevent the failure that occurs on a single machine from affecting other machines.

6.5.11 HyperFlow

The main issue during SDN controller design was the trend of an increased number of switches. This trend increases traffic toward the centralized controller, which can become a bottleneck. The scientific community proposed making a few replicas physically distributed in different locations [169]. HyperFlow represents the first SDN solution with a distributed control plane designed for OpenFlow protocol. It acts as a logically centralized environment despite distributed architecture with different controllers. SDN network with implemented HyperFlow uses OpenFlow switches as forwarding elements, NOX controllers as decision elements, and an event propagation system for cross-controller communication (Fig. 6.32).

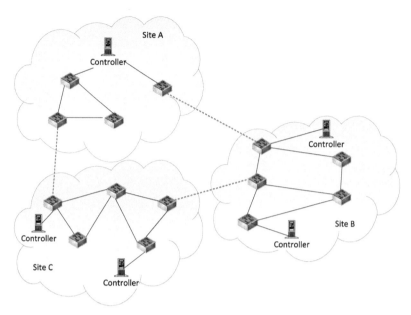

Figure 6.32. HyperFlow network [169].

Each controller has the same network view and runs the same software. It is responsible for a group of OpenFlow switches and directly manages their traffic. Indirectly, it can program or query the rest of the switches through communication with other controllers. In case of the controller's failure, the connected switches must be reconfigured to connect to the nearby controller. We must note that different controllers have different orders of events. For this reason, HyperFlow defines the authoritative controller as one responsible for ensuring the correct operation in disputed cases.

6.5.12   SMaRtLight

SMaRtLight is designed as a Floodlight controller extension to solve the network's fault tolerance issues and to enable changes such as one-to-one mapping between the OpenFlow switch and data store connection and the possibility of data store caching. This controller deals with failures on switches, controllers, or links in the data path or between the controller and OpenFlow switch. The primary controller is responsible for fault tolerance, while other controllers are backups. It stores application-related data in shared storage, implemented through a Replicated State Machine (RSM) [159]. In case of a failure on the primary controller, a new primary controller takes over and gets a complete data update from shared storage (Fig. 6.33).

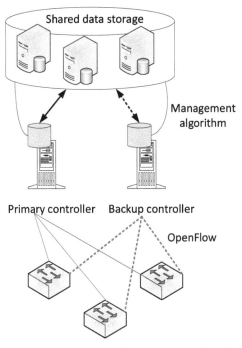

Figure 6.33. SmaRtLight SDN network [159].

Figure 6.33 shows the architecture of the SMaRtLight SDN network with Open-Flow switches directly connected to a controller but not to shared storage. Controllers are located between the data plane and shared data storage. For the system to function correctly, the following must be fulfilled:

- Switches are connected to both controllers and have not crashed; they work properly.
- The controller is connected to the database server and has not crashed; it works properly.
- Shared data storage is connected to each database server and runs recovery protocols.

6.5.13   Onix

Building a common control plane, which could provide different control functions, such as access control, routing, or traffic engineering, is one of the goals of SDN. Creating such a platform is accompanied by challenges, such as providing various functionalities for management in different contexts [159]. The Onix controller represents an open-source platform developed to provide a flexible and scalable environment capable of controlling network behavior through centralized software-based controllers. The prerequisite for that is a high level of programmability, which this platform provides using programmable interfaces, allowing the creation of custom applications and control for the network behavior. Its modular architecture can be customized and extended based on specific networking requirements, such as reliability, to handle system failure and simplify the structure for building management applications. Onix instances can be written in multiple languages like C++, Python, and Java.

6.5.14 ONOS

The Open Network Operating System (ONOS) represents an open-source SDN controller that provides centralized management and network control. Its goal is to provide high availability, scalability, and performance while introducing new applications and services to the network. The key characteristics are decoupling the control plane from the data plane and allowing centralized management and dynamic network configuration. Besides the OpenFlow protocol, it can use other southbound APIs to communicate with network switches and routers, enabling programmability and automatic network management (Fig. 6.34). We must note that ONOS is used in various network environments, including data centers, carrier networks, and enterprise networks [170].

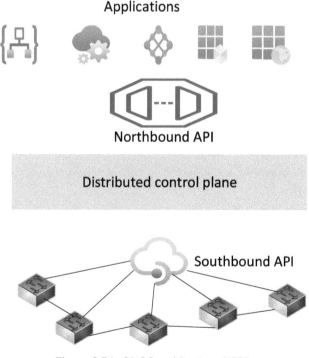

Figure 6.34. ONOS architecture [170].

Figure 6.34 shows the logically centralized but physically distributed controller architecture, which has implemented the following two configurations:

- Prototype 1 focuses on building architecture with a global network view and providing fault tolerance and scalability,
- Prototype 2 focuses on improving the system performance with the desired number of remote operations and the time required to process them. The aim is to allow agility and adaptability in network operations.

6.5.15   PANE

The Policy-based Architecture for Networked Environments (PANE) controller aims to provide greater visibility and control over the network to make a required resource reservation. It implements API between the user and the control plane to simplify network control and visibility and enable conflict resolution among users and their requests [159]. In this sense, the PANE controller assigns privileges to users while the request conflict is solved using the conflict resolution operator and the hierarchical flow table. It introduces the principal role in the network, which is assigned to end users or, more specifically, their applications. The principal exchanges the request, query, and hint messages to control resources, such as bandwidth or access, acquire information about the network states, and indicate the future demands of the system. Its authority is limited, so PANE introduces the concept of the share, representing a combination of principals, privileges, and flow groups. This concept implies building the tree of shares, where each share indicates which principal can publish which message for which flow. The tree's creation does not mean defining any new policy while combining them; creating a policy tree in hierarchical flow tables is possible.

6.5.16   Distributed Controllers-summary

Distributed SDN controllers provide scalability and resilience by decentralizing the control plane and consist of multiple controllers that function together to manage and enhance network scalability. These controllers also improve fault tolerance because if one controller fails, others can seamlessly take over its responsibilities, ensuring network service continuity. Reduced latency, efficient load balancing, and optimized performance result from controllers' locations, which are closer to the managed network segments. Table 6.3 gives a summarized review of the type, advantages, and limitations of distributed SDN controllers.

Table 6.3. A summarized review of distributed SDN controllers.

SDN controller	Type	Advantages	Limitations
Fleet	It focuses on scalability and fault tolerance.	Scalable architecture distributing control tasks across nodes, fault-tolerant design, and high availability suitable for large-scale networks.	It may require more resources due to its distributed nature, potentially complex to set up and manage.
Onix	It focuses on scalability and flexibility.	Scalable architecture supporting distributed control, designed for high performance and extensibility, enabling fine-grained control over network behavior.	It may have a steeper learning curve and is more suited for advanced users or specific use cases requiring detailed network control.
SMaRtLight	Intent-based distributed SDN controller.	Focuses on translating high-level intents into network policies, providing abstraction and simplification of network management based on business objectives.	Complexity in defining intents and policies, potentially challenging to align high-level objectives with detailed network configurations.
Onos	Open-source controller with a focus on performance and scalability.	Strong community support, scalability across distributed nodes, features designed for carrier-grade networks, and support for diverse use cases.	It may require more expertise for deployment and management compared to simpler controllers.
HyperFlow	High-performance controller optimized for large-scale networks.	Focusing on scalability and performance, suited for managing extensive network environments efficiently and supporting diverse applications.	Complexity and potential resource requirements, due to its focus on high performance, might be less straightforward for smaller deployments.
Pane	It focuses on network virtualization and isolation.	Specialized in network virtualization, offering features for creating and managing isolated virtual networks within a larger infrastructure.	Specific use case focus might not be as versatile for general SDN deployments without a strong emphasis on network virtualization.

6.6   SDN Implementations

SDN has numerous practical implementations across different network domains because it centralizes network intelligence and enables greater programmability, which implies building a more flexible and scalable environment. Cloud providers have recognized the advantages of SDN and widely use this technology despite the proprietary character of their platforms and components [171]. Large network operators have also begun implementing SDN in their access networks. Furthermore, they proceed with implementation cautiously, primarily using hybrid solutions. Today, SDN is increasingly being applied in enterprises as well. Besides technical challenges, enterprises' financial capabilities dictate the SDN adoption speed. For these reasons, enterprises implement SDN via managed edge services from the cloud. They connect on-premises clusters running edge workloads with clouds running scalable data center workloads.

6.6.1   Network Virtualization

The idea of using SDN to create virtual networks came after detailed insight into modern cloud networks. Scientists and professionals identified the need to create, manage, and modify computer environments without the administrator's actions. The key principle of SDN based on separating the control from the data plane brings the possibility of exposing a single API entry point to create, modify, and delete virtual networks. This way, using the same automation systems to provide computing and storage capacity and build virtual networks in the cloud is possible. The development and widespread implementation of network virtualization is strongly associated with developing different resource virtualization techniques and represents a process that is impossible to separate. The cloud providers have understood this process correctly and recognized the need to automate network provisioning, especially in data centers. Deployment in data centers initiated further development and emergence of container-based technology and software solutions such as Dockers and Kubernetes.

Network virtualization technology aims to programmatically provide network services so that virtual networks become lightweight objects (the objects that have less data or process less data), created and modified on demand, with a full set of services (Fig. 6.35). This approach opens further advances in networking and brings the possibility of creating virtual networks without limitations. This way, it is possible to create fine-grained, isolated microsegments according to specific requirements, such as distributed clusters, and to implement a new strategy for security. This strategy implies implementing security measures as an inherent part of the network and preventing the attack from spreading beyond the micro-segment.

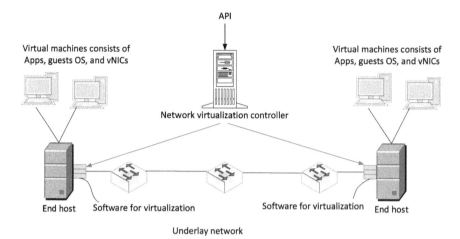

Figure 6.35. An example network virtualization system.

Figure 6.35 shows a network with the SDN controller as a central point responsible for network virtualization. It exposes a northbound API to create and modify virtual networks. Further, its role is to create and send instructions to program the flow table of virtual switches. Virtual switches run in hypervisors installed at hosts. They perform packet forwarding according to rules from flow tables. We can integrate controller and virtual switches using proprietary signaling methods or open interfaces. Integration focuses on connecting virtual machines and containers, usually implemented as an overlay among the servers.

6.6.2   Switching Fabrics

SDN has the predominant use case in data centers, where cost reduction and improving feature velocity play an important role. The providers aim to move from proprietary to bare-metal switches built using silicon chips. They want to perform software control of the switching fabric as the architecture that interconnects their servers and redirects the data coming in on one of the ports out to another of its ports. Switching fabric represents a two-tier design built according to the leaf-spine network topology. Providers use this topology to overcome the limitations of the traditional (three-tier) networks and improve performance (Fig. 6.36).

In traditional networks, providers usually establish redundant paths to avoid traffic loss in case of network failure. They implement the Spanning Tree Protocol (STP), which always has two or more potential traffic routes, which implies that if the primary route fails, STP will use a backup route. The STP is not an adequate solution for data centers because its mechanism can result in heavy loads. To overcome this limitation, providers implemented a two-tier leaf-spine topology

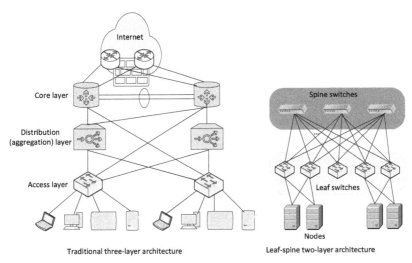

Figure 6.36. The example of traditional (three-tier) and leaf-spine network architecture.

consisting of leaf and spine switches, as shown in Fig. 6.36. The leaf switches represent the access layer and provide end points' connections to the data center. In practice, leaf switches are located in racks (two per rack) and have connections to each server in the rack. On the other side, these ToR switches are connected to multiple spine switches to provide redundancy, where the number of connections varies from used switch models. Spine switches should not have a mutual connection because leaf switches have connections with each spine switch. Today, leaf-spin topology represents a common architecture used in data centers because it provides scalability, high bandwidth, and low latency.

SDN can be implemented in a leaf-spine topology to introduce higher programmability, which implies more efficient management, flexibility, and automation. SDN controller has a key role because it simplifies the implementation of any changes in data centers. It enables building more efficient policy-based management, allowing granular control and policy deployment across the network (e.g., to provide security and QoS). Further, with centralized control, optimizing traffic flows, enabling traffic rerouting, and optimizing network paths based on real-time conditions is possible within data centers. SDN can enable the automation of many data center functionalities. It is an important goal for providers because of automatic resource provisioning, device self-configuration, and dynamic resource allocation. Finally, a higher level of programmability is a prerequisite for implementing custom applications that can interact with the data center infrastructure and solve specific data center requirements. In some SDN implementations, a leaf-spine switching fabric based on SDN with implemented a collection of control applications is often called SD-Fabric.

6.6.3   Traffic Engineering for WANs

Implementing advanced technologies, such as IoT, cloud computing, and Industry 4.0, creates many issues in traditional networks. More efficient traffic engineering is one of them, where solving two tasks is very important. The first refers to measurement and real-time traffic analysis, and the second concerns defining mechanisms for traffic routing, which should improve resource utilization and provide desired QoS requirements [172]. The existing mechanisms propose IP-based and MPLS-based traffic engineering. IP-based traffic engineering solves the multipath traffic load balance problem by optimizing the IP routing (e.g., a neighborhood search algorithm) to avoid network congestion [173]. However, this mechanism has two potential drawbacks:

1. Using link weights for routing algorithms (e.g., OSPF protocol) cannot split traffic equally, which implies the inability to use network resources fully.
2. Any change in the network requires a particular time to build the new network topology, which can cause congestion and degradation of network performance.

Sometimes, providers use Multiprotocol Label Switching (MPLS) to solve these two problems despite MPLS complexity and high-performance overhead, which is undesirable in data centers [174]. The deployment of MPLS in data centers is complex primarily due to the configuration of Label Distribution Protocol (LDP) sessions, the creation of label-switched paths (LSPs), and the management of routers and switches. Also, MPLS adds overhead by encapsulating packets with labels, increasing packet size, and requiring additional processing power, memory, and network bandwidth. This way, many challenges can occur related to troubleshooting, operational maintenance, and scaling in larger computer environments.

SDN functionality changes traffic engineering in the network from the foundation because it centralizes control and enables dynamic, programmable traffic management. The key point is the SDN controller, which makes it possible to route packets in real time, perform traffic prioritization, and build policy-based management. This way, it is possible to optimize resource utilization by implementing adaptive traffic routing and policies that ensure critical applications get the required priority. With programmatic management, SDN enables the automation and orchestration of network tasks and allows granular control over WAN infrastructure, significantly improving its efficiency, flexibility, and responsiveness (Fig. 6.37).

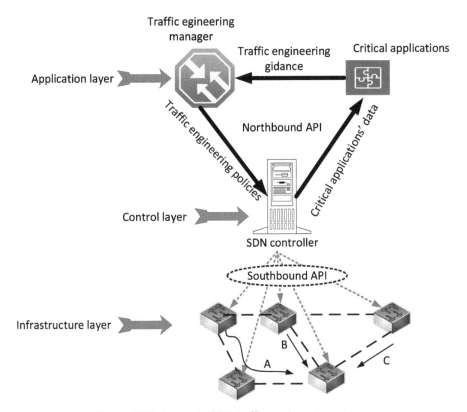

Figure 6.37. Dynamic SDN traffic engineering system.

Figure 6.37 shows a dynamic mechanism for traffic engineering in SDN-based networks, where a central algorithm looks at all three flows simultaneously and tries to place them optimally. For this purpose, the SDN controller monitors and analyzes traffic in real time and collects network status information to make traffic routing decisions. It provides global consideration of traffic applications, and in this way, granular traffic scheduling is possible. The SDN controller generates instructions sent to OpenFlow switches, which can have multiple flow table pipelines, making flow management more flexible and efficient.

6.6.4   Software-defined Wide Area Network (SD-WAN)

Traditional WANs' static, insufficiently flexible architecture cannot respond to modern, increasingly dynamic networking trends and meet user QoE requirements. It is necessary to simplify networking operations, optimize management, and introduce more programmability in WANs. For this reason, scientists and professionals implement SDN functionality into WANs and change their architectures to improve management and optimize performance. By introducing the key principles of SDN, WANs gain centralized control and visibility over the complete WAN, creating prerequisites to significantly increase reliability, scalability, and security. For example, traditional WANs use MPLS, wireless, broadband, and VPNs to enable secure access to enterprise applications, services, and resources. With implemented SDN technology, they can create and update security rules and routing policies in real time as network requirements change.

SD-WAN technology allows enterprise networks to extend over large geographical distances, efficiently monitor WAN connections' performance, and manage traffic to maintain high rates and optimize connectivity. Each device is centrally managed, with routing based on application policies. Combining this with zero-touch provisioning (the automated process of device configuration without interaction with a user, except for physical device connection to the network) makes it possible to perform deployment and configuration automation, reducing complexity, resource utilization, and costs [175]. Network management is simplified because the control is detached from the hardware to the centralized software. This way, there is no need to manage the device individually (Fig. 6.38) [176].

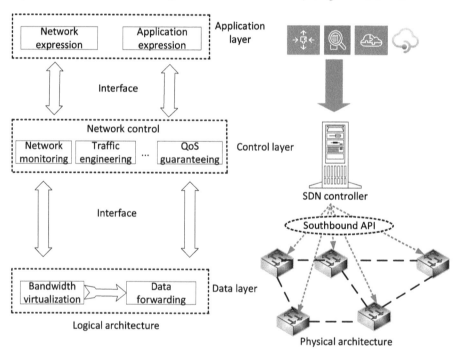

Figure 6.38. Logical and physical architecture of SD-WAN.

Figure 6.38 shows the three-layered logical and physical architecture of SD-WAN, which includes the data, control, and application layer. Bandwidth virtualization and packet forwarding are functions performed at the data layer. Bandwidth virtualization based on the abstraction of network links at one location aims to provide efficient resource utilization. The result of virtualization is a pool of resources that are available for each application and service. OpenFlow switches forward data according to the control layer instructions. We must note that many functions are implemented and managed at the control layer independently. It is possible to connect or chain these functions and, in this way, create complex services and increase the SD-WAN flexibility. The application layer enables providers to define their specific requirements through network and application expression, which can translate high-level requirements into compliant network configurations.

6.6.5   Access Networks

In traditional networks, the access layer (network) consists of special-purpose hardware devices, such as passive optical networks (PONs) or radio access networks (RANs). Therefore, the real challenge is transforming them into their merchant silicon/bare-metal counterparts so the software can control them. In practice, the academic community and large network operators invest huge resources and efforts to develop and implement software-defined PON or RAN networks, sometimes called CORD (Central Office Re-architected as a data center) initiative. The main idea is to isolate the packet forwarding engine from the control plane and implement control as software on commodity hardware. For example, we have an SDN-Enabled Broadband Access (*SEBA*) solution, depicted in Fig. 6.39.

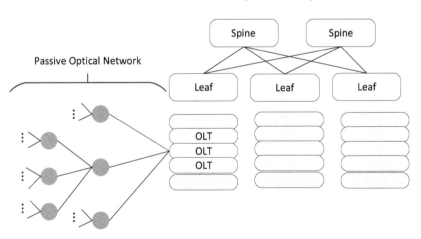

Figure 6.39. SDN-Enabled Broadband Access [171].

The cluster shown in Fig. 6.39 represents a combination of servers and access devices connected by a switching fabric (built using OpenFlow switches) and controlled by an SDN controller. In this architecture, functionality, such as a broadband network gateway originally provided by the legacy hardware, can be programmed into the switches instead of as VNF. This solution represents an example of VNF off-loading, where it is possible to move packet processing from the servers into the switches.

6.6.6 Network Telemetry

Traditional monitoring performs reading different fixed counters, such as received or transmitted packets or sampling subsets of packets. SDN goes further and introduces an In-band Network Telemetry (INT) solution. This solution's base is the forwarding pipeline's programming, aiming to collect network state during packet processing. INT implies encoding instructions from the controller into packet header fields and then processing them by OpenFlow switches through the forwarding pipeline. These instructions explain to the device what state to collect and how to write it into the packet, and they can be embedded either in regular data packets or in special probe packets. The INT also implements traffic sinks, whose task is to retrieve and report the collected information, which are the results of previously mentioned instructions.

6.7 SDN and NFV Integrations

SDN and NFV are complementary technologies that can enhance network management, flexibility, and efficiency. There are many use cases with a strong demand to provide network flexibility, scalability, efficiency, and service delivery in various domains and scenarios. We would like to point out the following use cases where it is useful to implement SDN/NFV architecture:

- on-demand and Application-specific Traffic Steering,
- middleboxes virtualization,
- virtualized customer's premises equipment,
- wireless, and
- mobile networks.

6.7.1 On-demand and Application-specific Traffic Steering

Traffic steering represents the possibility of directing users' requests to the appropriate service/content sources in accordance with the available networking resources and capabilities on the client and server side, user permissions, and location. Users can have different requests, such as a video streaming service that requires strict performance. In these cases, it is necessary to enable on-demand and application-specific traffic steering, which could ensure more efficient resource usage and better QoE for the user. In the SDN/NFV architecture, the role of SDN is to enable

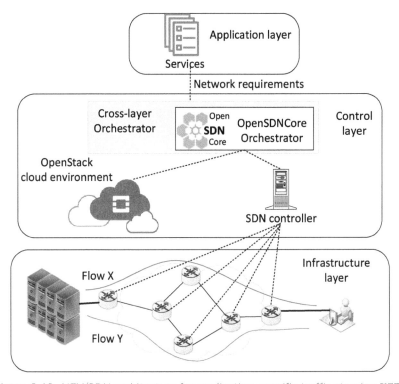

Figure 6.40. NFV/SDN architecture for application-specific traffic steering [177].

efficient traffic steering between VNFs, providing dynamic service chaining. By decoupling control from the data plane, SDN enables the exchange of information between the application and network layers, allowing traffic routing through virtualized network functions (like firewalls or load balancers) flexibly, as shown in Fig. 6.40 [177].

The SDN/NFV architecture presented in Fig. 6.40 contains a cross-layer interface between the application and network layer [178]. This interface enables the deployment of network services with on-demand and application-specific traffic steering. The key component is the Cross-Layer Orchestrator, which serves as an NFVO and VNFM to manage the lifecycle of services in the OpenStack cloud environment and WAN domains based on OpenFlow. In a production environment, this component can be implemented over the OpenSDNCore orchestrator using Java programming language.

6.7.2 Middleboxes Virtualization

Today, we often encounter middleboxes in enterprise networks whose deployment aims to improve performance (e.g., traffic shaping or load balancing), provide security functionalities, and deep packet inspection for incoming and outgoing traffic. However, hardware-based middleboxes have certain limitations, such as high operational costs caused by management complexity (proprietary solutions need to be deployed, configured, and managed individually) and significant capital costs (CAPEX). Practically, to implement new network functions, one or more middleboxes must be bought. The reason is the inflexibility of proprietary hardware, which creates vendor lock-in and limits innovation.

By implementing SDN/NFV architectures, we can significantly reduce costs and expedite the delivery of network functions. This approach offers elasticity and dynamic service chaining, paving the way for a more efficient and adaptable network infrastructure. NFV efficiently manages virtual middleboxes, while SDN facilitates the interconnection between VNFs, enabling the delivery of network services through Service Function Chaining (SFC). Among the various solutions available, the one that stands out is Glasgow Network Functions (GNF). GNF excels in deploying and managing container-based network services across diverse cloud environments, as illustrated in Fig. 6.41 [179].

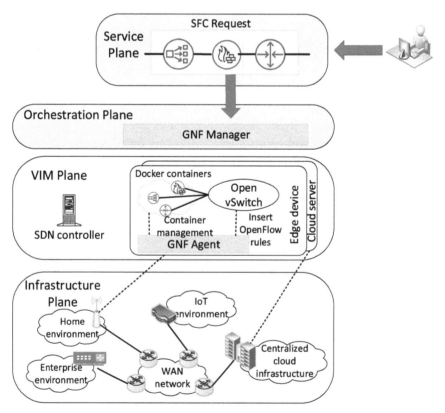

Figure 6.41. The GNF platform [177].

Figure 6.41 provides a comprehensive view of the Glasgow Network Functions (GNF), which is composed of four distinct planes. The first plane, the infrastructure plane, contains all the physical resources of the network and computations. It incorporates NFV centralized cloud infrastructures with edge devices such as CPEs, virtual routers, and IoT gateways. The subsequent planes, VIM, and orchestration are responsible for resource orchestration. At the VIM plane, the GNF agent is deployed on all cloud servers and edge devices, enabling local VNF instantiation using the Docker engine for rapid deployments and low resource utilization. It also facilitates local traffic steering management through virtual switches and OpenFlow rules. GNF leverages the SDN controller for network connectivity in the NFVI. At the orchestration plane, the GNF manager receives NFV service requests and performs the necessary operations using the SDN controller and GNF agent instances.

6.7.3 Virtualized Customer Premises Equipment

In many cases, customer premises equipment (CPE) can present a problem for providers due to maintenance costs, management difficulties, and the impossibility of performing remote upgrades. As a solution, we can see the virtualization of functions associated with CPE, where creating virtual CPE (vCPE) is challenging due to problems related to network services instantiation in distributed infrastructures (e.g., using multiple NFVI-PoPs). In this case, it is a rational solution to implement VNFs in the service provider's cloud platform (cloud CPE) or the on-premise CPE, depending on latency and available resources. Such a scenario implies implementing SDN for communication management on the cloud, CPE, and WAN [180].

Figure 6.42 presents a service-oriented SDN/NFV architecture for provider networks, offering a range of generic network services that can be selected by providers (DHCP and NAT) or end users. The benefits of this architecture lie in its flexibility. Network services can be implemented in a distributed manner, either in the provider data center or the CPE, and both solutions are based on a three-layer architecture [180]. The service layer application (SLApp) empowers different providers and end users to choose their network services, providing a mechanism for authentication and a high-level data model for defining flexible network services known as the Service Graph (SG). The key component at the orchestration layer is the Global Orchestrator (GO), which manages the Forwarding Graph (FG) received from SLApp. In this way, it is possible to deploy network services according to the VNF requirements and infrastructure capabilities. The key component at the orchestration layer is the Global Orchestrator (GO), which manages the Forwarding Graph (FG) received from SLApp. In this way, we can deploy network services according to VNF requirements and infrastructure capabilities. By using GO, it is

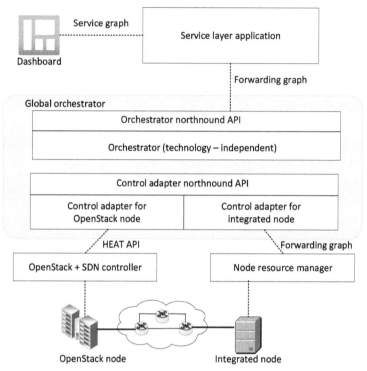

Figure 6.42. An SDN/NFV architecture design for vCPE [177].

possible to implement multiple control adaptors and coordinate different infrastructures (e.g., OpenStack and integrated node).

In network service deployment, the integrated node and the OpenStack node
play distinct roles. The integrated node, which represents the CPE, receives a Forwarding Graph (FG) from the Global Orchestrator (GO) via the node resource
manager (NRM) using REST API. The NRM's task is to instantiate all VNFs,
which can be done using Docker containers, DPDK process, or hypervisor. It uses
an extensible Data-Path daemon (xDPd) to create an OpenFlow switch and its
corresponding controller for each FG. On the other hand, the OpenStack node
represents the provider data center, with OpenStack or other cloud platforms for
network service deployment. In this setup, a hypervisor is responsible for VNF creation, while the controller and virtual switches handle the traffic steering.

6.7.4   Wireless Network

The surge in wireless communications' popularity reflects new demands, including
mobility support, programmability, rapid network service delivery, performance,
and security. However, the management and configuration of today's large WiFi

networks often prove complex and inflexible in solving application requirements or user needs. As a real production solution, OpenSDWN, a software-defined wireless networking architecture, emerges to address these challenges efficiently. OpenS-DWN combines the advantages of SDN, NFV, and wireless, offering a robust NFV/SDN approach through the implementation of per-client access points (Aps) and virtual middleboxes [181].

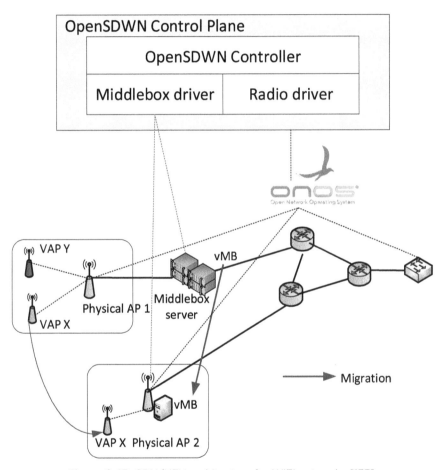

Figure 6.43. SDN/NFV architecture for WiFi networks [177].

Figure 6.43 presents a comprehensive view of the proposed architecture, featuring the creation of a Light Virtual Access Point (LVAP). This LVAP leverages SDN applications to abstract certain functions of the 802.11 AP, such as authentication, handoff, and client associations. In this setup, a physical AP supports the establishment of multiple LVAPs, one for each client. Each LVAP serves as a dedicated link between its client and infrastructure. The architecture also allows for the implementation of a firewall as a virtual middlebox, either on a middlebox server or at the access point. Integration with LVAPs is facilitated through virtual networks. A service differentiation mechanism (DPI-based) endeavors to identify and classify flows, redirecting traffic to the appropriate virtual middleboxes (vMB). The OpenSDWN controller orchestrates all these functions, enabling seamless mobility with the migration of both LVAPs and vMBs among APs.

6.7.5   Mobile Networks

In mobile networks, mobile edge computing (MEC) or multi-access edge computing provides IT and cloud computing within the Radio Access Network (RAN). ETSI performs standardization through Group Specification (GS) MEC [182, 183]. Operators deploy a set of computer and storage resources (e.g., data centers, clusters, etc.) at the edges of mobile networks to assist the core data center in supporting computing and communication (Fig. 6.44) [184].

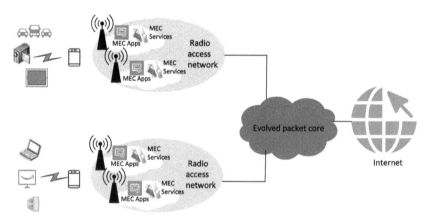

Figure 6.44. SDN/NFV architecture for Mobile edge computing [177].

Figure 6.44 shows the SDN/NFV solution for MEC, which is important to enable 5G networks according to 5G-PPP. The focus of this solution is to deliver services closest to the users and to fulfill certain requirements (bandwidth, delay, jitter, context awareness, and mobility) of critical applications, such as IoT or augmented reality. In practice, we see the implementation of such a solution in the EU H2020 SELFNET project [185], a significant initiative in the field of MEC and 5G networks. The SELFNET project proposes the design and implementation of an autonomic management framework for 5G networks, incorporating cloud computing and artificial intelligence. The goal is to reduce operational costs and improve the QoE of the end users. This way, it is possible to solve issues related to self-protection against distributed attacks, self-healing in case of network errors, and self-optimization of the network traffic.

The approach proposed in a SELFNET project implies building a federated cloud infrastructure. This infrastructure consists of multiple edge NFVI-PoP and a core NFVI-PoP that provide the resources needed for VNFs' execution (VNFs support some management elements and network services). In such architecture, SDN controllers are responsible for connectivity between edge NFVI-PoPs and the core NFVI-PoP through the creation of virtual networks.

6.8   Conclusion

SDN and NFV are technologies that implement and manage network services more efficiently. We should implement these technologies together to utilize their benefits. NFV provides portable virtual network functions, while SDN enables more efficient resource management and orchestration, and together, they ensure the building of flexible, scalable, and agile infrastructures. These two technologies suit various network environments, such as enterprise networks, data centers, campus networks, and service provider networks. Their implementation can help reduce the time required to implement new services, simplify the implementation process, and reduce costs.

From the perspective of data centers, the issue of managing a heterogeneous computer infrastructure consisting of a large number of servers and virtual machines is very important. With SDN and NFV, it is possible to simplify the virtualization process, enable greater mobility by automatically migrating virtual machines, and increase the utilization of available hardware and bandwidth. Higher energy efficiency is an important indicator of their implementation because it can reduce electricity consumption, especially in the data center, and significantly reduce maintenance costs.

The possibility of SDN, NFV, and cloud integration significantly benefits LAN and WAN environments. This integration is particularly interesting for service providers with increasingly complex user demands. It is useful for services that must meet different Service Level Agreements (SLAs) regarding availability, scalability, and security. For example, it is possible to provide a minimum recovery time and enable optimal traffic redirection without affecting user services. More details about the mentioned integration will be presented in the next section.

DOI: 10.1561/9781638283591.ch7

Chapter 7

NFV Implementation in the Cloud

Cloud computing is a modern computing concept that combines utility computing, on-demand services, grid computing, and software-as-a-service. It brings business models used to deliver IT capabilities (software, platforms, hardware) as a service request, scalable and elastic. This new trend in computing enables the exposure of IT resources as a service on the Internet with the supply of new mechanisms that allow providers to give users access to a virtually unlimited number of resources. Cloud providers offer billing mechanisms to use these resources based on their consumption.

NFV implementation is of great importance for cloud computing because it allows the creation of networks that are more agile and responsive. It is a process that enables the transition from traditional hardware-based to software-based (virtualized) network functions. This process begins with the identification of network functions that are suitable for virtualization, continues with the selection of an appropriate cloud provider, and completes with the design and deployment of VNFs on the cloud infrastructure. The crucial tasks in this process are building the virtual environment, orchestrating VNFs, providing strong security measures, and dynamic resource allocation. NFV implementation brings many advantages to the cloud, such as improved flexibility, scalability, and cost-effectiveness. Its lifecycle consists of testing, incremental deployment, and continuous improvements in cloud performance. This section aims to highlight the importance of cloud technologies in modern computing and point out the advantages obtained by the implementation of the NFV concept.

The integration of these technologies is of great benefit to society as a whole. It helps to overcome numerous issues in a fast and efficient way, even in crises. As an example, we can mention the COVID-19 pandemic, where the implementation of such solutions enabled educational institutions to respond quickly and ensure the continuity of the educational processes [186]. Generally, in these cases, it is necessary to redesign the network architecture to provide optimal network resource utilization as fast as possible. It is necessary to examine the capabilities of existing IT infrastructure and examine the possibilities to connect cloud platforms and support work in virtual space. Implementations of cloud and NFV technologies imply the transition of information anytime, anywhere, through networks.

7.1   Introduction to Cloud

IT infrastructure represents the basis of every modern system, whose crucial task is to support various services and applications in heterogeneous environments. It can be defined in different ways, so for network administrators, it represents a set of network devices, while for developers, IT infrastructure represents a platform for application development. In essence, IT infrastructure means a combination of hardware and software that should enable the realization of various business processes. For this reason, providers and enterprises pay special attention to its design.

The development and implementation of solutions related to the availability, scalability, efficiency, and security of the IT infrastructure are a priority for a provider or a company infrastructure design. Traditional computer networks based on hierarchical organization can only respond to increasingly complex user requirements to a specific extent [187]. Figure 7.1. shows a design of traditional network infrastructure and its basic characteristics – hierarchy and redundancy. However, the static nature and insufficient level of programmability greatly complicate infrastructure management and make it more complex [188]. Further network softwarization has been imposed as a logical solution to overcome these shortcomings.

Many definitions of cloud computing exist in the literature. Scientists and professionals often use the definition of the USA National Institute of Standards and Technology (NIST), which defines the cloud as a computing model that allows users ubiquitous and appropriate access to shared infrastructure on demand, with minimal interaction with the service provider [189]. This definition includes five basic cloud characteristics:

- on-demand self-servicing – users can get resources without direct interaction with the service provider,

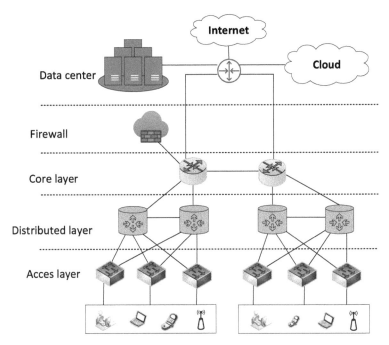

Figure 7.1. Traditional network infrastructure.

- broad network access – users can access resources using standard computer networks' mechanisms,
- resource pooling – all available resources are pooled and assigned to users according to requirements; while users are not aware of the exact resource location,
- rapid elasticity – high level of scalability, given that resources are elastically provided following user requirements and
- service measurement – monitoring and reporting on used resources.

There are many definitions of cloud computing, which indicates that it is a new concept of computing. This concept, based on advanced technologies, such as virtualization and clustering, came to market parallel with the global economic crisis when enterprises focused on core activities and cost reduction. The pay-as-you-go service pricing principle was applied to respond to the technological and financial requirements, which means paying only for the resources and period they used. This way, cloud users do not have to invest in infrastructure to be able to implement their services or offer them to other users. The ability to quickly allocate the necessary resources at the user's request makes this process very simple and scalable. The fact that services in the cloud are mostly web-oriented means that access can be achieved through different user devices, such as desktop and laptop computers or mobile phones [130].

7.2   The Fundamentals of Cloud Computing

The traditional business concept implies the delivery of finished products to users. In cloud computing, providers build appropriate services and deliver them according to specific user requirements. Besides the service, the access method is also important to users. Cloud computing provides users with the required resources at the right time without knowledge of resource location. Users do not need to be familiar with the concepts of cloud computing or have additional expertise in the field of computing to be able to use this technology (Fig. 7.2) [130].

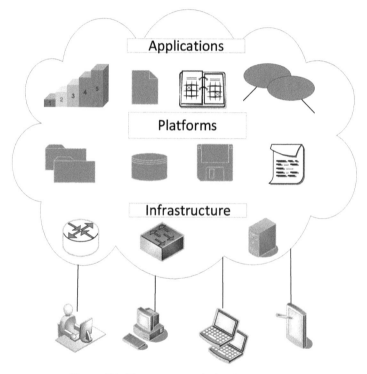

Figure 7.2. The concept of cloud computing.

It is necessary to ensure a high level of abstraction of physical resources to achieve flexibility, efficiency, and scalability within the network infrastructure. Creating a shared, dynamic, and highly scalable virtual environment makes it possible to host many different, resource-demanding applications and their data. To create such an environment, implementing technologies such as virtualization, which separates software from hardware, and clustering, which enables the grouping of servers into a unified physical resource, is of the greatest importance. Further, it is possible to implement multitenancy, allowing multiple users to use one instance of an application (tenants are logically separated). Resource and cost-sharing represent a completely different principle compared to the traditional approach, where building a separate application or service instance for each user is necessary.

The cloud computing concept brings benefits related to cost reduction. It enables efficient resource usage by implementing the following rules:

- users can access resources at any time and from any location,
- only the required resources can be used,
- only a minimal presence of network devices at the user's location is possible, and
- rapid response to new resource demands.

7.3   Cloud Architecture

Knowledge of cloud architecture is a key element of its deployment, and combining all the components and technologies required for cloud computing is essential. Well-designed cloud architecture is a prerequisite for achieving many benefits. For this reason, organizations usually start migration to the cloud with a lift-and-shift approach, where on-premises applications shift to the cloud with minimal modifications. Applications' final deployment and running depend mainly on cloud architecture, which defines the integration of the components and resource pool creation, sharing, and scaling.

The following components represent the foundation of cloud architecture:

- A frontend platform – contains the user devices (laptop or desktop computer, mobile phone, web browser, and others) that enable interaction with the cloud and access to appropriate services.
- A backend platform – consists of many components that build the cloud, such as computing resources, storage, security mechanisms, and management.
- A cloud-based delivery model – implies three types of cloud delivery models: Software-as-a-Service (SaaS), Infrastructure-as-a-Service (IaaS), and Platform-as-a-Service (PaaS).
- A network (internet, intranet, or intercloud) – connects the frontend and backend cloud architecture components and enables data transfer between them.

As mentioned, backend platform components are important in creating cloud architecture. The backend software has the task of providing access and fulfilling users' requirements. These requirements usually refer to accessing cloud resources such as storage, applications, and development environments. An efficient service that takes care of resources and applications running on them requires a suitable running environment. The cloud runtime uses virtualization technology and hypervisors to create this environment (hypervisors represent all user services, servers, and networking), including data storage. Data storage is of great importance for the cloud because the operation of applications depends on it. For this reason, flexible, scalable storage services that can store and manage vast amounts of data in the cloud represent an imperative.

The most important backend component is infrastructure. It contains the hardware and software components required for systems to run smoothly and implies real-time service and data management according to user requirements. Efficient communication between the backend and frontend cloud architecture components is a prerequisite for dynamic resource allocation. Finally, the wider deployment of cloud computing brings security challenges. It is very important to implement security solutions and provide service visibility, prevent data loss and downtime, and ensure redundancy (perform backups, debugging, and implement virtual firewalls).

A simple way to understand cloud architecture is to group cloud components at various layers (Fig. 7.3).

Cloud computing architecture has a hierarchical organization consisting of three layers:

- The hardware layer is the lowest and is responsible for managing physical resources. This layer is implemented first and represents the basis of the data center's functioning.
- The virtualization layer is the middle layer, containing two sublayers: infrastructure and platform. Different virtualization techniques implemented at the infrastructure sublayer (e.g., virtualization of the network, storage, server,

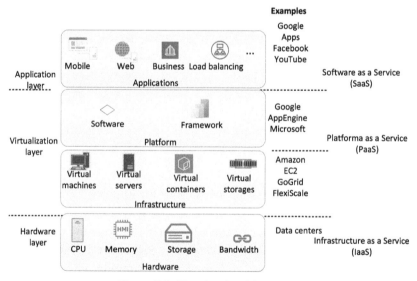

Figure 7.3. The cloud architecture.

and others) provide dynamic resource allocation, which is the base of cloud computing architecture. The platform sublayer is above the infrastructure layer and includes operating systems and suitable environments for application development.

- The application layer is the highest in the architecture and includes the applications available to users and network services.

It is very simple to conclude that cloud computing architecture is modular. Each layer is separated from the layers above and below, ensuring each operates independently. Also, a similarity with the Open Systems Interconnection (OSI) network model can be observed (not a strict dependence on it). The architecture modularity enables support for different application requirements while reducing management and maintenance costs [130].

7.4   A Cloud-based Delivery Model

Cloud computing has changed businesses' usage of technology in many enterprises. The enterprises gain the capability to implement remote work efficiently and scale infrastructure on the click, which represents significant improvements in infrastructure and its management. The first step in choosing a solution for a cloud is understanding the differences between the three common types of cloud delivery models. According to the network resource usage method, it is possible to identify the following models of service delivery [190]:

- *Software as a Service* (SaaS),
- *Platform as a Service* (PaaS) and
- *Infrastructure as a Service* (IaaS).

Figure 7.4 shows the relationship between services, applications, and cloud models. Infrastructure and platform resources are delivered based on user requirements. Each layer of the architecture can be implemented as a service of the layer above it. Similarly, each layer can be viewed as a user of the layer below it.

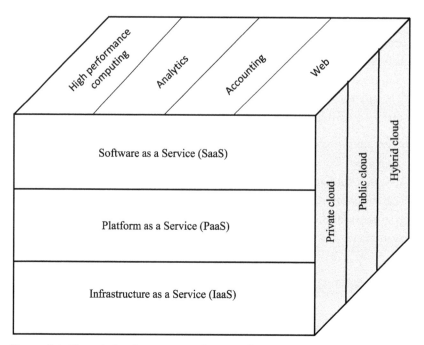

Figure 7.4. The relation between services, applications, and the cloud models.

7.4.1 Software as a Service

The SaaS model enables the use of finished applications, where the provision of complete hardware and software infrastructure is the cloud provider's responsibility [191]. The user leases certain software from the provider and pays according to resource and service consumption (*pay-per-use* principle). Users can access the services using any device, a simple interface such as a web browser, and the internet.

This way, users do not possess, manage, or maintain the infrastructure (servers, routers, switches, storage, and others) required to use the software, but that is the responsibility of the cloud providers (Fig. 7.5). Since the user does not have to own or maintain network equipment, this model represents a suitable solution for small and medium-sized enterprises. They can achieve large savings related to equipment but also get licensed software necessary for business processes.

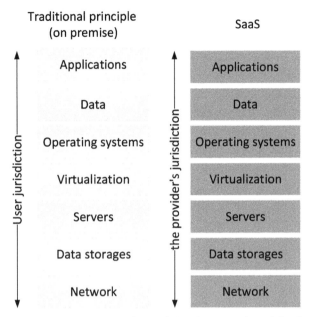

Figure 7.5. The jurisdictions in the traditional approach and SaaS model.

Figure 7.5 shows a comparative presentation of the conventional approach and the SaaS model. The advantages of applying the SaaS model are the following [130]:

- Optimal utilization of resources.
- Much faster access to new technologies and applications.
- More efficient debugging process.
- Possibility to expand and adapt applications to new business conditions easily.
- Improving the security, performance, and availability of applications.
- There are low initial costs and cost reductions since maintenance is the provider's responsibility.

Business processes are a good example of SaaS model implementation. In practice, the following business applications are often used:

- *Customer Relationship Management* (CRM),
- *Enterprise Resource Planning* (ERP) and
- *Human Resources Management* (HRM).

Today, there are many commercial solutions based on the SaaS model, such as Google Apps, Cisco WebEx, Microsoft Office 365, and Dropbox.

7.4.2   Platform as a Service

The PaaS model enables the creation, running, and management of applications using different development tools on the provider's platform. Users manage the applications and have a certain level of access privileges but do not have full rights to administer the hardware, network, or operating system [191]. They can deploy the applications without having to deal with the licensing costs and complexity of deploying and maintaining the underlying hardware and software infrastructure (e.g., servers, storage, and networking).

PaaS is a comprehensive environment that provides both the development platform and the infrastructure for running the application. It includes services and tools that should provide development, testing, implementation, hosting, and maintenance of the applications, all using a web interface for access. By implementing the multitenancy principle, PaaS allows multiple users to use applications at the same time. Also, PaaS provides scalability, allowing applications to scale up or down easily based on demand. A standard set of tools in the PaaS model consists of:

- operating system,
- program environment,
- database and
- application or web server.

A comparative presentation of the traditional approach and the PaaS model of service provisioning is shown in Fig. 7.6.

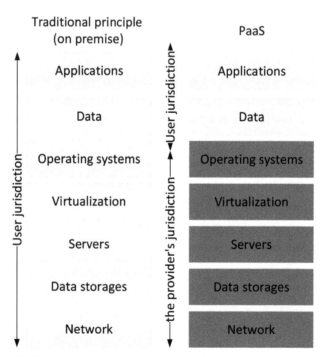

Figure 7.6. The jurisdictions in the traditional approach and PaaS model.

The benefits of PaaS deployment are:

- cost reduction as the users lease the platform (and not just the hardware),
- ability to implement own applications and complete control over them and
- simple integration with other systems.

Today, there are many commercial solutions based on the PaaS model, including Microsoft Azure (formerly known as Windows Azure), AWS Elastic Beanstalk, and Google App Engine.

7.4.3   Infrastructure as a Service

The IaaS model provides a virtualized infrastructure over the internet at the users' requests [192]. Users can manage data processing and storage, network, and other resources, whereby the user can create and use arbitrary software (operating systems and applications). They cannot manage the underlying cloud infrastructure but have full control over the operating system, data stores, and applications. In the IaaS model, payment for the service is made based on the consumption achieved, which is measured based on the time spent and the specific resources used. This cloud service model brings advantages, primarily to new users who are not obliged to invest in a complete network infrastructure.

A comparative presentation of the traditional approach and the IaaS model of service provisioning is shown in Fig. 7.7.

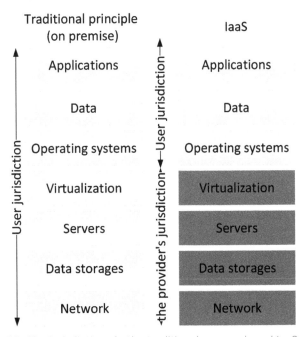

Figure 7.7. The jurisdictions in the traditional approach and IaaS model.

The advantages of IaaS deployment are:

- delivery of resources (e.g., CPU, network equipment, and data storage) as a service,
- full control over virtual machines,
- the multitenancy approach allows multiple users to coexist and use the same infrastructure resources,
- dynamic resource scaling according to requirements,
- costs based on the actual use of resources and
- focus on business development.

Today, there are many commercial solutions based on the IaaS model, such as Elastic Compute Cloud (EC2) and Rackspace.

7.5 Cloud Types

Today, cloud technologies are an integral part of computing in every enterprise. The reason is that clouds provide various services and secure data storage for customers with minimal costs. Each enterprise has specific needs that cloud services should fulfill. Despite many similarities, which primarily refer to the usage of virtualization and clusterization technologies, operating systems, management platforms, and APIs, we cannot see two identical cloud infrastructures in practice. Differences between them are primarily related to clouds' location and ownership. The main cloud computing types are private clouds, public clouds, hybrid clouds, and multi-clouds.

7.5.1 Public Cloud

A public cloud is a model of publicly available infrastructure with services (e.g., storage, computing power, and applications) that are hosted and managed on remote servers in data centers. Cloud services are delivered over the internet by network providers (Fig. 7.8). It is the widely used service delivery model for many reasons. From a financial perspective, enterprises do not have to invest in the infrastructure, and payment for services is made based on resource usage. Further, from a technical standpoint, the cloud providers manage the entire infrastructure, and the maintenance and building of new capacities are under their jurisdiction. Users can access the cloud infrastructure and use services on a pay-as-you-go model whereby they believe that the cloud possesses an unlimited set of resources. Essentially, that is not true because users acquire this interpretation through implementing the fast elasticity mechanism (after the termination of use, resources are returned to the pool and assigned to another user if necessary).

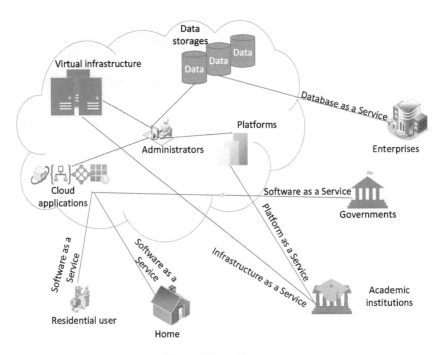

Figure 7.8. Public cloud.

As previously stated, the complete cloud infrastructure is under the provider's jurisdiction. In many cases, providers can decide to distribute their infrastructure over several locations due to redundancy. So, cloud providers are responsible for making different decisions, such as service delivery policies, prices, and billing models. Despite the many advantages of the public cloud, there is a potential problem with data and network security, which, in some cases, could affect the efficiency of the business model [124]. Amazon EC2, Google AppEngine, Sales-Force, and IBM BlueCloud are examples of public clouds.

7.5.2 Private Cloud

A private (internal) cloud (Fig. 7.9) is a model that refers to a dedicated computer environment exclusively used by one user, such as an enterprise or some organization. It operates within the private (enterprise) data center, whereby the enterprise manages the entire infrastructure, as well as the applications that exist in the private cloud [126]. Sometimes, private clouds can also be at a special location, for example, in the computing centers that are responsible for them.

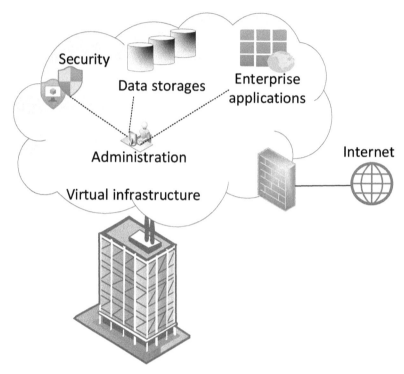

Figure 7.9. Private cloud.

Unlike public clouds that serve multiple organizations, the owners of private clouds have complete control over data, security, reliability, and quality of services. This way, private clouds can provide greater control, security, and customization because they allow enterprises to have more control over their data, infrastructure, and applications while leveraging cloud computing benefits such as scalability and flexibility. Private clouds represent the ideal solutions for users with specific security or performance requirements that public cloud services are unable to provide. However, such a solution still brings significant costs for enterprises since it is necessary to build and maintain the entire infrastructure. Besides enterprises, the private cloud model finds application in academic and research environments. There are many companies, such as Microsoft, Cisco, IBM, Amazon, and VMware, that provide private cloud services.

7.5.3 Hybrid Cloud

Hybrid clouds (Fig. 7.10) represent a unique architecture that is a result of a combination of private and public clouds, which remain separate entities. Mutual connections between them allow data and applications to be shared. Enterprises often decide on a hybrid cloud approach to leverage the benefits of both types of clouds while addressing specific business needs, security concerns, and regulatory require-ments. The key motives are the need to provide strictly confidential data that does not leave the enterprise's location and the requirement to avoid costs by using a large number of resources (e.g., for data processing or storage) for non-confidential data [130].

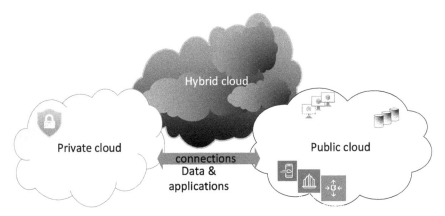

Figure 7.10. Hybrid cloud.

Figure 7.10 shows that confidential data and applications are hosted in a pri-vate cloud environment, which provides more control, security, and customization. Other data and applications are hosted in a public cloud, offering scalability, cost-effectiveness, and accessibility. The hybrid cloud design requires special attention, with careful separation of public and private parts and the definition of different privilege levels for other services. The integration between private and public clouds often requires the implementation of specialized technologies that ensure secure communication and data movement between them. API-driven architectures, vir-tual private networks (VPNs), and orchestration tools are commonly used to man-age hybrid cloud configurations. We must note that orchestration is essential for managing and optimizing hybrid cloud environments, where organizations use a combination of on-premises infrastructure and cloud services.

7.5.4 Multi-clouds

Multi-cloud (Fig. 7.11) refers to using services from different cloud providers at the same time. This way, a multi-cloud environment enables the building of a flexible environment for each workload, which can be private, public, or a com-bination of both cloud environments [175]. The creation of resource and service policies independently of vendors offers the possibility of implementing solutions that best suit specific enterprises' needs and minimize vendor lock-in. In practice, multi-cloud solutions can use technologies like Dockers, Kubernetes, Terraform, or Pulumi with the aim of providing a greater level of flexibility and portability to migrate, build, and optimize applications across multiple clouds and computing environments. However, the management of multiple clouds can be complex from the integration, security, and data management aspects. Users should track, secure, and manage their workloads consistently across all environments from a single interface. It is not a simple task because each provider uses different tools and APIs for cloud service management. To provide more efficient management, cloud providers must incorporate appropriate solutions directly into their products to enable the required level of visibility and efficient cost and configuration monitoring. We must emphasize the maintenance complexity that arises from the demand to navigate various service offerings, pricing models, and management tools offered by each cloud provider. Also, the coordination of updates, patches, and compliance measures across multiple platforms can be complicated. Generally, the complexity level depends on many factors, such as the scale of deployment, the diversity of services utilized, and the specific requirements of the organization. Some enterprises opt for automation and adopt standardized practices to mitigate complexities.

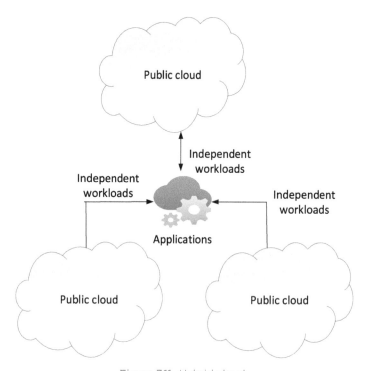

Figure 7.11. Hybrid cloud.

7.5.5   Cloud – Summary

We must emphasize that each cloud type has its advantages and weaknesses, and the choice depends on the enterprise's specific requirements and long-term goals. Table 7.1 shows a comparative view of the benefits, limitations, and use cases of previously mentioned types of clouds.

Table 7.1.   Benefits, limitations, and use cases of different cloud types.

Cloud type	Benefits	Limitations	Use cases
Public cloud	Cost-effective – the pay-as-you-go model reduces upfront infrastructure costs. Scalability – easily scale resources up or down based on demand. Accessibility – accessible from any location with an internet connection. Reliability – is provided redundancy and high availability.	Security – data security can be a concern due to shared infrastructure. Dependency – relies on the provider's infrastructure and service availability. Compliance challenges with specific regulations.	Ideal for temporary workloads. Easily deploy and scale web apps. Collaboration tools – shared documents, emails, and collaboration suites.
Private cloud	Offers more control and security over data. It is tailored to specific organizational needs. Easier adaptation to specific compliance regulations.	Higher upfront investment and maintenance costs. It is not as flexible in scaling compared to public clouds. Requires skilled personnel for management.	Industries like healthcare or finance have strict data and privacy requirements. Hosting applications with specialized requirements.
Hybrid cloud	A blend of public and private clouds offers flexibility in workload placement. Scale resources by leveraging both cloud environments. Use public cloud for less sensitive data and private for critical workloads.	Management and integration can be complex. Data movement between public and private clouds can introduce security risks.	Disaster recovery – utilize the public cloud for backup and recovery. Seasonal workloads – scale into the public cloud during peak times.

(*Continued*)

Table 7.1. Continued

Cloud type	Benefits	Limitations	Use cases
Multi-cloud	Reduces vendor lock-in and enhances flexibility. Avoids reliance on a single provider's capabilities or outages. Leveraging different providers for unique services.	Different cloud platforms might not seamlessly integrate. Requires robust management and monitoring tools.	Ensuring high availability by distributing across multiple providers. Utilizing different providers to meet specific compliance standards in other regions.

Issues such as high costs, security and compliance concerns, and vendor lock-in can cause enterprises to give up on moving entirely to the public cloud. In these cases, some enterprises even repatriate their workloads back to on-premises infrastructure. However, it is a real rarity because enterprises typically choose to build their cloud using open-source platforms. For them, open-source cloud platforms are a better choice than a proprietary cloud platform, primarily considering the costs that arise due to license payments. Further, by implementing open-source platforms, enterprises gain the possibility to choose between many frameworks, tools, and services. Besides openness, the open-source platforms should deliver advantages such as guarantees in terms of SLA, testing, and integration offered by proprietary solutions. In practice, there are many open-source platforms, such as OpenStack, OpenNebula, CloudStack, and Eucalyptus.

7.6   OpenStack

OpenStack is an open-source platform that emerged on the market in July 2010 as an initiative launched by NASA and Rackspace [193]. This platform is a collection of various software tools used for the creation and management of both public and private clouds, with the aim of providing users access to remote computing resources and applications run as services on reliable virtual servers. OpenStack provides IaaS through a set of interrelated services, such as computing, storage, networking, identity, and others. Users can choose to install part or all services, where each service has an API to enable overall integration. Generally, OpenStack has a highly modular architecture, which allows the integration of different components based on users' needs. Many virtualization solutions can be implemented, such as ESX, Hyper-V, KVM, LXC, QEMU, UML, Xen, and XenServer; components can be integrated based on users' needs. This way, it is possible to build a flexible environment adaptable to various applications (the entire code can be modified and adapted as needed). Besides flexibility, scalability for different infrastructure sizes is the next characteristic of OpenStack, which implies the deployment of up to 1 million physical machines, up to 60 million virtual machines, and billions of stored objects [194]. It provides horizontal scaling very easily, which means that some tasks can run concurrently and serve different numbers of users by just spinning up more instances [195]. We must emphasize that OpenStack is often used for a validation testbed in case it is necessary to adopt and develop the new standards.

OpenStack deployment consists of many services (components) whose goal is to provide an API to access infrastructure resources (Fig. 7.12). It is the following services [193]:

- Shared services,
- Compute services,
- Hardware lifecycle services,
- Storage services,
- Networking services,
- Workload provisioning services,
- Application lifecycle services,
- API proxy services,
- Web frontend services and
- Orchestration services.

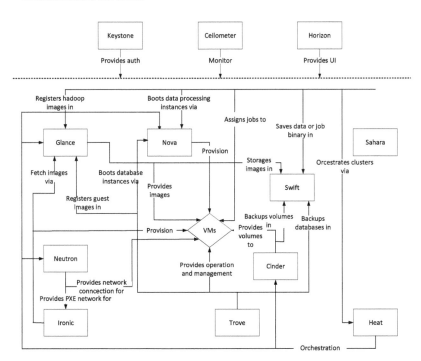

Figure 7.12. The relationships among the OpenStack services.

Figure 7.12 shows the conceptual architecture, which includes OpenStack services as independent parts authenticated through a shared Identity service. The services communicate through public APIs, except in cases where it is necessary to use privileged administrator commands. Each service can use at least one API process, which is responsible for listening to the API requests, preprocessing them, and passing them to other service parts. Communication between processes takes place through an Advanced Message Queuing Protocol (AMQP) message broker (e.g., RabbitMQ, MySQL, MariaDB, and SQLite), and any change of service state is stored in a database. Users can access OpenStack via the web interface implemented by the Horizon dashboard or via command-line clients and by issuing API requests through tools like browser plug-ins [193].

7.6.1   Shared Services

Shared services in OpenStack represent components that different tenants can use. Their role is to provide centralized functionalities for them. This service group contains identity service, placement service, image service, and key management.

Identity service (Keystone) must be installed within an OpenStack environment first because it provides authentication and management of user accounts and role information [193]. It means that this service enables users to access other OpenStack services based on their assigned roles and permissions and integrate with existing backend directory services like LDAP.

The Placement service provides a list of available resources across the cloud, such as CPU, memory, or storage, providing a complete insight into the available capacity and utilization of computing resources. It assists in the process of resource allocation (e.g., for a new virtual machine) and determines the appropriate host with the required resources. This service interacts with the Nova compute service by exposing RESTful API and aims to provide information about available resources before Nova makes decisions about where to place workloads [193]. The placement service matches resource requirements with the available resources on the compute nodes and provides the information needed for optimal resource allocation and efficient infrastructure utilization.

The Image service (Glance) provides a catalog and repository for disk images, including operating system images and snapshots [193]. Its primary task is discovering, registering, and retrieving VM images by exposing RESTful API. This way, it is possible to analyze VM image metadata and retrieve the actual image, which later can be used as a template for deploying new virtual machines.

The key management service (Barbican) provides a centralized system for the storage, provisioning, and management of encryption keys, certificates, passwords, and other sensitive data used in cloud applications. It focuses on security and compliance and ensures confidentiality and appropriate, sensitive data management by offering a set of functionalities, including secret storage, key generation, certificate management, and a RESTful API for seamless interaction. In this way, other OpenStack services can securely access and utilize cryptographic keys and sensitive data, supporting the overall security of the cloud infrastructure.

7.6.2   Compute Services

The Compute (Nova) and Container (Zun) services are the next group of OpenStack services. Nova service represents the core of this platform [193]. It is responsible for the lifecycle management of virtual instances (virtual machines) because it handles the provisioning and management of computing resources within cloud infrastructure. This service aims to provide a scalable and flexible environment for the creation and management of virtual machines according to user requirements (e.g., launching, scheduling, or terminating virtual machines). It runs on top of existing Linux servers as a set of daemons whose task is to provide appropriate service. Sometimes, in literature, OpenStack Compute (Nova) is defined as a cloud computing fabric controller used for the deployment and management of virtual instances. Communication with other OpenStack services is required for the establishment of basic functions. For example, the interactions with services such as Glance (for accessing and managing images), Neutron (a service for networking), and Cinder (a service for storage resources) enable the efficient orchestration of many processes (e.g., resource allocation according to user demands). The efficient management of computing resources as a prerequisite for IaaS service is provided by Nova's modular architecture and robust APIs. However, Nova has limited support for containers.

For this reason, OpenStack includes Zun service as a component focused on container management. Zun provides APIs that enable users to create, manage, and delete containers within cloud infrastructure. It means that Zun service provides orchestration and management of containerized workloads, like Nova's service for virtual machines. So, users can interact with containers without directly interacting with the container runtime. Like Nova, Zun communicates with other OpenStack services like Keystone for authentication, Neutron for networking, and Cinder for persistent storage, offering a seamless experience for deploying and managing containers alongside traditional virtual machine workloads.

7.6.3   Hardware Lifecycle Services

The Hardware lifecycle group of OpenStack services consists of bare metal provisioning service (Ironic) and lifecycle management of accelerators (Cyborg) [193].

Ironic is designed to provide and manage physical bare-metal servers instead of virtual machines and is used in cases when users require direct access to the underlying hardware resources without the virtualization layer. Ironic uses *Preboot Execution Environment* client-server interface (PXE), *Parallel method invocation* computational concept (PMI), or some vendor-specific remote management protocols to create a unified interface for a heterogeneous set of servers. At the same time, Ironic establishes an interface for Nova service that allows physical servers to be managed as virtual machines. This way, it supports various deployment methods, including local disk images, network-based deployment, and integration with hardware management interfaces. In some cloud environments, hardware accelerators such as *Field-Programmable Gate Arrays* (FPGAs), GPUs, or *Data Processing Units* (DPUs) are utilized to boost the performance of specialized workloads.

Cyborg represents an OpenStack service focused on providing a framework for managing them within an OpenStack environment. Also, it allows users to allocate accelerators to instances managed by Nova to improve the performance of specific workloads. So, Cyborg provides APIs for requesting, provisioning, attaching, and disconnecting accelerators to instances, making it easier for users to utilize these resources as needed.

7.6.4   Storage Services

The next OpenStack service group is a storage service, which consists of the object (Swift) and block (Cinder) storage services and a Manila-shared file system. Swift provides highly available, scalable, and redundant object storage, which is suitable for the cost-effective storing of large amounts of unstructured data [193]. It has a distributed architecture composed of commodity hard drives without a central control point, where objects can be written to many storage devices. For data replication and integrity across the cluster, the OpenStack software is responsible (if one node fails, OpenStack software replicates data from other nodes). Swift is usually used for backups, archives, and content distribution, where objects and metadata are created or modified by using the Object Storage API. This API, implemented as a set of REST web services, supports the standard (non-serialized), JSON, and XML serialized response formats.

Unlike Swift, Cinder is a block storage service that provides persistent storage to Nova virtual machines, Ironic bare metal hosts, and containers in OpenStack [193]. Cinder supports a range of storage backends like Ceph and LVM (Logical Volume Manager), providing flexibility in storage choices. Cinder has component-based architecture, which is highly available because it can scale to very serious workloads. Also, Cinder provides support for process isolation to avoid cascading failures, and failures should be easy to diagnose, debug, and repair. End users use this service to create and manage storage using the Horizon user interface and command line tools or directly by using the REST APIs. Further, Open Stack uses a shared file system service (Manila), which allows multiple users and applications to access shared file storage concurrently by using the Network File System (NFS) or Common Internet File System (CIFS) protocol. It is useful, especially for applications that require shared access to files as needed, enabling features like snapshots for backup, cloning, and scaling storage resources.

7.6.5   Networking Services

In OpenStack, the networking service (Neutron) is responsible for providing network connectivity as a service within a virtual infrastructure consisting of networks, subnets, routers, switches, and all cloud components and services managed by the Nova service [193]. The key task of Neutron is to implement an API that will allow providers to deploy different networking technologies with the aim of providing network connectivity and addressing in the cloud. This way, providers can configure and manage a variety of network services, such as firewalls, NAT, or VPNs (Fig. 7.13).

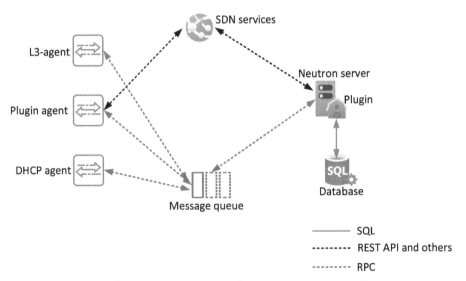

Figure 7.13. The OpenStack Networking components [193].

Figure 7.13 shows the OpenStack Networking diagram consisting of the following components [193]:

- Neutron API server – supports L2 networking and management of IP addresses and enables routing between L2 networks and gateways to external networks.

- Networking plug-ins and agents – they run on each compute node with the aim of accommodating different network devices and software, and this provides flexibility to OpenStack architecture and deployment. Also, it includes integration with various OpenStack components, such as Keystone (for authentication and authorization of API requests), Nova (to plug each virtual NIC on the VM into a particular network), and Horizon (the web-based graphical interface used for creation and management of network services).
- Messaging queue – used for API operations completion by managing RPC requests between the Neutron server and Neutron agents that run on each hypervisor.
- DHCP agent – provides DHCP services to tenant networks.
- L3 agent – enables L3/NAT forwarding for external network access of VMs on tenant networks and requires message queue access.
- SDN services – provides additional networking services to tenant networks.

By implementing Neutron, it is possible to configure different network topologies and instruct other OpenStack services like Compute to attach virtual devices to these networks' ports. This way, Neutron provides flexibility in networking by enabling the creation of different network types, including:

- Provider networks – leverage the existing physical infrastructure and are typically used for connecting instances to external networks or the internet.
- Self-service networks – the creation of virtual networks aims to provide more isolation and flexibility within OpenStack.

Load balancing is an important feature for OpenStack networking because it is necessary to provide scalable and on-demand load-balancing functionality. Octavia is the OpenStack component that provides load balancing as a service (LBaaS), allowing users to manage and distribute incoming application traffic across multiple virtual machines, containers, or bare metal servers [193]. This component is suitable for applications that require high availability and scalability. It can analyze the state of backend servers and ensure that incoming requests come to operational instances (Octavia monitors the application's state and can remove or add servers automatically). Users can define listeners and pools to manage incoming traffic and distribute it to backend servers based on criteria such as protocols, ports, and load-balancing algorithms. Octavia can be deployed as a standalone instance or integrated with other OpenStack services like Nova and Neutron.

OpenStack can enable DNS-as-a-service functionality within the cloud using the Designate component [193]. It implies a programmatic approach, which gives users the possibility to provision and manage DNS domains and records programmatically. This way, users can create, manage, or delete DNS domains along with various record types like A, AAAA, CNAME, and more, enabling the association of domain names with corresponding resources. Integrated with Open-Stack services (e.g., Nova or Neutron), Designate supports multi-tenancy, providing secure DNS management. It is achieved through DNS management segregation, which has a key role in effective and secure DNS design in large environments. It means that DNS servers within the OpenStack deployment have distinct roles, with each server dedicated to a single role. With its RESTful API and high availability configurations, Designate streamlines DNS management, enabling automation and integration and ensuring the reliability of DNS services in an OpenStack environment.

7.6.6   Workload Provisioning Services

Magnum is the OpenStack service that is responsible for the deployment and management of container orchestration engines, such as Kubernetes, Docker Swarm, and Apache Mesos [193]. Its goal is to simplify their deployment and operation, allowing users to manage containerized applications efficiently. Magnum enables users to choose the COE that best suits their application requirements. For example, Magnum can orchestrate an image of an operating system that contains Docker and COE and run it in either virtual machines or bare metal in a cluster configuration. Moreover, it is able to manage complete container orchestration engine life-cycle management, integrated with other OpenStack services.

We must note that Magnum is integrated with other OpenStack components, such as Keystone (for users' authentication and authorization) and the OpenStack dashboard (providing a graphical user interface). Only authorized users and services can interact with the Magnum service via RESTful API in a programmatic way. Users can create, update, and delete container clusters and perform various operations related to container orchestration. They use cluster templates and specify configuration parameters that can be relevant to the cluster infrastructure or the particular COE (e.g., the orchestrator type, number of nodes, node flavors, networking options, and others). Another important feature of Magnum is support for multi-tenancy, which implies that different OpenStack components can create and manage container clusters independently. This way, each component has its own set of resources for running containerized workloads. Magnum integrates with Neutron to provide network connectivity for container clusters, which includes configuring network connectivity within the cluster and exposing services externally.

Many enterprises that use OpenStack have the requirements to simplify the deployment and management of data processing frameworks, such as Hadoop, Apache Spark, or Apache Storm. Sahara is an OpenStack service that can complete these requirements by defining configuration parameters such as the framework version, cluster topology, node hardware details, and others [193]. Secure access to Sahara resources and operations is very important. Sahara integrates with Keystone for user authentication and authorization. Only users with permissions can define cluster configurations using templates and specifying parameters such as the Hadoop version, node count, and others. It is possible to scale clusters up or down based on workload demands dynamically (users can add or remove nodes to adjust the size of the cluster). Also, it is possible to integrate Sahara with another OpenStack service and allow different OpenStack services to create and manage their Hadoop clusters independently. This way, providing multi-tenancy Sahara ensures that OpenStack services have their own set of resources for running big data processing workloads. It is possible to integrate Sahara with other OpenStack services like Cinder or Swift, which aims to provide users with additional storage options for their data processing needs.

Trove is a service that relies entirely on OpenStack and provides Database as a Service. Its task is to simplify the provisioning, management, and scaling of relational and non-relational databases, allowing users to deploy their database instances easily without the need for great database administration skills [193]. Trove supports various database engines, including MySQL, PostgreSQL, MongoDB, Cassandra, and Couchbase, and exposes a RESTful API for programmatic interaction with users. Users choose the database engine that best suits their application requirements.

Database service allows resource isolation and automates complex administrative tasks such as deployment, configuration, patching, backups, restorations, and monitoring. Users can provision and manage database instances using a self-service approach. It implies that they can create, modify, and delete database instances through the Trove API or the OpenStack dashboard (Fig. 7.14).

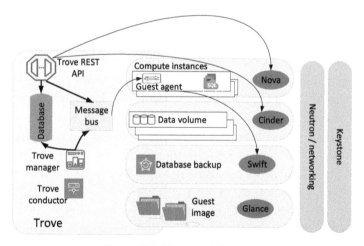

Figure 7.14. Trove architecture.

Figure 7.14 shows integration with OpenStack services for orchestration that enables users to define and manage complex database deployments using appropriate templates, which provide the uniform creation and management of database instances. These database instances are possible to create and manage independently because Trove supports a multi-tenancy approach and allows different OpenStack services to create and manage their database instances. Besides integration with Keystone, which performs users' authentication and authorization, Trove integrates with OpenStack services for monitoring and logging because users must have insights into the performance and health of their database instances and with Neutron for networking.

7.6.7 Application Lifecycle Service

The Application lifecycle management service represents a non-standard OpenStack component, which consists of different tools that together enable the management of various stages of an application's lifecycle within an OpenStack environment. Masakari is an OpenStack service that focuses on ensuring the high availability of instances and applications running on hosts in the OpenStack cloud. Its primary goal is to automate the recovery process in case of failures, minimizing downtime for applications running on the cloud. By automating the recovery process, Masakari reduces the impact of potential failures and ensures continuity of service (Fig. 7.15) [193].

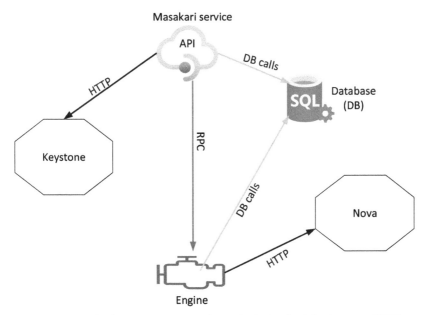

Figure 7.15. The key components of a typical Masakari deployment [193].

Figure 7.15 shows the Masakari architecture, which is composed of an engine and two API servers, each performing different functions. To interface with users, Masakari exposes a REST API, while internally, Masakari communicates via an RPC message-passing mechanism. The task of API servers is to process REST requests (it typically refers to reading/writing in the database) and send RPC messages to the Masakari engine. The engine runs on the same host where the Masakari API is running and has a manager that is listening for RPC messages. This engine is responsible for making responses to the REST calls. Generally, the Masakari continuously monitors the instances or VMs by listening for failure events (e.g., hardware failures, hypervisor failures, or any other critical issues affecting the instance's availability). When a failure event is detected, the role of Masakari is to identify the affected instances and to notify the suitable recovery method to perform the necessary actions for failover or recovery. It implies actions such as restarting the VM on another host, migrating it to a different host, or performing other recovery operations to restore service.

The next component of the Application lifecycle management service is Murano [193], which enables the application's deployment and management in an OpenStack environment to be simplified. It offers an application catalog, tools, and APIs to facilitate the packaging, deployment, and lifecycle management of applications on an OpenStack cloud. The key features of Murano include:

- Application Catalog – contains metadata and deployment instructions, making it easier to deploy complex applications with their necessary components and configurations.
- Application Catalog management – users can create and define application topologies and configurations through a visual environment or YAML-based templates. This way, it is possible to make a description of multi-tier applications and their relationships, specifying components, dependencies, and configurations.
- Lifecycle management – supports application lifecycle management operations such as applications scaling (vertically or horizontally based on changing resource needs), updating (configuration and integration), and monitoring their state and performance.

The Murano architecture consists of the Murano command-line client, Murano dashboard, Murano API, Murano engine, and Murano agent (Fig. 7.16).

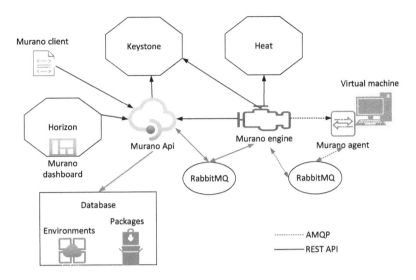

Figure 7.16. Interaction between Murano components.

Figure 7.16 shows the interaction between Murano components. Operations, such as software installation and configuration, can be executed remotely on users' servers through an AMQP queue to the Murano agent. The communication can be configured on a separate AMQP instance to ensure that the servers are isolated. Murano enables integration with various OpenStack services and supports extensibility through custom plugins and components. Murano interacts with these services using their REST API through their Python clients, with the aim of preventing the reimplementation of the existing functionality. Further, Murano automates the deployment process of applications by utilizing Heat, OpenStack's orchestration service. It leverages Heat templates to define and deploy the necessary resources, integrating with other OpenStack services like Nova (compute), Neutron (networking), and Cinder (block storage) as needed for the application.

The next service within this service group is Solum [193], which is responsible for providing easier cloud service consumption and integration with the application development by automating the source-to-image process and simplifying app-centric deployment. It is dedicated to integration with various OpenStack services, like Heat (for orchestration) and Nova (for computing), to facilitate the deployment and management of applications. The goal of Solum implementation is to automate the deployment process by abstracting the complexity of infrastructure setup and application deployment, streamlining the process for developers. Moreover, it supports multiple programming languages and application frameworks, providing a flexible platform for different types of applications.

Freezer is a component of the application lifecycle management service group focused on backup, restoration, and disaster recovery services within OpenStack

(Fig. 7.17) [193]. Its goal is to protect various resources such as virtual machines, volumes, images, shared file systems, and databases. It means that the Freezer possesses the following features:

- Agentless architecture – operates in an agentless mode, utilizing existing OpenStack services and APIs to perform backup and restore operations without requiring additional software on the target resources.
- Incremental backups – optimizes backup operations by only storing changes made since the last backup, thus reducing storage requirements and backup time.
- Multiple backup levels – enables users to perform full, incremental, and differential backups based on their specific requirements.
- Support for various workloads – supports different OpenStack services and resources, including Nova instances, Cinder volumes, Glance images, Swift objects, Manila shares, and databases like MySQL, PostgreSQL, and MongoDB.
- Backup destinations – allows backups to different locations such as local file systems, Swift object storage, NFS, or other compatible storage systems.
- Disaster recovery – provides the means to restore resources and data from backups in case of system failures, data corruption, or other undesirable events.

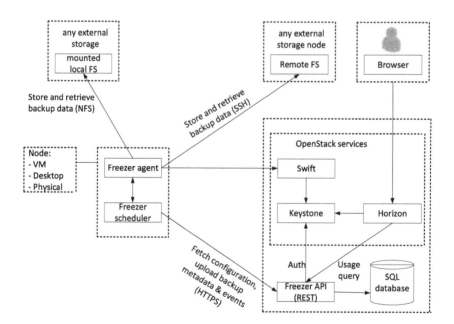

Figure 7.17. Freezer architecture [193].

Figure 7.17 shows the key components of Freezer architecture and the interaction between them [193]. The web interface is used to interact with the Freezer API for configuration. Its task is to provide features from Agent CLI and scheduler configurations, such as multi-node backup synchronization, metrics, and reporting. The Freezer scheduler represents a client-side component running on the data backup node. It has daemons for data retrieval from the Freezer API and jobs execution (e.g., backups, restore, admin, and other actions). These actions are performed by running the Freezer agent as multiprocessing Python software on the client side. It has a wide range of options to execute optimized backups according to the available resources. The Freezer API stores and provides metadata to the Freezer web UI and the scheduler. Also, it is used to store session information for multi-node backup synchronization. The Freezer API uses a backend database to store and retrieve metrics, metadata session information, and job status.

7.6.8   API Proxy Services

Sometimes, users can be required to use an EC2-compatible API within an OpenStack environment. For this purpose, OpenStack provides an EC2 API compatibility layer through the nova-api-ec2 service (EC2 API proxy) and allows users to interact with the OpenStack cloud using the EC2 API, which is the same API used by Amazon EC2. It is possible to provide a similar interface for instances and other resources, and users can use standard EC2 command-line tools, SDKs, or libraries to interact with OpenStack. The main benefit represents the easy migration of workloads between OpenStack and Amazon EC2.

Even though the EC2 API compatibility layer allows the use of EC2-compatible tools, there exist some differences or limitations compared to using native OpenStack APIs. The native OpenStack APIs use Keystone and provide consistent and comprehensive access to each OpenStack service for users, which can use OpenStack-specific resource naming and identifiers. The EC2-compatible API in OpenStack is a compatibility layer that can facilitate work in the OpenStack environment for users familiar with the Amazon EC2 API. The differences exist in resource naming, functionality, and documentation compared to the native OpenStack APIs.

7.6.9   Web Frontend Services

Horizon is the web-based dashboard interface, which is a standard part of the OpenStack ecosystem. It provides a visual interface that complements the command-line tools and APIs available for managing resources. Its goal is to simplify resource deployment and management and to provide an overview of various OpenStack services (Fig. 7.18).

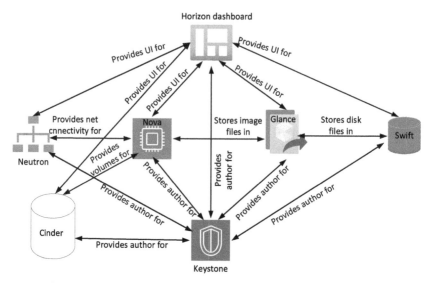

Figure 7.18. Horizon relations with basic OpenStack services [196].

As depicted in Fig. 7.18, by using the Horizon dashboard, it is possible to manage services, including adding users and setting up role-based access controls. This dashboard enables users to launch and manage virtual machine instances, view images available in the cloud, and perform actions such as starting, stopping, and deleting instances. It represents a convenient tool that helps users manage networks, routers, subnets, and security groups through the Neutron service (e.g., to configure network components, mutual communications between instances, and between instances and external networks). Generally, Neutron is created to support the NFV concept and can deploy virtual machines that provide common network services. OpenStack seeks to support plugin implementations of the virtual machines for network services and allow cloud users to request a VM and configure parameters, such as desired hardware and others, to choose a VM image from a list of options in the Glance repository, and to monitor all VMs [196].

Further, Horizon allows users to manage block storage volumes (Cinder) and object storage containers (Swift), which includes creating, attaching, and detaching volumes and managing object storage resources. Finally, Horizon provides necessary information about resource usage and enables monitoring and other OpenStack services typically manage metrics. Finally, Horizon provides essential information about resource usage and enables other OpenStack services to manage metrics and perform resource monitoring. It can be customized to fit the specific needs of an OpenStack deployment.

Skyline is an OpenStack dashboard optimized by UI and user equipment, which has a modern technology stack and ecology. It is easier for developers to maintain and operate by users and has higher concurrency performance. This component is under development.

7.6.10   Orchestration Services

The main component of OpenStack's orchestration services is the Heat component, which is responsible for resource orchestration. It uses declarative template formats through an OpenStack-native REST API to define the design and automate the deployment and scaling of resources. Heat orchestration templates (HOTs) describe cloud applications in text files to be readable and writable by humans and managed by control tools. This way, Heat establishes the relationships between particular resources, whereby it gains the possibility to call out to the OpenStack APIs to create all desired infrastructure in the correct order to launch applications completely (Fig. 7.19). It implies the creation of most OpenStack resource types (e.g., virtual instances, volumes, security groups, and other resources) as well as the implementation of some more advanced functionalities, such as high instance availability and autoscaling.

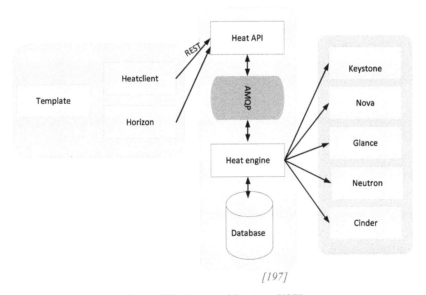

[197]

Figure 7.19. Heat architecture [197].

Despite the primary role of managing infrastructure, HOTs can be used for integration with software configuration management tools such as Puppet and Ansible. Operators can customize Heat's capabilities by installing plugins. For template processing, templates are responsible for the Heat engine, which interacts with other

OpenStack services and aims to create and configure resources and manage the overall orchestration process. The ceilometer is the telemetry and metering service in OpenStack, which can be used to collect and store data about the resources and usage during the orchestration process.

Senlin is an OpenStack service that is responsible for cluster orchestration and management, providing a framework for creating, scaling, and maintaining groups of interconnected resources (clusters). The core component is Senlin Engine, which receives users' requests from the Senlin API (RESTful API) and interacts with the underlying OpenStack services to create, scale, update, and delete clusters. Users make requests that contain profiles and policies. For example, a profile in Senlin defines the properties and configurations of an individual resource (virtual instance) within a cluster, such as nodes or storage volumes. We must note that a cluster is a group of interconnected nodes managed by Senlin, which can be scaled dynamically. The cluster's behavior is defined using policies, where users define conditions for scaling actions.

Mistral is an OpenStack service that is responsible for workflow automation. It implies the definition, execution, and management of workflows, allowing users to automate complex tasks and processes. Mistral supports the creation of workflows through a domain-specific language and provides integration with other OpenStack services. This way, it is possible to establish seamless coordination and execution of tasks across different cloud resources. It is particularly useful for orchestrating multi-step processes, handling dependencies between tasks, and automating repetitive operations in OpenStack environments. Those steps often represent interactions with components distributed across different machines (e.g., real machines, virtual machines, or containers). Mistral provides capabilities to automate such processes, where users can design, execute, and monitor workflows, enhancing the efficiency and consistency of cloud operations within an OpenStack infrastructure.

Zaqar is an OpenStack service whose main task is to enable messaging and notification for cloud applications. In practice, Zaqar serves as a multi-tenant messaging service, which enables communication between OpenStack components and services. It supports the publish-subscribe and message queue patterns and allows applications to send and receive messages asynchronously. The architecture is scalable and reliable, and it can be integrated with other OpenStack services (e.g., ova, Neutron, and Swift) to facilitate communication between different cloud applications. Further, it can simplify the development of distributed and loosely coupled open-stack applications, creating a unified messaging platform that is able to provide efficient interaction between different cloud services.

Blazar is an OpenStack service that enables efficient resource management through reservation-based leasing. It allows the reservation of hosts, storage, and network resources for a certain time, ensuring dedicated access and predictability in a multi-tenant OpenStack environment. Users can define leases with specific resource requirements, and it automates resource allocation. The system supports event triggers, enabling automated actions based on specific conditions during the lease period. This reservation mechanism is useful in cases where users require dedicated resources, enhancing planning and predictability in resource utilization within OpenStack.

AODH is an OpenStack service that provides alarming and metering services for cloud environments (Alarm Orchestration as a Service). In combination with the Ceilometer, it provides telemetry and metering service, which can be used in OpenStack for alarm creation based on collected metrics. Users can define rules and thresholds based on these metrics, generating alarms when certain conditions are fulfilled. These alarms can trigger automatic actions or notifications, enabling users to respond proactively to potential issues in their environment. AODH helps to monitor resource state and performance, supporting a more responsive and automated approach to managing cloud infrastructure.

7.7   OpenStack Design

Designing an OpenStack infrastructure implies scheduling and configuring different components in a private or public cloud. The goal is to create a scalable and efficient environment with a range of other services. However, before providers decide on a certain type of cloud, they must analyze financial aspects because, with the increase in cloud infrastructure complexity, the costs of cloud building and maintenance get more significant. They must estimate costs increasing as their cloud scales and opt for solutions that minimize capital expenditure at all layers of the stack. The usage of cloud brokerage tools should allow the deployment of the workloads to the most cost-effective platform, and the utilization of dependable commodity hardware and freely available open-source software components can decrease overall costs.

Besides the financial aspects, designing an OpenStack cloud requires a proper understanding of the user's requirements, such as providing computing power, storage capacity, and network capabilities. It requires determining the best possible configuration (e.g., private, public, hybrid, or multi-cloud) that suits business objectives. So, if we want to make an appropriate design, we must understand the logical architecture and implement the following OpenStack modules:

- daemons – usually run as background processes except on Linux platforms where they run as a service,

- scripts – they are used for virtual environments installation and tests running, and
- command-line interface – enables users to submit API calls to OpenStack services through commands.

Based on users' requirements, providers choose the OpenStack deployment model, which includes single-node, multi-node, and high-availability configurations. The deployment quality implies planning the cloud infrastructure carefully. It is necessary to plan the physical or virtual infrastructure, consider factors like server hardware, storage capacity, power equipment, and network requirements, and decide on the number and type of nodes for computing, storage, and networking services. Generally, providers are responsible for designing adequate network architecture, which can consist of storage, backend, and computing resources, and therefore must consider factors like high availability and scalability. They must provide a networking service that can allow full control over the creation of virtual network resources to tenants. To accomplish this goal, OpenStack uses tunneling protocols that establish encapsulated communication paths over existing network infrastructure to segment tenant traffic (e.g., tunneling over GRE or encapsulating with VXLAN and VLAN tags).

Further important considerations for the design of OpenStack are how to implement secure identity and access management. In this sense, the implementation of Keystone can support the configuration of user interfaces and API access and guarantee high availability for critical components. Security is an important challenge for OpenStack design because providers must implement robust solutions for key areas. Besides functions provided by Keystone, security measures should include network (e.g., firewall rules and encryption for data in transit) and hypervisor security. For these reasons, designers must consider how to include the best practices and possibilities in OpenStack design and secure virtual machine images by scanning for potential vulnerabilities. It is necessary to implement a proactive approach to patch management, consistently updating OpenStack components and dependencies to mitigate potential vulnerabilities and improve overall security. As a further measure, it is necessary to implement monitoring and logging tools for prompt incident detection, secure API access through authentication mechanisms, and regularly audit configurations. Ensure documentation is comprehensive, conduct thorough testing, and prioritize security best practices. By managing these concerns, providers can create a robust and scalable OpenStack environment tailored to users' requirements.

7.8   NFV Implementation in OpenStack

NFV, a technology designed to virtualize and consolidate network services in standard servers, switches, and storage, offers a significant gain in agility, scalability, and cost-effectiveness compared to traditional networks. OpenStack, an open-source cloud computing platform, serves as a good infrastructure for implementing NFV use cases. Typical NFV implementation use cases in OpenStack are:

- VNF deployment – involves implementing networking functions such as firewalls, load balancers, routers, and switches as virtual machines or containers within the OpenStack environment.
- Chaining multiple VNFs to create complex network services – OpenStack's Neutron networking service allows users to define service chains by connecting VNF instances in a specific order to process network traffic flows.
- Dynamic scaling – OpenStack's orchestration service, Heat, can automatically scale VNF instances up or down in response to changes in network traffic or performance metrics.
- Resource orchestration – OpenStack's resource orchestration capabilities enable the automated provisioning, configuration, and management of VNF instances, including auto-scaling, auto-recovery, and lifecycle management of VNFs.
- Integration with SDN – OpenStack integrates with SDN controllers such as OpenDaylight to provide SDN capabilities within the NFV environment.
- Support for virtual tenant networks (VTNs) – OpenStack provides support, allowing NFV operators to securely isolate and manage multiple VNF instances for different tenants or customers within the same infrastructure.
- Performance optimization – provides features for optimizing the performance of VNFs, such as CPU pinning, NUMA (Non-uniform memory access) awareness, and DPDK integration, to ensure high throughput and low latency for network traffic.
- Service assurance and monitoring – OpenStack offers a range of monitoring and logging services, such as Ceilometer and Aodh, that provide real-time insights into the performance and availability of VNF instances.

OpenStack, a versatile and scalable platform, empowers operators to efficiently deploy, orchestrate, and manage virtualized network services. It's a tool that puts users in control of their NFV implementation, allowing them to adapt and scale as needed.

7.8.1   VNFs Deployment in OpenStack

Deploying VNFs in OpenStack involves several steps to create, configure, and manage the virtual instances of network functions [198]. This process begins with the preparation of an OpenStack environment. It implies ensuring that the OpenStack environment is properly configured with the necessary computing, networking, and storage resources. Practically, we must set up compute nodes (hypervisors), configure Neutron networking for tenant isolation and connectivity, and provision appropriate storage for VM images and data. The next step is to create a VM image, which contains the software stack for the desired VNF. This image typically includes the operating system, required dependencies, and the specific VNF application software.

Further, it is necessary to define a flavor in OpenStack that specifies the compute, memory, and disk resources for the VNF instance. Flavors allow the definition of different resource profiles to serve the requirements of different VNFs. To launch a VM instance based on the VM image and prepared flavor, we should use the OpenStack dashboard or CLI. It means specifying the required network connectivity, such as the Neutron network and subnet to which to attach the instance. The next step is to configure networking for the VNF instance according to users' requirements (assigning IP addresses, configuring VLANs or VXLANs, setting up routing, and configuring security groups to control traffic access). If the VM instance is up and running, it is necessary to install and configure the VNF software inside the VM. This step may involve running scripts or configuration files provided by the VNF vendor to set up the required services and parameters.

By following these steps, we can deploy VNFs in an OpenStack environment and leverage NFV's flexibility and scalability to deliver network services efficiently. Lifecycle management of the deployed VNF instances, including scaling up or down based on demand, upgrading or patching software versions, and decommissioning instances when they are no longer needed, is also possible. OpenStack's orchestration service, Heat, can be used to automate lifecycle management tasks through templates and workflows.

7.8.2   The OpenStack Integration with SDN

NFV is used with cloud networks and combined with SDN to provide sufficient power for virtualization and control over network functions. This integration increases the reliability and security of cloud networks and provides features like resiliency, load balancing, and QoS in cloud services. From the OpenStack perspective, it is possible to integrate SDN and improve network services. It is possible to manage Nova services with a separate Neutron service for networking and virtualize the Neutron service by integrating SDN into OpenStack. SDN provides several novel applications such as resiliency, load balancing, and QoS in cloud services to improve the user experience, make it better and more flexible, and enhance cloud service.

An OpenStack multinode environment can be created with one controller node and compute nodes with Neutron-Nova services, which combine control and data plane. After that, it is possible to implement a separate private network with an interface and subnets to load instances with it. For SDN integration with OpenStack, it is necessary to use an SDN framework, such as OpenDaylight (Fig. 7.20) [199].

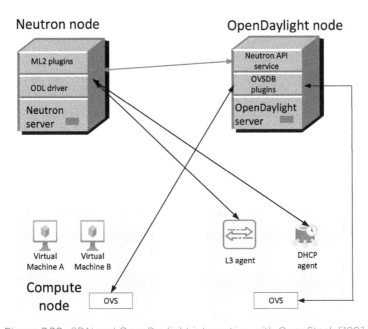

Figure 7.20. SDN and OpenDaylight integration with OpenStack [199].

Figure 7.20 shows the implementation of ODL with SDN, which includes the following techniques:

- Neutron ML2 plugins – a framework in OpenStack neutron service for work with open vSwitch, Linux Bridge, and L2 agents (L2 devices work with Neutron ML2 driver in OpenStack for package forwarding and routing policy),
- OVS – switch designed for massive network automation through programmatic extension, still supporting network interface protocols (e.g., NetFlow, CLI, LACP, and others),
- ODL driver – it acts as an interface between OVSDB and ML2 plugins and uses the OpenFlow protocol for network communication.

In the context of cloud networking, NFV brings significant advantages. It enhances network services by integrating SDN and OpenStack cloud. For instance, we can integrate NFV in OpenContrail distribution [199]. NFV plugins with Neutron ML2 successfully install all Contrail packages in the cloud controller node and configure them with the SDN controller. It is important to note that OpenContrail consists of an OpenContrail virtual router and an OpenContrail controller. The virtual router acts as a forwarding plane run on a hypervisor of the virtual server. At the same time, the controller serves as an interface between northbound APIs, which have a virtualized server used as a virtual router and connected with one central gateway router. The integration with OpenStack multinode environment and SDN with Contrail release involves downloading Contrail distribution and extracting it on the controller, then installing the dependency of contrail release and setting up with Neutron to use NFV. Finally, it is necessary to modify the plugin file and activate NFV in Neutron services.

SDN with a decoupled control plane and the use of the OpenFlow protocol makes it possible to manage a network dynamically with implemented NFV [200]. Cloud orchestrators have the OpenStack application, which can be managed by an SDN controller using the OpenFlow protocol with SSL. All the network devices are connected to a central controller to provide double-link resiliency and security using the NFV and firewall. Network devices connected with virtual routers manage dynamic traffic forwarding using a virtual NFV hypervisor router and isolated network called switch stack (Fig. 7.21) [199].

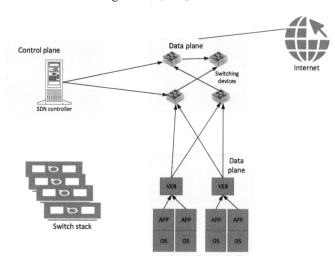

Figure 7.21. Open Stack architecture with implemented SDN and OpenDaylight [199].

Figure 7.21 shows the cloud network directly connected with switching devices on the data plane that can manage network routing and cloud network traffic forwarding. Virtual switching is created using NFV, and the whole network function is isolated using OpenContrail. The SDN controller is useful because it has an OpenFlow mechanism for cloud flow control of service and load balancing using dynamic request management. So, complete network traffic is managed using the central SDN controller, which is more stable, secure, resilient, and efficient than the previous networking techniques.

7.8.3   Support to VTNs

NFV implementation in OpenStack brings many benefits, such as customization of logical networks according to service requirements, on-demand provisioning allowing resource scaling up or down as conditions change, and network resource isolation for improved reliability and security. A use case that implies the implementation of NFV/SDN functionalities in OpenStack environments aims at the creation of SDN-enabled VTNs. VTNs are virtual networks deployed to different tenants in an isolated way, independently of underlying physical network resources. This way, it is possible to support specific QoS and SLA requirements, which represent a trend for SDN usage in the creation of virtual networks (Fig. 7.22) [201].

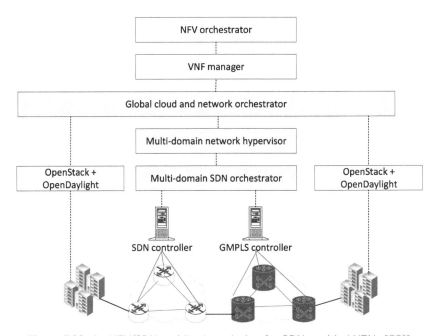

Figure 7.22. An NFV/SDN architecture design for SDN-enabled VTNs [201].

Figure 7.22 shows that infrastructure SDN controllers are used to create VTNs, while a new tenant SDN controller is responsible for their management. When an SDN-enabled VTN deployment takes place, the respective tenant SDN controller should be manually installed and configured on a dedicated server. This way, NFV and SDN integration can enable the virtualization of tenant SDN controllers and provide fast and dynamic VTN provisioning. Further, we can deploy SDN-enabled VTNs over multiple data centers and WAN domains, and the goal is to provide geographically distributed cloud services with specific QoS and SLAs. In this context, NFV is used to virtualize tenant SDN controllers (e.g., OpenDaylight) [201], control the underlying SDN-enabled VTNs, and provide fast and dynamic VTN provisioning. OpenStack serves as the VIM for each data center, and an OpenDaylight controller is used to connect a virtual tenant SDN controller to its respective VTN. The multidomain SDN orchestrator (MSO) mechanism is needed to create the VTNs. The MSO creates an abstraction over multiple domains, including different transport network technologies, thus enabling the composition of end-to-end services over heterogeneous WAN networks. Also, the multidomain network hypervisor can be used for the creation of end-to-end SDN-enabled VTNs over the abstraction provided by MSO. Using the global cloud and network orchestrator, a VIM mechanism, this architecture integrates geographically distributed data centers and multiple WAN domains, providing a unified cloud and network operating system for the creation of end-to-end NFV services over VTNs.

7.9   Conclusion

NFV represents a technology that enables the implementation of network functions on virtual infrastructure instead of traditionally on dedicated hardware appliances. Its role in OpenStack is to enable the virtualization of network functions using the compute (Nova) and networking (Neutron) services. Nova is responsible for the management and orchestration of virtual machines, and from an NFV perspective, this component ensures the deployment and management of virtualized resources for running VNFs. Neutron enables the creation and management of virtual networks and connecting VMs and has a crucial role in providing network services by connecting VNFs. Deployment of VNFs in OpenStack is simplified by using an orchestration service (Heat), which can automate the resource provisioning. A higher level of programmability in OpenStack is provided by integration with SDN, where the SDN controller has a key role. Its task is to improve programmability and OpenStack's compatibility with existing NFV-MANO frameworks. The OpenStack platform provides interoperability, adhering to open standards and APIs that facilitate interoperability between different VNFs and NFV infrastructure components. This way, it is possible to optimize performance (such as low latency and high throughput) by implementing specific NFV solutions. Overall, OpenStack serves as a flexible and scalable foundation for building and managing virtualized network infrastructures.

DOI: 10.1561/9781638283591.ch8

Chapter 8

Service Chaining in Modern Computer Environments

In the previous sections, we explained the fundamentals of NFV technology and its role in creating a new network design. We especially emphasized the importance of service and resource orchestration for the automation of numerous activities in modern computing environments. The benefits of NFV have been considered through its implementation in modern network architectures, which have already become a standard in computing. The benefits of NFV implementation are considered through the implementation of modern networking techniques that have already become a standard in computing. This section aims to combine all the fundamentals mentioned above and expose integration between NFV technology and service chaining in modern computer environments. This integration is the instrument of modernizing and optimizing network infrastructure because it allows the dynamic creation of service paths and the virtualization of network functions. Its results are improved flexibility, scalability, and resource efficiency in the network services delivery. The crucial considerations refer to the possibility of introducing a significantly higher level of network programmability, which should enable virtualized network functions to work together on network service implementation and improve performance in a virtualized environment.

8.1   Service Chaining Strategies

Service chaining in a traditional network refers to the process of traffic forwarding through a predefined sequence of services or functions in a specific order. It is a standard concept implemented using physical and logical interconnections of network devices such as firewalls, load balancers, proxies, and others. The goal of service chaining is to ensure that the network traffic passes through the necessary services sequentially to achieve objectives such as security, optimization, or monitoring.

In practice, numerous challenges arise from the rigid nature of traditional networks, where each change to the path based on traffic classification or any addition or removal of new network functional blocks requires chain modification or even complete altering. For example, adding a new function requires the implementation of new hardware, which represents a time and resource-demanding process. Sometimes, it is possible to use overlay networks and solve some physical networks' limitations regarding service chaining. The required hardware already exists, and it is necessary to perform traffic path rerouting. This solution brings configuration complexity and depends on the underlying infrastructure (Fig. 8.1).

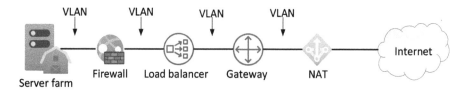

Figure 8.1. Service chaining in the traditional network [202].

In Fig. 8.1, we show an example of service chaining in a traditional network, where traffic from a typical web server should reach the Internet. Packets pass through a gateway (typically providing NAT services) towards a firewall and then to the server farm. Typically, each link in the chain is a logically separated path, e.g., a VLAN. Lack of application-level granularity, support for different transport mediums, or the interconnection between other overlays is another challenge for efficient service chaining in traditional networks. The existing overlay techniques are not able to facilitate the transmission of the application-level information along the data path and its utilization by the intermediate or end nodes (these nodes cannot influence the packet processing decisions).

The existence of large-scale data centers in networks requires the dynamic creation of service chains. This way, it is possible to reduce the management and configuration costs of service deployment as well as the connection complexities of a huge number of network devices. By implementing NFV and SDN technologies in networks, middleboxes are replaced with VMs, enabling dynamic service chaining.

New and innovative services can be implemented in a flexible and fast manner and allow traffic forwarding in accordance with specific flow requirements only through desired network functions (Fig. 8.2) [202].

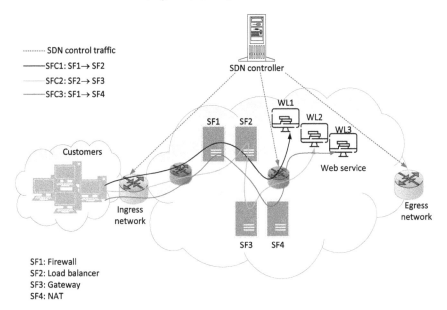

Figure 8.2. Dynamic service chaining [204].

As shown in Fig. 8.2, the first request aims to provide access to critical data from the server and needs only a firewall and load balancer. The SDN controller is responsible for creating an adequate service function chain in which traffic will pass through only the firewall and load balancer. The second request aims to enable access to a web application that might have a gateway for secure communication between on-premises and cloud environments and a load balancer to distribute incoming web traffic across multiple servers for improved reliability and performance. The SDN controller will create a separate service function chain (SFC) in which traffic will pass through the gateway and load balancer. The third request will pass through the firewall and NAT to provide a comprehensive security solution while efficiently managing IP address utilization. Firewalls handle security policies, while NAT handles the translation of IP addresses.

Dynamic service chaining brings many advantages, mainly related to the suited utilization of available resources. These advantages are [202]:

- A high level of flexibility regarding end-to-end service provisioning because the SDN controller can configure the different service chains for a new customer by implementing a new policy.
- Decreasing capital and operational costs – the SDN controller forwards packets to essential network functions and eliminates network over-provisioning.

- A better experience for users (individuals, businesses, or any entities that utilize the network services) – by implementing NFV and SDN, it is possible to provide scalable, dynamic, flexible, and automatic service function chaining in accordance with users' requirements.
- A selective increase of capacity (elasticity) – if traffic requirements increase only for a particular chain, it dynamically leads to an increase in the capacity of network functions presented in this chain.

8.2   Standardized Architecture for SFC Deployment

The goal of contemporary communications is to create a flexible and efficient network architecture that can adapt to different workloads while ensuring the correct deployment order of the required services. These services must be inserted dynamically, with minimum or no disruption to the existing network. By combining SFC with dynamic cloud scaling, it is possible to achieve an agile and flexible network architecture that can respond dynamically to new business requirements and customers' requests. In this sense, SFC techniques should carry information from applications and be able to interpret that information.

To solve the requirements for cloud scaling, the Internet Engineering Task Force (IETF) makes great efforts to propose an architecture for service chaining. Its key task is to define a methodology that can provide the uniform implementation of service chaining across the network. Fig. 8.3 shows the precise insight of the proposed SDN-based SFC architecture and its components grouped into control and data plane [203].

Before describing the interaction between control and data plane components, it is necessary to explain their roles and particular terms as follows:

- An *SFC-enabled domain* represents a network or its region that implements SFC.
- *Service Function* (SF) – represents a network function, such as firewall, NAT, DPI, IDS, and others, that is able to provide a value-added service to traffic flows.
- *SFC Classifier* – an entity that classifies traffic flows according to classification rules defined in an SFC Policy Table. It runs as an application on an independent (physical or virtual) platform placed on a data path or on top of a network controller.
- *SFC Policy Table* – contains classification rules, where each rule consists of traffic parameters (e.g., MAC addresses) for matching and appropriate actions identifying the SFC and the service functions that should apply to the traffic.

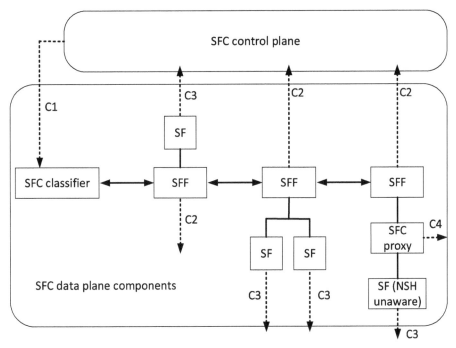

Figure 8.3. A typical SFC architecture [203].

- *SFC Header* – a header embedded into a packet by the SFC Classifier aims to facilitate packet forwarding along the SFC path.
- *SF Node* is any node within an SFC-enabled domain that contains one or multiple SFs.
- *Service Function Instance* (SFI) – indicates a service instance on a service node, such as a firewall, a load balancer, and others.
- *Service Function Forwarder (SFF)* – responsible for providing service layer forwarding in such a way that it receives packets carrying the SFC header and forwards them to the associated SF instances according to the information contained in the SFC header.
- *SF Proxy* – represents a network element used when the network service cannot process the SFC information and is placed before a legacy SF node in the traffic path to and from this SF. Its role is to facilitate the operation of legacy SF nodes by removing the SF header and sending de-encapsulated traffic to the SF based on information from the SFC header. Once the service is processed and the packet is sent back to the SF proxy, then it reinserts the SF header and path information and forwards the packet to the SFF for the subsequent steps.
- *SFC encapsulation* – represents a method for insertion of additional header information in the data frame after the classifier identifies the traffic to be

forwarded to the service chain path. There are multiple possible encapsulation headers and existing overlay techniques, such as Layer 3 Virtual Private Network (VPN) or segment routing (SR) [1].

- *Network Service Header* (NSH) – an IETF standard for SFC encapsulation [204, 205], which provides a protocol-agnostic mechanism for describing and implementing service paths within a network by appending a header to packets. This header consists of information about the service path and the payload in the form of metadata. The metadata is used in the design-making process for the service path selection and any other special handling the packet may need [1].

The control plane has a key role regarding the management of SFC and SF instances, mapping SFC to a service function path (SFP), configuring forwarding rules at the data plane components, and adjusting the SFP according to the status of SF instances and overlay links. It has four interfaces [203] for communication with the data plane components, which are used as follows:

- C1 interface – enables communication between the SFC control plane and the SFC classifier. It allows the implementation of SFC classification rules in classifiers, which are responsible for binding incoming traffic to service function chains and SFPs according to these rules.
- C2 interface – provides transmission of SFF reports (containing the connectivity status of attached SFs) to the SFC control plane.
- C3 interface – ensures transmission of collected packet-processing statistics from the Network Service Header (NSH)-aware SFs to control plane, which uses these statistics to adjust the SFPs dynamically.
- C4 interface – ensures transmission of statistics collected from NSH-unaware SFs via SFC proxy to the control plane, which uses these statistics to adjust the SFPs dynamically.

SFC classifier, SFF, SF, and SFC proxy are the main components of the data plane. The SFC classifier differentiates incoming traffic into flows by using the target application and other predefined requirements. It tags each flow by adding an SFC header (which contains the SFP ID) to each flow packet header. The SFP is the real path whose ID is related to an SFC and identifies the ordered set of conceptual SFs that must be implemented to the particular flow.

Performing a set of actions (e.g., load balancing) on incoming packets that may belong to one or a certain number of SFPs is the task of the SF (each SF may consist of multiple distributed instances). The role of SFF is to send incoming packets to SFs according to the defined SFPs. It uses and inserts SFP-specific information in an additional packet header (SFP packet encapsulation). The largest number of SFs are not capable of recognizing the SFC packet headers (NSH), and therefore, it is necessary to implement an SFC proxy between SFF and SFs. SFC proxy is responsible for stripping off the SFC header from the packet and forwarding it to the SFI running on the legacy SF node. When the legacy SF node returns the packet to the proxy, the proxy shall correlate the packet with the SF Chain and add back the SFC header.

8.3   SDN/NFV-based Architecture for SFC Deployment

In modern computer networks, the emergence of new technologies and communication types (e.g., IoT and M2M) causes an increasing demand for Internet services. The static service chaining model in traditional networks requires to be optimized to provide internet services in terms of reducing CAPEX and OPEX. For this reason, adding new functionality to conventional networks is a very complex task. It is necessary to combine technologies such as NFV and SDN to overcome the limitations of the static SFC model. NFV is a paradigm for network service provisioning that separates the network functions from the physical infrastructure, enabling VNF implementations as modular software on commercial servers. This way, SFC builds an application-specific network overlay that determines the placement and ordering of network functions in a specific service chain. We must note that different solutions for VNF placement at physical infrastructure, VNF instances scheduling to run on the servers, and optimal chaining mechanisms for traffic steering in the network have direct influences on the QoS.

The network architecture based on the NFV and SDN technologies contains orchestration, control, and data plane (Fig. 8.4). The orchestration plane is responsible for creating SFC strategies, which should enable the control of the global network according to different traffic types and user requests. So, it is responsible for the end-to-end management and network service orchestration in the administrative domain. Each domain has a network-level manager called the SDN controller, responsible for network connectivity management. This controller adds flow rules into the switches' OpenFlow tables with the aim of orchestrating different VNFs. According to an adopted SFC strategy, the SDN controller performs the mapping of VNFs and virtual links onto a substrate network and creates an SFP [202].

Figure 8.4 shows the extended ETSI NFV architecture for SFC deployment. The SFC orchestrator is a key component integrated with the existing network architecture, whose task is to provide SFC deployment in cloud environments effectively and flexibly. It means that the SFC orchestrator is responsible for the coordination, configuration, and management of the SFC processes. Its primary role is to enable network traffic to span a specified sequence of service functions in the correct order to satisfy service requirements. For this reason, the SFC orchestrator must

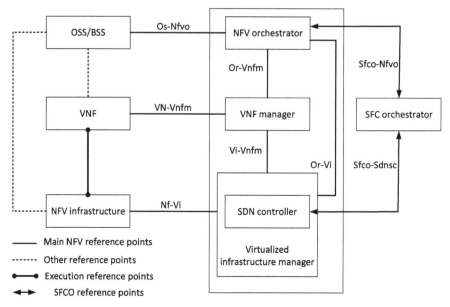

Figure 8.4. Extended ETSI NFV Architecture for SFC [202].

communicate with the NFVO, which manages operations such as instantiation, deletion, and scalability of network functions using VIM. It provides the NFVO with the necessary information to instantiate and manage the service functions in the correct order.

Practically, the SFC orchestrator manages interconnections of various VNFs to fulfill specific service requirements. It often works together with policy engines to implement policies that are designed for classifiers and SFFs and dictate the behavior of the service chain. SFC orchestrator supports the dynamic adaptation of service chains based on network conditions, service requirements, or policy updates and ensures flexibility and responsiveness to evolving network requirements. For this purpose, it must include monitoring and analytics to track the performance of the service chain, detect anomalies, and collect data for reporting and optimization.

In networks with implemented SDN functionality, it is necessary to establish interaction between the SFC orchestrator and SDN controller to program the underlying network infrastructure. The SDN controller provides flow rules in the flow table of switches for efficient traffic steering through the service functions. For communication with the NFVO and SDN controller, the SFC orchestrator uses the new *Sco-Nfvo* and *Sfco-Sdnc* components (interfaces), respectively. The key functional blocks of the SFC orchestrator are the SFC manager and SFC catalog. The SFC manager is responsible for communication with the SDN controller and NFVO, and it significantly affects SFC deployment and its management. Also, it enables the addition, deletion, and update of the SFC operations and the creation of a new SFP on top of the SDN controller. The SFC catalog is a database that stores all information regarding SFP, SFC, and SFC classifier rules [202].

The successful SFC deployment mainly depends upon activities such as:

- instantiation and deletion of operation and
- scaling input/output operations.

One of the important tasks that all components of ETSI NFV architecture (such as NFVO, VNFM, and SDN controller) should fulfill is to provide the dynamic deployment of SFC. NFVO should extract and launch VNFGG and provide various SFPs that define the specific order of SFs. It sends the request to the VNFM to initiate and delete the VNFs according to a particular SFC request. After executing the request, the VNFM is responsible for sending an acknowledgment back to the NFVO. NFVO receives the acknowledgment and creates a Name Server (NS) record. NFVO sends this record to the SFC orchestrator and informs it about addition and deletion operations. The SFC orchestrator parses the VNFFGs received from NFVO in the NS record and consequently creates flow rules of SFP for the SDN controller. The SDN controller adds flow rules to the flow table and reports to the SFC orchestrator about the successful operation of the SFC [202].

For scaling, there is a set of autoscale policies defined at the VNF level. The component responsible for monitoring uses a threshold value defined in these policies to identify changes when parameters (e.g., the average amount of CPU load or memory utilization) increase/decrease regarding threshold value and generate alarms. The task of NFVO is to check the scale input/output of action and then request VNFM to instantiate or delete the VNFs. After execution, the VNFM sends an acknowledgment back to NFVO. When NFVO receives the acknowledgment, it creates an NS record for the SFC orchestrator. This record is required for the SFC orchestrator because it must update the SFP and SFC in accordance with the scaling operation. Further, the SFC orchestrator must calculate the effective SFP and create flow rules for the SDN controller. The SDN controller uses these rules to program flow tables at switches and reports to the SFC orchestrator about successful scaling operations.

8.4 Virtual Network Embedding (VNE)

Network virtualization is a transformative technology for modern networks, whose primary entities are virtual networks. SFCs, like any other virtual network, are the result of combining active and passive network elements (network nodes and network links) on a substrate network. By virtualizing the node and link resources of a substrate network, we unlock the potential to create multiple virtual network topologies. Despite their diverse characteristics, we can co-host them on the same physical infrastructure. This flexibility, enabled by different methods of resource virtualization, allows for the management and modification of networks in a highly dynamic and adaptable manner. Moreover, by introducing network virtualization, we divide the management and business roles of service providers into three groups:

- The virtual network providers, which collect virtual resources from one or more infrastructure providers,
- The virtual network operators are responsible for installing, managing, and operating the virtual networks according to the needs of the service providers and
- The service providers are free of management and concentrate on business by using virtual networks to offer customized services.

The main resource allocation challenge is embedding virtual networks in the substrate network [206]. The idea is to perform dynamic mapping of virtual resources onto physical hardware, with the aim of achieving the maximal benefit from existing hardware. This approach leads to the self-configuration and organization of networks, which is necessary for the customization of end-to-end services. The optimal resource allocation, crucial for various objectives from QoS, economic benefits, or survivability over energy efficiency to the security of the networks, is ensured by the embedding algorithms [207]. Implementing network virtualization makes it possible to use these algorithms to allocate virtual resources optimally on a physical infrastructure. The virtual network operator uses embedding algorithms to decide which virtual resources to request from the virtual network provider. The virtual network provider then instantiates them using the substrate resources of infrastructure providers (Fig. 8.5).

Figure 8.5 shows that virtual network embedding deals with the allocation of virtual resources in nodes and links. Thus, it is necessary to solve the virtual node mapping, allocate virtual nodes to physical nodes, and perform virtual link mapping to paths connecting the corresponding nodes in the substrate network. In virtual network embedding, the optimization goals and constraints are crucial for the quality of the embedding solution. We must emphasize that common optimization goals are:

- efficient resource utilization (e.g., CPU, memory, bandwidth, and storage) and reduction of operational costs,
- latency minimization by placing virtual network elements closer to each other in the physical network,

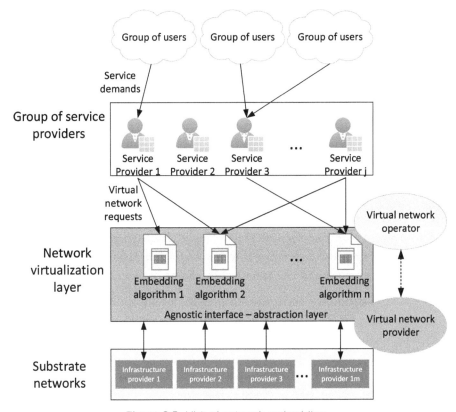

Figure 8.5. Virtual network embedding.

- bandwidth optimization by ensuring sufficient bandwidth availability for each virtual link,
- energy efficiency by consolidating virtual resources onto a smaller number of physical nodes and dynamically adjusting resource allocation based on workload demand,
- implementation of redundancy, backup paths, and failover mechanisms to mitigate the impact of node or link failures and increase fault tolerance and reliability,
- load balancing through network traffic distribution evenly across physical resources to prevent overloading of individual nodes or links.

Ensuring that the physical infrastructure has sufficient resources (CPU, memory, bandwidth) is not easy because resource constraints may vary based on the type of virtual network functions and services [207]. Further, it is crucial to emphasize that the embedding solution must respect the underlying physical network topology, as this is a significant requirement. The solution should also satisfy virtual network connectivity requirements. Meeting the QoS requirements specified by the virtual network, including latency, jitter, packet loss, and throughput, is very important because any failure can lead to degraded performance and user dissatisfaction. Security and isolation also introduce some constraints because the provider hosts multiple virtual networks belonging to different tenants on the same physical infrastructure. Each tenant may have distinct security requirements and may be running applications with sensitive data. In such a multi-tenant environment, it is crucial to ensure that the resources allocated to one tenant's virtual network are isolated from those of other tenants to prevent potential security breaches or data leaks. Finally, design embedding algorithms and techniques that can be able to adapt dynamic changes in network conditions (e.g., workload fluctuations, network failures, and resource additions/removals) must be flexible and scalable to support large-scale virtualized environments.

The problem of virtual network embedding is challenging, and there is a wide range of approaches and techniques aimed at finding efficient solutions under various optimization goals and constraints [208]. Some of them include:

- Greedy algorithms – these algorithms make locally optimal decisions at each step, leading to an overall solution [209]. For example, the first fit algorithm, which assigns virtual nodes to physical nodes iteratively based on resource availability, and the shortest path algorithm, which maps virtual links onto physical links with the shortest path length, are prime instances of the successful implementation of Greedy algorithms.
- Integer linear programming – treats VNE as an optimization problem with binary decision variables representing the mapping of virtual nodes and links [210]. Objective functions and constraints are defined to optimize various objectives and satisfy resource constraints. However, these approaches are computationally expensive for large-scale instances.
- Heuristic algorithms – these algorithms, such as genetic algorithms, simulated annealing, and particle swarm optimization, offer efficient solutions by exploring the solution space using iterative search procedures [211]. They are particularly valuable in their ability to find near-optimal solutions in large-scale virtual network embedding instances, providing a sense of reassurance in their practicality.
- Machine learning – can be used to predict optimal VNE mappings based on historical data, network characteristics, and performance metrics [212].

8.5   Challenges for Service Function Chaining

The implementation of dynamic service chaining brings several benefits, but it also comes with many challenges. One of the challenges is related to dedicated topology. For the implementation of network functions, the network topology represents a core component. The dependency between the implementation of network functions and network topology limits redundancy, scalability, and resource utilization. Also, dedicated network topology impacts the complexity of network configuration required for SFC deployment. Any change in service chains (service addition or deletion) causes a modification in the chain's order and network topology. Accordingly, it is necessary to change the chain's configuration, which produces additional complexity. As the number of services and the complexity of service chains increase, maintaining scalability becomes crucial. Providing that the system can handle a growing number of service instances and adapt to changes in network scale without compromising performance is challenging. That is the reason why the provider wants to keep network topology the same once they have installed, configured, and deployed the network.

The next challenge is related to the dynamic ordering of service functions. The number of services in each SFC is independent of others, but currently, SFCs are rigid because they are built based on manual configuration. In traditional networks with implemented static chains, packets pass through the chain, even though some requests require only a subset of services. It is the reason for implementing dynamic service chaining using NFV and SDN technologies. The replacement of traditional middle-boxes with VMs enables packet forwarding through desired network functions according to specific requirements. Adapting service chains dynamically based on changing network conditions, user requirements, or service policies can be complex. In this sense, the SDN controller has a key role in creating chains dynamically and forwarding traffic intelligently to a particular network function based on the label, such as VLAN, source MAC address, or network service header (NSH) [202]. Ensuring that the network can quickly and seamlessly reconfigure service chains in real-time is a challenge.

The task of placing Service Function Chains (SFCs) with survivability constraints is complex. It involves ensuring that the mapped SFCs remain functional and operational even in the presence of failures or network disruptions. This challenge is particularly crucial in critical network environments where uninterrupted service delivery is essential (e.g., in fog networks) [212]. We want to emphasize the following several aspects of this challenge:

- Survivability constraints specify the level of resilience required for the SFCs. It includes ensuring that backup resources or paths are available to reroute traffic in case of failures, maintaining certain levels of service availability, and minimizing service disruptions during failure recovery.
- Failure scenarios include link failures, node failures, and even multiple simultaneous failures. Each of them may require different survivability mechanisms and placement strategies to ensure continued service operation.

- Resource redundancy involves provisioning backup resources or redundant SFC instances to handle failures. However, it increases the costs of resource utilization and the complexity of managing redundant resources.
- Failure detection and recovery enable the identification and beginning of recovery procedures. Usually, it includes traffic rerouting along backup paths, activating standby resources, or dynamically reconfiguring the SFC placement to bypass the failed components.
- Dynamic adaptation provides answers to changing network conditions and traffic patterns. These mechanisms can continuously monitor the network and adjust the placement of SFCs accordingly to optimize resource utilization while meeting survivability requirements.
- Optimization trade-offs ensure a trade-off between survivability and other optimization objectives, such as minimizing resource usage or reducing latency. Balancing these incompatible objectives requires sophisticated optimization algorithms that consider multiple factors and constraints simultaneously.
- Standardization and best practices define guidelines for designing survivable network architectures and services. These standards can ensure interoperability and compatibility with existing networking technologies.

Solving the challenge of placing SFCs with survivability constraints requires a comprehensive understanding of network architecture, resilience mechanisms, and optimization techniques. The focus, in this case, is on developing efficient algorithms, protocols, and architectures to ensure reliable and resilient service delivery in dynamic and heterogeneous network environments.

Different vendors may implement various service functions or orchestrators. Ensuring interoperability between diverse components is crucial to avoid vendor lock-in and promote flexibility in choosing network equipment. However, introducing service functions and their chaining can create security challenges, especially if multiple service functions process sensitive data. VNFs can be vulnerable to security attacks, and the whole service function chain can fail. For this reason, it is necessary to provide a stable and robust SFC architecture. Providing integrity, confidentiality, and secure communication between service functions is crucial for protecting network traffic.

In certain scenarios, the deployment of SFCs extends across infrastructure managed by distinct providers [213]. This expansion introduces a significant level of complexity and a multitude of challenges, primarily due to the following factors:

- Different infrastructure providers have strict policies regarding the disclosure of confidential information about their network architecture, performance metrics, and resource availability. It limits the visibility and information sharing necessary for effective SFC placement and management.

- Each provider has its proprietary network technologies, management systems, and APIs, which lead to interoperability challenges when integrating SFCs across heterogeneous environments.
- Coordinating resource allocation and sharing across multiple provider domains while respecting each provider's policies and constraints requires implementing mechanisms for negotiating resource requirements, enforcing service level agreements, and managing resource contention in multi-domain environments.
- Different providers may have divergent policies and governance models regarding network access, traffic management, and service delivery. For this reason, it is necessary to harmonize these policies and ensure compliance with regulatory requirements.
- In the event of failures or disruptions, ensuring quick detection, isolation, and recovery while spanning multiple provider domains requires robust fault management mechanisms and coordination between providers.
- Billing and settlement processes across multiple providers for SFC usage add complexity. It involves accurately measuring resource consumption, aggregating usage data across provider domains, and facilitating fair and transparent settlement mechanisms.

Overcoming these challenges necessitates a high degree of collaboration among various stakeholders, including service providers, network operators, regulatory bodies, and standardization organizations. The importance of standardization efforts, such as IETF documents and industry consortia, cannot be overstated. These initiatives aim to develop common frameworks, protocols, and interfaces for inter-provider SFC deployment. Furthermore, the potential of innovative technologies like blockchain and federated learning to provide secure and decentralized coordination in multi-provider SFC environments should be a topic of future research.

The optimal mapping of SFC to the substrate network also represents a challenge because it is necessary to strategically implement service functions in the networks to achieve optimal performance, efficiency, and resource utilization [214]. The reason for VNF placement or SFC resource allocation problems is that defining, managing, and enforcing policies that control traffic, load balancing, and other aspects of service chaining can be complex. Ensuring consistency and coherence in policy management across different services and network segments is challenging. We must note that service chaining introduces additional processing steps, potentially impacting network performance and introducing latency.

Optimizing the performance of individual service functions and ensuring that the overall service chain meets performance requirements are also important challenges.

8.5.1   Optimal Placement of SFC – Use Cases

Models of SFC optimal placement are mechanisms for optimizing various network parameters, such as allocated bandwidth, end-to-end delays, or deployment cost. It's important to note that the SFC is important for more than just network services. Its architecture is also crucial for transport services, multimedia services, and application services. The goal of optimal SFC placement is to bring significant benefits, including reduced delays, minimized network capacity requirements, efficient allocation of user demands to service functions, and effective routing of traffic through different service functions, all with a strategic focus on resource allocation. Scattered and multiple instances of service functions direct user requests to move through various service functions, forming dynamic service chains [215]. The SFC model must be flexible to accommodate the dynamic user demands and service policies (e.g., users sometimes change their position rapidly, and the service policy can vary based on latency). In this sense, the placement of SFC should perform automatically, saving significant time and reducing operational costs. However, automation includes the implementation of different optimization strategies to choose the optimal parameter values and improve end-to-end performances. In some cases, the optimization models are not scalable to larger networks, so it is important to develop approximation algorithms for better scaling. This approach results in a reliable carrier-grade SFC model, enabling high availability and fault tolerance.

So, one reason for the SFC placement optimization is to achieve savings in network link capacities (Fig. 8.6) [214].

Figure 8.6 shows a regional office for a hypothetical application service provider, with its service accessible to users via the Internet. The service is composed of three virtual functions (e.g., firewall, proxy server, and business logic) in a specific order. Depending on the deployment locations of these virtual functions, the packets traverse different links and, finally, different paths. It represents a common scenario in today's networks, given the distributed nature of physical resources and end users. The path (indicated by the dashed red line in Figure 8.6) represents the optimal solution, demonstrating how SFC placement optimization can save link capacities and reduce delays. Errors in service placement can lead to additional delays, complex reconfigurations, and increased OPEX and CAPEX. This fact highlights the urgency and necessity of implementing SFC placement optimization strategies.

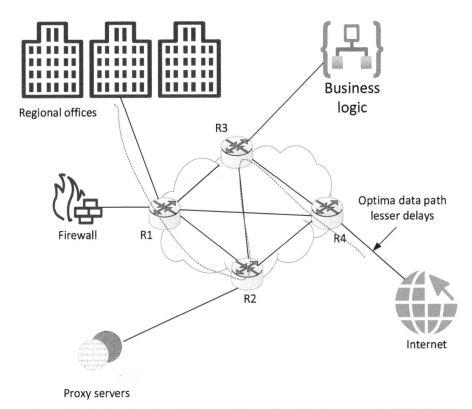

Regional offices

Firewall   R1

Business logic

R3

Optima data path lesser delays

R4

R2

Internet

Proxy servers

Figure 8.6. Savings in network link capacities with optimal placement of SFC [214].

In certain cases, a cloud service provider may choose to offer distributed micro-datacenter (micro-cloud) capabilities to its mobile users. These micro-clouds, strategically located at the edges, are equipped with web servers for fast updates to the users, representing a concept already in use at the cellular base stations in 5G/6G networks [216]. This approach has some challenges. For example, the database servers and resource-intensive computing servers remain in the core cloud locations, causing user requests to traverse to multiple clouds for fulfillment (Fig. 8.7).

Figure 8.7 shows that a user from user base 1 must follow the path represented by the solid black line (as it requires access to the database or the computing servers). In contrast, a user from user base 2 has to follow the path represented by the dotted line (as it only needs a fast response from the web server). The selection of these paths is crucial and depends on the type of services offered to the end users. Proper service chains must be formed and operated across multiple clouds at the application level. This scenario is particularly relevant in the case of technologies like IoT, which handle massive amounts of data where packets traverse through multiple applications or services [217]. The use of SFC as a dynamic steering tool for IoT-related big data underscores its importance.

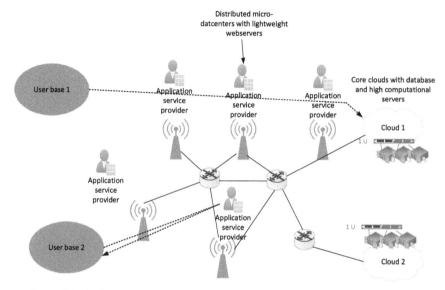

Figure 8.7. SFC use case at the application level across multiple clouds [214].

8.6   Conclusion

The SFC implies packet forwarding along a predetermined sequence chain of VNFs and represents a common service in networks with implemented NFV and SDN. Since there are multiple VNF instances, it is necessary to select and place the required VNF instances in the correct order to fulfill the routing of SFC flows. So, in modern networks, NFV provides the virtualized infrastructure. At the same time, SFC should be installed as a dynamic path for traffic flow through virtualized network functions, creating a customizable and efficient service delivery framework.

It is necessary to provide an appropriate framework for NFVO to design efficient NFV management and orchestration. This framework should allow the creation of the sequential forwarding of network traffic through a predefined set of service functions to fulfill specific service requirements. Generally, SFC orchestration is a component of a larger network architecture that includes NFV and SDN functionality. Its focus is to solve tasks such as defining and managing VNFFGs, which represent the order and connection points of different VNFs. Interaction between SFC and NFV orchestrators has the goal of ensuring the correct instantiation and lifecycle management of VNFs. SFC orchestration also involves policy enforcement, dynamic adaptation to changing conditions, and coordination with SDN controllers for efficient traffic steering. This way, it is possible to optimize service delivery, improve network efficiency, and provide flexibility in defining and adapting service chains based on growing requirements.

DOI: 10.1561/9781638283591.ch9

Chapter 9

NFV and Network Slicing

The network slicing concept has occurred because of advancements in computing and the emergence of NFV technology. It enables the partition of a physical network into many logical networks, where each one provides tailored services for a certain application scenario. Such logically isolated networks represent flexible network entities, which can be customized for different use cases using the same physical infrastructure simultaneously. The main challenge in the slicing is related to the separation of the existing large monolithic network functions implemented on legacy hardware into multiple software-based modular network functionalities with variable granularity [218]. Legacy hardware is designed as cohesive devices and does not possess the flexibility required for network slicing. For this reason, it is necessary to provide solutions that can enable the seamless separation of network functions, such as the integration of virtualized instances into existing hardware. The successful transition to a sliced network architecture means allowing dynamic and efficient allocation of resources while preserving the functionality of legacy systems.

Today, NFV and network slicing represent key technologies in the field of modern networking that have significant roles in the development and optimization of advanced networks. In essence, they are complementary technologies that contribute to the evolution of flexible, efficient, and customizable networks, especially in the context of emerging 5G/6G networks and the increasing variety of services and applications. By implementing these technologies, operators get the opportunity to create customized service chains and deploy, scale, and interconnect network functions dynamically in response to varying service demands. Further, the idea of 5G/6G networks is to provide flexible chaining of cloud-native functionalities on demand in the form of different network slices supporting various requirements. The integration of NFV and network slicing brings numerous benefits, such as resource optimization, service customization, faster deployment of new services, the opportunity to build scalable infrastructure according to different demands, and cost efficiency.

9.1   Network Softwarization

Network softwarization represents a leading trend in networking that aims to transform networks by introducing more programmability into networks. This trend implies the deployment of software-based solutions and wider implementations of NFV and SDN technologies, which provide the appropriate level of flexibility and modularity required for the creation of slices as logical (virtual) networks on one physical infrastructure. In essence, network slices represent E2E logical networks created on-demand that are mutually isolated [219]. Slices have independent control and management, and they are flexible in responding to specific requirements that refer to appropriate use cases. The 3GPP (3rd Generation Partnership Project) defines network slicing as a technology that allows the operator to create networks customized to deliver optimized solutions for various scenarios that require different requirements. (Fig. 9.1) [220].

The goal of network softwarization is to create a new design and implement more programmability in different network segments, such as RANs, transport networks, mobile-edge networks, and network cores. It is not an easy task because each network segment has different requirements and technical characteristics, so the levels of softwarization are different [221].

Network slicing emerges because of the need to manage different verticals with different applications, going from broadband services to critical applications such as industrial networks. In any of these scenarios, it is necessary to implement custom-designed solutions and perform network slicing. The next-generation mobile networks (NGMN) alliance recognizes the core network as the first step of network slicing. It sees the core network as a collection of 5G/6G network functions combined to fulfill specific use cases and avoid all unnecessary functionalities. In practice, with network slicing implementation, providers introduce more flexibility in their networks, and each service has a different dedicated core network slice created to guarantee QoS accomplishment. Further, network slicing implies having

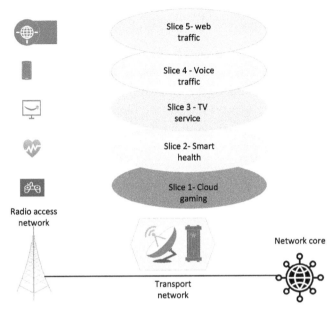

Figure 9.1. Network slicing.

ad-hoc U/C (user/control) plane functionalities for each use case, which increases the scalability and reduces the signaling overhead and latency by means of avoiding all unnecessary functionalities. Each network slice, corresponding to a specific use case, incorporates unique functionalities in the user and control planes to fulfill the specific requirements of that use case (e.g., a network slice designed for intelligent cars requires ultra-low latency communication to support real-time data exchange for features like autonomous driving).

Network slicing represents a solution that provides network softwarization and enables the robust management of multiple verticals simultaneously. The central place has the core network design using VNFs and following the SDN/NFV architectural principles [221]. We must note that VNFs run in virtual machines on standard servers deployed at different network sites based on specific service requirements. For example, network slices can use core network and service VNFs based on the required storage capacity and latency of the requested service.

Network softwarization is only possible with the deployment of software-based solutions in transport networks. In practice, there is a clearly stated requirement to respond to 5G/6G RANs needs. For this reason, it is necessary to implement transport networks as a platform where different user and network services can be accommodated. Such transport networks imply using appropriate interfaces in SDN/NFV infrastructures that should enable easy implementation of resource discovery and optimization mechanisms in the control plane. The main task of such programmable transport networks is to provide tightly coupled interactions with the RAN. It is a prerequisite for efficient coordination of functions such as mobility and load balancing.

One of the important requirements for modern networks is to move applications and network functions closer to the end-user. It means extending data centers to the network edge and network edge virtualization that should leverage SDN, NFV, and information-centric networking (ICN). The main idea is to create a smart and content-oriented edge that can fulfill high-demanding requirements such as throughput and an improved QoE. Such softwarized network edge includes high bandwidth, low latency, location awareness, and real-time insight into radio network information. Further, the implementation of software-based solutions into the network edge aims to collect information in real-time and make efficient use of available resources by reducing the traffic volume directed to the network core.

Network softwarization implemented using NFV and SDN technologies is fundamental for programmable networks. They enable the decoupling and abstraction of network functions and provide the required level of network efficiency, reliability, and service flexibility. New management and network services require more than the utilization of open APIs and numerous Software Development Kits (SDKs). It is necessary to make further progress in network softwarization, which mainly leads to building a more flexible core infrastructure that can fulfill more complex QoS requirements. In practice, it is necessary to follow modern trends in networking, such as network cloudification manifested in specifications for SDN and 5G mobile edge or multi-access edge computing. When the network runs on the cloud, operators can be innovative and offer new, cost-effective, and dynamic QoS management. Customization and optimization of network slices is one of the solutions that defines a new slice organization by grouping similar services in a single slice (Fig. 9.2) [24].

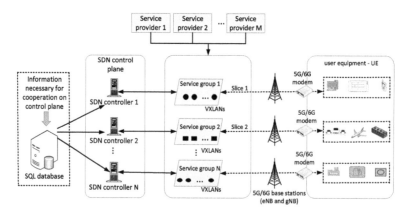

Figure 9.2. 5G/6G multi-slice environment [24].

In Fig. 9.2, we show the previously mentioned service group organization of network slices. Different providers that offer the same service are grouped into a single slice. For isolation between them, it is necessary to use the existing network segmentation mechanisms, such as VLAN or VXLAN. This way, it is possible to provide a high level of scalability since the number of slices is not limited. The proposed solution uses VXLANs that ensure separate providers that offer the same service group (each slice can contain up to 224 different providers belonging to a single service group) [24]. Users can access other slices and choose technical and cost-effective solutions and service providers that offer the desired services.

Virtualization and deployment of its different techniques have special importance when it comes to smart environments that should be created in 5G/6G networks. These environments require uninterrupted connections when users dynamically change location and move from one network to another [222]. It represents a great challenge, which can be accomplished at the L3 layer by establishing full interoperability and integration of heterogeneous networks, which is necessary for the continuity of communication sessions. Although SDN technology with the utilization of virtual IP addresses solves the problem, there is an issue related to the implementation of its homogeneous environment. The reason is cost, given the enormous investments in existing networks. Slicing and deployment of the optimal set of SDN features is a solution that provides full L3 mobility and includes a common controller to manage the IP address translations.

9.2 Network Slicing Concept and Key Principles

The NGMN (next-generation mobile network) alliance is a forum founded by world-leading mobile network operators that first introduced the term network slicing [223]. Its main goal is to perform changes within next-generation network infrastructure, service platforms, and devices with the intention to satisfy end-user demand and expectations. This forum defined network slices as E2E logical networks that can run on a physical or virtual infrastructure, mutually isolated, with independent control and management that is possible to create on demand. Each slice can span multiple domains, including radio access networks, core networks running on distributed cloud infrastructure, and transport networks supporting flexible allocation of VNFs. As a self-contained and programmable logical structure, the slice can adapt to changing requirements and provides a multi-service and multi-tenant approach. So, each slice can fulfill the specific requirements of different services, applications, or user groups. It is necessary to emphasize that slice as a virtualized end-to-end environment can be opened for third parties, which differentiates network slicing from network sharing (Fig. 9.3) [221, 224].

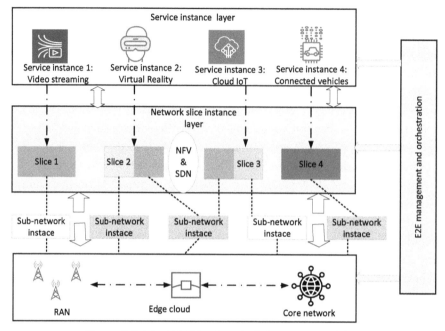

Figure 9.3. The NGMN network slicing concept [224].

Figure 9.3 shows that NGMN slice capabilities consist of the following three layers:

- Service Instance Layer (SIL) – represents each service (e.g., end-user service or business service) provided by the network operator or by third parties.
- Network Slice Instance (NSI) – provides the network features that the service instance requires. NSI may be composed of one or more sub-network instances, which another NSI may share.
- Resource Layer (RL) – provides all virtual or physical resources and network functions that are necessary to be used for NSI creation.

Besides 3GPP, the ITU, like other standardization bodies, defines network slicing from its perspective. The ITU sees network slicing as the key concept in network softwarization, whose task is to enable the creation of logically isolated network partitions (LINP) by combining multiple virtual resources, isolated and equipped with a programmable control and data plane. It means that ITU observes network slicing as a mechanism that allows network operators to customize each slice based on the specific needs of the services or applications it serves. Further, ITU treats slice isolation as a method to ensure that the performance, security, and other characteristics of one slice do not affect others.

Network slicing is also necessary to observe from a business perspective. Each slice represents a particular combination of network resources, functions, and tools required to satisfy a specific business case (service), including OSS, BSS, and DevOps operations. In practice, it is possible to identify two types of slices:

- Internal slices – network partitions used for internal providers' services, where providers retain full control and management of them and
- External slices – network partitions used for customer service hosting. They appear to the customer as dedicated networks/clouds/data centers.

The goal of network slicing is to design a logical entity that can offer end-to-end service characteristics containing RAN, core network, and transport network components. It implies that each slice has its set of parameters, such as latency, bandwidth, reliability, and security features, to fulfill the different service requirements. Basic principles that describe network slicing and its operation on 5G/6G networks are the following:

- Orchestration and automation – these are necessary to provide efficient management and control of the slice creation, modification, and deletion. In this sense, the orchestration systems should enable the coordination of resources across the network to deliver the desired slice features.
- High reliability, scalability, and isolation – the main goal is to ensure performance guarantees and security for each tenant. The efficient scaling of resources is provided to fulfill the requirements of new use cases or increased user demand. The isolation mechanism ensures that the traffic of one slice remains separate and secure from other slices.
- Programmability – simplifies the provisioning of services, manageability of networks, and integration and operational challenges, especially for supporting communication services. Dynamic resource allocation allows efficient use of network resources and ensures that each slice receives the necessary resources when needed.
- Slice customization – network slicing enables each network operator to customize each slice based on the specific needs of the services or applications it serves.
- Network resources elasticity – it is possible to implement an effective and non-disruptive reprovisioning mechanism and scale up/down allocated resources. This way, providers offer users the desired SLA regardless of their location.
- Hierarchical abstraction – involves the organization of different abstraction levels within a network infrastructure, with the aim of providing efficient management of virtualized network slices tailored to specific service

requirements. At the top level, there is a high-level abstraction representing overall service needs, followed by individual network slices that encapsulate specific use case characteristics, and finally, the lowest level dealing with the physical and virtual resources.

9.3   ONF Network Slicing Architecture

Open Networking Foundation (ONF) defines the SDN architecture as dynamic, manageable, cost-effective, and adaptable for the high-bandwidth, dynamic nature of modern applications. By decoupling control from the data plane, SDN enables the creation of a programmable control plane and the abstraction of the underlying infrastructure for applications and network services. Such an approach is in accordance with the key principles of the 5G/6G network slicing, which should provide the fast and cost-effective deployment and adaptation of services to changing market demands. Therefore, the SDN technology can be observed as a tool that allows providers to achieve the key principles of network slicing.

Besides the SDN controller, the key components of SDN architecture are infrastructure resources and network functions that enable the fulfillment of service requirements. The main component is the SDN controller, which performs an intermediary role between clients and resources, acting as a server and client simultaneously. In practice, the SDN controller operates via client and server contexts, respectively, to enable server-client communications [219]. The term client context refers to information required for a controller to perform its tasks successfully. For example, the resource group is information that the controller uses to provide the resources required for successful service delivery to customers. Further, customer support comprises information that the controller requires to provide appropriate support for customer operations, including different policies that regulate customer rights and their interactions with the controller. The server context comprises information required for the controller's interaction with resources specified in a resource group (Fig. 9.4).

Figure 9.4 shows the process by which the set of resource groups accessed through server contexts transforms to those defined in separate client contexts. As a key component, the SDN controller is responsible for the virtualization (abstraction and aggregation/partitioning) of the underlying resources. The goal is to provide a specific resource group for client needs according to the information contained in its client context. Further, the SDN controller performs orchestration and optimally delivers the selected resources to different resource groups. The administrator is responsible for the controller's configuration, which includes the creation of server and client contexts and the implementation of their associated policies. So, it is easy

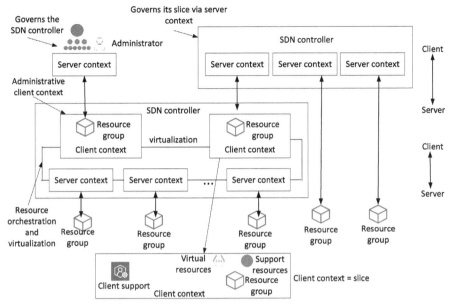

Figure 9.4. ONF SDN network slicing architecture [219].

to conclude from this figure that SDN supports slicing because the client context provides the required virtual resource group and control logic that forms a slice.

9.4 Management and Orchestration

Increasing the number of slices affects the complexity of network management. Therefore, it is important to implement a solution for 5G/6G slice management and orchestration based on the usage of the enhanced existing NFV MANO framework (Fig. 9.5).

Figure 9.5 shows a solution for 5G/6G slice management and orchestration based on the enhanced NFV MANO framework. MANO orchestrates the allocation of physical and virtual resources (e.g., computing, storage, radio, and network resources) to satisfy the specific requirements of each network slice. It ensures isolation between different network slices to maintain the security and performance of each slice. Moreover, it provides dynamic scaling of resources to adapt to changing demand and traffic patterns in real-time. We must emphasize the importance of inter-slice coordination, where MANO has the task of managing dependencies and interactions between different network slices that represent E2E logical structures consisting of 5G/6G RAN slices, 5G/6G TN (transport network) slices, and 5G/6G CN (core network) slice subnets [24]. Each of these subnets may consist of further subnets; for example, the RAN subnet decomposed further into fronthaul,

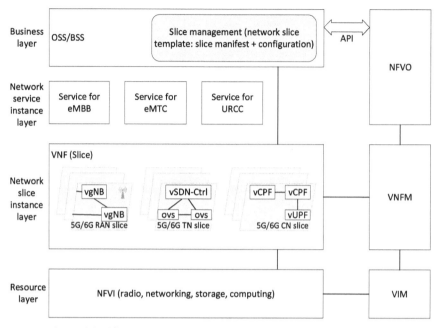

Figure 9.5. Slice management and orchestration architecture [218].

midhaul, and RAN network functions. So, it is necessary to ensure that changes or issues in one slice do not adversely affect others.

The MANO system is responsible for creating, modifying, and deleting network slices based on the service providers' and users' requirements. It can be performed by defining the slice parameters, resource allocation, and associated policies. Also, MANO manages the configuration of VNFs and physical resources to ensure that each slice achieves its performance objectives. The MANO system manages the activation and deactivation of network slices dynamically based on demand, traffic patterns, and service-level agreements. It is easy to notice the enhancement of the existing OSS/BSS system with the slice MANO functionality, which uses the capability exposed by NFV orchestration for network service and VNF lifecycle management. Policy management, monitoring, and analytics are capabilities of network slice instances (NSIs) whose implementation is also in charge of MANO. Efficient policy management implies implementing QoS policies for each network slice to guarantee performances such as low latency, high throughput, or reliability. Monitoring these performances for each network slice and collecting data on key metrics is necessary to enable the slices to fulfill their defined KPIs. The enhanced NFV MANO framework also includes slice template management and NSI life cycle management divided into four phases (Fig. 9.6).

Designing is the first phase in Fig. 9.6 and includes the abstraction of network capabilities into modular network function components (NFC) and the creation

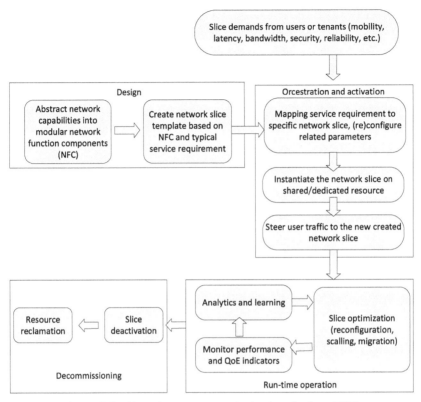

Figure 9.6. Lifecycle management of network slices [218].

of network templates. This phase implies creating a catalog of NFCs, which must contain the building blocks of network slices. A network template is created from one of the available NFCs and must consider functional and performance requirements from users or tenants. Finally, the forwarding graph must be created based on the appropriate NFC and associated relationships [218].

Orchestration and activation are integral processes in the network slicing implementation, which represent the next phase. The main task is to map service and performance requirements to a slice template using users' or tenants' requirements. The template also must contain parameters that closely describe the specific deployment to achieve the required performances (e.g., capacity and QoS). It is possible to chain related NFCs via virtual connections defined in the forwarding graph.

Run-time assurance is the third phase, which comprises continuous monitoring and analytics. These processes include real-time tracking of slice-specific metrics, fault detection, and resolution, providing end-to-end visibility into virtualized and physical components. By monitoring resource utilization, security events, and user experience, it is possible to optimize network slices and proactively manage potential issues through predictive analytics and closed-loop automation.

Decommissioning is the last phase, which refers to the process of retreating or shutting down a specific network slice, temporarily or permanently. This activity enables the management of resources efficiently, adapting to changing demands, and optimizing the overall performance of the 5G/6G infrastructure. The decommissioning process involves several key steps, including identifying the network slice for decommissioning, notifying relevant stakeholders, ensuring a smooth transition of services to other slices or parts of the network, releasing allocated resources, updating orchestration systems, and validating that the decommissioning does not adversely impact other slices or services.

9.5 Network Slicing Use Case in Network with Implemented NFV and SDN

The network slicing concept allows many slices to run on a common NFVI. This deployment includes multiple tenants who can manage a set of slices. Figure 9.7 shows a single level of recursion, where tenants directly serve the end users. Each slice consists of VNFs created and chained in the appropriate order to provide the particular network service that the slice should deliver to users. Network slicing deployment includes, as previously mentioned, the slice creation and a run-time phase, which comprises the connection of different functional blocks within each slice.

Figure 9.7 shows the tenant's access to NFVI resources from different infrastructure providers. The first provider has the task of providing resources for two NFVI-PoPs, while other providers are responsible for SDN-based WAN transport networks used to communicate these NFVI-PoPs. Further, VIMs manage virtual machines in NFVI-PoPs and underlying hardware. The infrastructure controllers interact with the SDN and NFV components (VIM and the WAN infrastructure manager) to dynamically allocate, configure, and control the physical and virtual resources required for each network slice. VIMs and WAN infrastructure managers are SDN applications that delegate tasks related to network management to their underlying infrastructure controllers. The tenants can manage a set of network slices independently, where each slice comprises an OSS, a tenant controller, and a network service orchestrator. The OSS applications instruct tenant controllers to manage VNFs placed in appropriate slices.

It is necessary to note that from the ETSI perspective, two functions perform resource (the RO) and network service orchestration (NSO) [219]. The task of ROs is to manage NFVI resources through VIMs, while NSO performs the lifecycle management of network services using the capabilities provided by the RO and the VNFMs. The NFVI resources provided by different infrastructure providers are

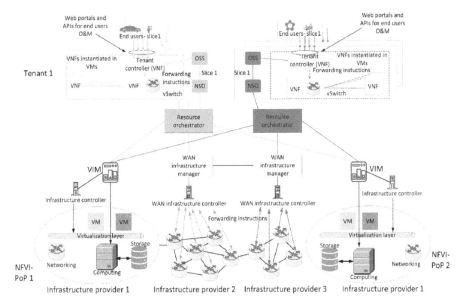

Figure 9.7. Network slicing deployment in a common framework, integrating both SDN and NFV [219].

available for all tenants. Tenants lease virtual resources from infrastructure providers according to previously signed business agreements. Access and resource reservation are the tasks of ROs that interact with VIMs and WAN infrastructure managers (WIMs) through their exposed interfaces. Interaction is also possible between different WIMs. This way, it is possible to establish communication between RO and a particular WIM through another WIM. It is necessary to emphasize that components such as VIM, RO, NSO, or controllers are independent software applications that need separate access, configuration, and management. Their relationships can be established by using the APIs that each of them provides.

Network slicing allows the creation of isolated and customized slices tailored to the service requirements, such as enhanced mobile broadband (eMBB), massive machine type communication (mMTC), or ultra-reliable low latency communication (URLLC). In this sense, resource management is important for efficient allocation and resource utilization within each network slice. Its dynamic character enables it to fulfill the specific requirements of different slices and perform activity at the infrastructure and tenant levels. From the infrastructure perspective, slice-agnostic VIMs and WIMs provide virtual resources for tenants, while ROs should deliver these resources to the corresponding slices at the tenant level. VIMs and WIMs must have precise information about the availability of the resources (i.e., their current usage) from the domain of their jurisdiction. Their decisions are based on real-time demand and variable requirements of different slices and tenants. This way, it is possible to ensure that slices and tenants receive all the necessary resources when needed.

Network slicing allows the creation of slices on a shared physical infrastructure. Ensuring the security and privacy of each slice is crucial to prevent unauthorized access, data integrity violations, and other potential threats. For these reasons, each functional block and manageable resource (e.g., VNF) has its security mechanisms, ensuring operation within desired parameters and controlling access to unauthorized entities. Strong authentication mechanisms are necessary to verify the identity of users and devices within a network slice. Data in transit and at rest within network slices should be encrypted to protect against unauthorized access and remain confidential and secure as it travels through the network. Ensuring the security of VNFs is also essential to prevent the exploitation of vulnerabilities and attacks. Network slicing implementations must comply with relevant privacy and security regulations and other local data protection laws. Compliance ensures that user rights and privacy are respected. Privacy protection measures, such as data anonymization and compliance with privacy regulations, are required to safeguard user privacy.

9.6   Conclusion

NFV represents an architectural framework that transforms traditional, hardware-based network functions into software running on standard servers, enhancing flexibility and reducing costs. On the other hand, SDN complements NFV by providing a programmable and centralized approach to network management. It separates the control plane from the data plane, allowing dynamic and centralized control over network resources. SDN facilitates efficient resource utilization, network programmability, and adaptation to changing traffic patterns.

Network slicing enables customization, efficient resource allocation, and improved service quality by tailoring virtual networks to specific use cases. NFV includes the underlying technology that facilitates the dynamic deployment and management of these VNFs, contributing to the development and optimization of modern networks. Together, NFV, SDN, and network slicing enable the transition to more flexible, adaptive, and efficient network architectures that can meet the diverse and evolving demands of 5G and beyond. They contribute to faster deployment, improved resource utilization, and enhanced service quality in the increasingly complex and dynamic nature of modern networks.

References

[1] R. Chayapathi, S. F. Hassan, and P. Shah, *Network Functions Virtualization (NFV) with a Touch of SDN: Netw Fun Vir (NFV EPub_1)*. Addison-Wesley Professional, 2016.

[2] N. Veljković, "I mreža se virtuelizuje," *PC Press*, Mar. 2017, [Online]. Available: https://pcpress.rs/i-mreza-se-virtuelizuje/.

[3] Ž. Bojovic, V. Šenk, D. Dobromirov, and P. D. Bojovic, "Intervendor Working of VoIP Networks," *J. Inst. Telecommun. Prof.*, vol. 5, no. 5, pp. 26–32, 2011.

[4] Ž. Bojovic, E. Secerov, D. Dobromirov, and V. Šenk, "Maximizing the Profit of Telecom Telcos by a Novel Traffic Scheduling Policy," *Elektron. Ir Elektrotechnika*, vol. 113, no. 7, pp. 67–72, 2011.

[5] D. Vujošević, P. D. Bojović, J. Šuh, G. Martić, and Ž. Bojović, "The course on modern 5G/6G networks: A step toward understanding a flexible network core," *Comput. Appl. Eng. Educ.*, vol. 31, no. 2, pp. 301–323, 2023.

[6] J. G. Herrera and J. F. Botero, "Resource allocation in NFV: A comprehensive survey," *IEEE Trans. Netw. Serv. Manag.*, vol. 13, no. 3, pp. 518–532, 2016.

[7] TechTarget, "Load Balancing." [Online]. Available: https://www.techtarget.com/searchnetworking/definition/load-balancing.

[8] L. Mo, "Reliability of NFV using COTS hardware," *ZTE Commun.*, vol. 12, no. 3, pp. 53–61, 2014.

[9] Ž. Bojović, J. Šuh, and P. Bojović, *Softverske tehnologije u računarskim mrežama sa velikim podacima*. Fakultet Tehničkih Nauka u Novom Sadu, 2021.

[10] M. K. Shin, Y. Choi, H. H. Kwak, S. Pack, M. Kang, and J. Y. Choi, "Verification for NFV-enabled network services," in *2015 International Conference*

on Information and Communication Technology Convergence (ICTC), IEEE, Oct. 2015, pp. 810–815.

[11] Ž. Bojović, Đ. Klipa, P. D. Bojović, I. M. Jovanović, J. Šuh, and V. Šenk, "Interconnected Government Services: An Approach toward Smart Government," *Appl. Sci.*, vol. 13, no. 2, p. 1062, 2023.

[12] European Telecommunications Standards Institute – ETSI, "Network Functions Virtualisation (NFV); Release Description; Release 3." 2023. [Online]. Available: https://www.etsi.org/deliver/etsi_gr/NFV/001_099/007/03.07.0 1_60/gr_NFV007v030701p.pdf.

[13] S. Lee, K. Levanti, and H. S. Kim, "Network monitoring: Present and future," *Comput. Netw.*, vol. 65, pp. 84–98, 2014.

[14] S. Herker, X. An, W. Kiess, S. Beker, and A. Kirstaedter, "Data-center architecture impacts on virtualized network functions service chain embedding with high availability requirements," in *2015 IEEE Globecom Workshops (GC Wkshps)*, IEEE, Dec. 2015, pp. 1–7.

[15] B. Yi, X. Wang, K. Li, and M. Huang, "A comprehensive survey of network function virtualization," *Comput. Netw.*, vol. 133, pp. 212–262, 2018.

[16] S. Ravidas, S. Lal, I. Oliver, and L. Hippelainen, "Incorporating trust in NFV: Addressing the challenges," in *2017 20th Conference on Innovations in Clouds, Internet and Networks (ICIN)*, IEEE, Mar. 2017, pp. 87–91.

[17] B. Han, V. Gopalakrishnan, L. Ji, and S. Lee, "Network function virtualization: Challenges and opportunities for innovations," *IEEE Commun. Mag.*, vol. 53, no. 2, pp. 90–97, 2015.

[18] STL partners, "NFV Architectural Framework: The ETSI architectural framework explained." 2017. [Online]. Available: https://stlpartners.co m/articles/telco-cloud/nfv-architectural-framework/.

[19] M. Ersue, "ETSI NFV management and orchestration-An overview." 2013.

[20] P. Veitch, M. J. McGrath, and V. Bayon, "An instrumentation and analytics framework for optimal and robust NFV deployment," *IEEE Commun. Mag.*, vol. 53, no. 2, pp. 126–133, 2015.

[21] M. Bouet, J. Leguay, T. Combe, and V. Conan, "Cost-based placement of vDPI functions in NFV infrastructures," *Int. J. Netw. Manag.*, vol. 25, no. 6, pp. 490–506, 2015.

[22] K. Pentikousis, C. Meirosu, D. R. Lopez, S. Denazis, K. Shiomoto, and F. J. Westphal, "Guest editorial: Network and service virtualization," *IEEE Commun. Mag.*, vol. 53, no. 2, pp. 88–89, 2015.

[23] N. T. Jahromi, R. H. Glitho, A. Larabi, and R. Brunner, "An NFV and microservice based architecture for on-the-fly component provisioning in

content delivery networks," in *2018 15th IEEE Annual Consumer Communications & Networking Conference (CCNC)*, IEEE, Jan. 2018, pp. 1–7.

[24] P. D. Bojović, T. Malbašić, D. Vujošević, G. Martić, and Ž. Bojović, "Dynamic QoS management for a flexible 5G/6G network core: a step toward a higher programmability," *Sensors*, vol. 22, no. 8, p. 2849, 2022.

[25] L. Cao, P. Sharma, S. Fahmy, and V. Saxena, "NFV-VITAL: A framework for characterizing the performance of virtual network functions," in *2015 IEEE conference on network function virtualization and software defined network (NFV-SDN)*, IEEE, Nov. 2015, pp. 93–99.

[26] OPNFV, "Bringing it home with Jerma: The 10th and final OPNFV release." 2020. [Online]. Available: https://www.opnfv.org/.

[27] M. I. Csoma, B. Koné, R. Botez, I. A. Ivanciu, A. Kora, and V. Dobrota, "Management and Orchestration for Network Function Virtualization: An Open-Source MANO Approach," in *2020 19th RoEduNet Conference: Networking in Education and Research (RoEduNet)*, IEEE, Dec. 2020, pp. 1–6.

[28] F. Slim, F. Guillemin, A. Gravey, and Y. Hadjadj-Aoul, "Towards a dynamic adaptive placement of virtual network functions under ONAP," in *2017 IEEE Conference on Network Function Virtualization and Software Defined Networks (NFV-SDN)*, IEEE, Nov. 2017, pp. 210–215.

[29] C. Zhang, H. P. Joshi, G. F. Riley, and S. A. Wright, "Towards a virtual network function research agenda: A systematic literature review of vnf design considerations," *J. Netw. Comput. Appl.*, vol. 146, p. 102417, 2019.

[30] D. Cotroneo, L. De Simone, and R. Natella, "NFV-bench: A dependability benchmark for network function virtualization systems," *IEEE Trans. Netw. Serv. Manag.*, vol. 14, no. 4, pp. 934–948, 2017.

[31] R. Cziva and D. P. Pezaros, "Container network functions: Bringing NFV to the network edge," *IEEE Commun. Mag.*, vol. 55, no. 6, pp. 24–31, 2017.

[32] X. Molero, F. Silla, V. Santonja, and J. Duato, "Modeling and simulation of storage area networks," in *Proceedings 8th International Symposium on Modeling, Analysis and Simulation of Computer and Telecommunication Systems (Cat. No. PR00728)*, IEEE, Aug. 2000, pp. 307–314.

[33] G. A. Gibson and R. Van Meter, "Network attached storage architecture," *Commun. ACM*, vol. 43, no. 11, pp. 37–45, 2000.

[34] J. Kempf, B. Johansson, S. Pettersson, H. Lüning, and T. Nilsson, "Moving the mobile evolved packet core to the cloud," in *2012 IEEE 8th International Conference on Wireless and Mobile Computing, Networking and Communications (WiMob)*, IEEE, Oct. 2012, pp. 784–791.

[35] L. M. Contreras, P. Doolan, H. Lønsethagen, and D. R. López, "Operational, organizational, and business challenges for network operators in the context of SDN and NFV," *Comput. Netw.*, vol. 92, pp. 211–217, 2015.

[36] G. M. Yilma, Z. F. Yousaf, V. Sciancalepore, and X. Costa-Perez, "Bench-marking open source NFV MANO systems: OSM and ONAP," *Comput. Commun.*, vol. 161, pp. 86–98, 2020.

[37] L. Mamushiane, A. A. Lysko, T. Mukute, J. Mwanġama, and Z. Du Toit, "Overview of 9 open-source resource orchestrating ETSI MANO compliant implementations: A brief survey," in *2019 IEEE 2nd Wireless Africa Conference (WAC)*, IEEE, Aug. 2019, pp. 1–7.

[38] M. Portnoy, *Virtualization essentials*, vol. 19. John Wiley & Sons, 2012.

[39] S. N. T. C. Chiueh and S. Brook, "A survey on virtualization technologies," Rpe Report, 142, 2005.

[40] Ž. Bojovic, Đ. Klipa, E. Šecerov, and V. Šenk, "Smart government-from information to smart society," *J. Inst. Telecommun. Prof.*, vol. 11, pp. 34–39, 2017.

[41] R. Rose, "Survey of system virtualization techniques," 2004.

[42] D. Stefanović, "I mreža se virtuelizuje," *Svet Kompjut.*, 2005, [Online]. Available: https://www.sk.rs/2005/08/sknt01.html.

[43] R. Morabito, J. Kjällman, and M. Komu, "Hypervisors vs. lightweight virtualization: a performance comparison," in *2015 IEEE International Conference on Cloud Engineering*, IEEE, Mar. 2015, pp. 386–393.

[44] R. Davoli and F. Pareschi, "Applying Partial Virtualization on ELF Binaries Through Dynamic Loaders," 2013.

[45] K. Koning, H. Bos, and C. Giuffrida, "Secure and efficient multi-variant execution using hardware-assisted process virtualization," in *2016 46th Annual IEEE/IFIP International Conference on Dependable Systems and Networks (DSN)*, IEEE, Jun. 2016, pp. 431–442.

[46] D. Kusnetzky, *Virtualization: A manager's guide*. O'Reilly Media, Inc., 2011.

[47] K. RahimiZadeh, M. AnaLoui, P. Kabiri, and B. Javadi, "Performance modeling and analysis of virtualized multi-tier applications under dynamic workloads," *J. Netw. Comput. Appl.*, vol. 56, pp. 166–187, 2015.

[48] L. Yan, "Development and application of desktop virtualization technology," in *2011 IEEE 3rd International Conference on Communication Software and Networks*, IEEE, May 2011, pp. 326–329.

[49] C. H. Chang, C. T. Yang, J. Y. Lee, C. L. Lai, and C. C. Kuo, "On construction and performance evaluation of a virtual desktop infrastructure with GPU accelerated," *IEEE Access*, vol. 8, pp. 170162–170173, 2020.

[50] G. Lai, H. Song, and X. Lin, "A service based lightweight desktop virtualization system," in *2010 International Conference on Service Sciences*, IEEE, May 2010, pp. 277–282.

[51] B. Goldworm and A. Skamarock, *Blade servers and virtualization: transforming enterprise computing while cutting costs*. John Wiley & Sons, 2007.

[52] S. Soltesz, H. Pötzl, M. E. Fiuczynski, A. Bavier, and L. Peterson, "Container-based operating system virtualization: a scalable, high-performance alternative to hypervisors," in *Proceedings of the 2Nd ACM SIGOPS/EuroSys european conference on computer systems 2007*, Mar. 2007, pp. 275–287.

[53] E. Bugnion, J. Nieh, and D. Tsafrir, *Hardware and software support for virtualization*, vol. 12. 2017.

[54] J. Gandhi, "Efficient memory virtualization," The University of Wisconsin-Madison, 2016.

[55] I. S. Ružić, "Virtuelne mašine," *Svet Kompjut.*, 2012, [Online]. Available: https://www.sk.rs/2012/12/sktr01.html.

[56] Red Hat, "What is network virtualization?" 2024. Accessed: Feb. 09, 2024. [Online]. Available: https://www.redhat.com/en/topics/virtualization/what -is-network-virtualization.

[57] M. G. Xavier, M. V. Neves, F. D. Rossi, T. C. Ferreto, T. Lange, and C. A. De Rose, "Performance evaluation of container-based virtualization for high performance computing environments," in *2013 21st Euromicro International Conference on Parallel, Distributed, and Network-Based Processing*, IEEE, Feb. 2013, pp. 233–240.

[58] M. Eder, "Hypervisor-vs. container-based virtualization," *Future Internet FI Innov. Internet Technol. Mob. Commun. IITM*, vol. 1, 2016.

[59] NetApp, "What are containers?" [Online]. Available: https://www.netapp.c om/devops-solutions/what-are-containers/.

[60] S. Ferry, "Kubernetes Application Containers: Managing Containers and Cluster Resources." [Online]. Available: https://developer.hpe.com/blog /kubernetes-application-containers-managing-containers-and-cluster-res our/.

[61] N. Dragoni, I. Lanese, S. T. Larsen, M. Mazzara, R. Mustafin, and L. Safina, "Microservices: How to make your application scale," in *Perspectives of System Informatics: 11th International Andrei P. Ershov Informatics Conference, PSI 2017, Moscow, Russia, June 27–29, 2017, Revised Selected Papers 11*, Springer International Publishing, 2018, pp. 95–104.

[62] L. Lei et al., "SPEAKER: Split-phase execution of application containers," in *Detection of Intrusions and Malware, and Vulnerability Assessment: 14th International Conference, DIMVA 2017, Bonn, Germany, July 6–7, 2017, Proceedings 14*, Springer International Publishing, 2017, pp. 230–251.

[63] I. Hrček, "Praktičan uvod u kontejner terminologiju." [Online]. Available: https://startit.rs/uvod-kontejner-terminologija/.

[64] A. Mouat, *Using docker: developing and deploying software with containers.* O'Reilly Media, Inc., 2015.

[65] D. Bernstein, "Containers and cloud: From lxc to docker to kubernetes," *IEEE Cloud Comput.*, vol. 1, no. 3, pp. 81–84, 2014.

[66] D. Jaramillo, D. V. Nguyen, and R. Smart, "Leveraging microservices architecture by using Docker technology," in *SoutheastCon 2016*, IEEE, Mar. 2016, pp. 1–5.

[67] P. Stanojevic, S. Usorac, and N. Stanojev, "Container manager for multiple container runtimes," in *2021 44th International Convention on Information, Communication and Electronic Technology (MIPRO)*, IEEE, Sep. 2021, pp. 991–994.

[68] Red Hat, "What is orchestration?" [Online]. Available: https://www.redhat.com/en/topics/automation/what-is-orchestration.

[69] S. Ballmer, *Seizing the Opportunity of the Cloud: The next wave of business growth.* London School of Economics, 2010.

[70] B. Burns, B. Grant, D. Oppenheimer, E. Brewer, and J. Wilkes, "Borg, omega, and kubernetes," *Commun. ACM*, vol. 59, no. 5, pp. 50–57, 2016.

[71] C. Carrión, "Kubernetes scheduling: Taxonomy, ongoing issues and challenges," *ACM Comput. Surv.*, vol. 55, no. 7, pp. 1–37, 2022.

[72] L. Larsson, W. Tärneberg, C. Klein, E. Elmroth, and M. Kihl, "Impact of etcd deployment on kubernetes, istio, and application performance," *Softw. Pract. Exp.*, vol. 50, no. 10, pp. 1986–2007, 2020.

[73] Cloud Native Computing Foundation, "Certified Kubernetes Software Conformance." [Online]. Available: https://www.cncf.io/certification/software-conformance/.

[74] A. E. Nocentino and B. Weissman, *SQL Server on Kubernetes: Designing and Building a Modern Data Platform.* Apress, 2021.

[75] S. Rana, "Getting Started With Kubernetes: Part 1: Setting Up Master - Node Architecture With Ubuntu 16.04." [Online]. Available: https://medium.com/@sarangrana/getting-started-with-kubernetes-part-1-setting-up-master-node-architecture-with-ubuntu-16-04-11f1e71d1aad.

[76] O. Yilmaz, "Extending the kubernetes api," in *Extending Kubernetes: Elevate Kubernetes with Extension Patterns, Operators, and Plugins*, Berkeley, CA: Apress, 2021, pp. 99–141.

[77] J. Baier, *Getting started with kubernetes.* Packt Publishing Ltd., 2017.

[78] S. Buchanan, J. Rangama, and N. Bellavance, *Introducing Azure Kubernetes Service: A Practical Guide to Container Orchestration.* Apress, 2020.

[79] E. Baker, "Kubernetes containers: A comprehensive runtime comparison." [Online]. Available: https://www.capitalone.com/tech/cloud/container-runtime/.

[80] M. Hausenblas and S. Schimanski, *Programming Kubernetes: developing cloud-native applications*. O'Reilly Media, 2019.

[81] Kubernetes, "ReplicaSet." [Online]. Available: https://kubernetes.io/docs/concepts/workloads/controllers/replicaset/.

[82] B. Burns, J. Beda, K. Hightower, and L. Evenson, *Kubernetes: up and running*. O'Reilly Media, Inc., 2022.

[83] DEV, "When to use Kubernetes deployments, pods, and services." [Online]. Available: https://dev.to/educative/when-to-use-kubernetes-deployments-pods-and-services-2p4h.

[84] A. Chawla, "Deployment Strategies In Kubernetes." [Online]. Available: https://auth0.com/blog/deployment-strategies-in-kubernetes/.

[85] H. Saito, H. C. C. Lee, and C. Y. Wu, *DevOps with Kubernetes: Accelerating software delivery with container orchestrators*. Packt Publishing Ltd., 2019.

[86] H. M. Gowda, "Configuring HPA (Horizontal Pod Autoscaler) on Kubernetes." [Online]. Available: https://hemanthmgowda.medium.com/configuring-hpa-horizontal-pod-autoscaler-on-kubernetes-a4856d2d10be.

[87] M. Niazi, S. Abbas, A. H. Soliman, T. Alyas, S. Asif, and T. Faiz, "Vertical Pod Autoscaling in Kubernetes for Elastic Container Collaborative Framework," *Comput. Mater. Contin.*, vol. 74, no. 1, pp. 591–606, 2022.

[88] G. Sayfan, *Mastering Kubernetes*. Packt Publishing Ltd., 2017.

[89] P. Leandro, "Kubernetes 101, part VII, jobs and cronjobs." [Online]. Available: https://dev.to/leandronsp/kubernetes-101-part-vii-jobs-and-cronjobs-12kg.

[90] Using a Service to Expose Your App, "Using a Service to Expose Your App." [Online]. Available: https://kubernetes.io/docs/tutorials/kubernetes-basics/expose/expose-intro/.

[91] N. Lamouchi, "Getting Started with Kubernetes," in *Pro Java Microservices with Quarkus and Kubernetes: A Hands-on Guide*, Berkeley, CA: Apress, 2021, pp. 291–307.

[92] M. Palmer, "Kubernetes Ingress with Nginx Example." [Online]. Available: https://matthewpalmer.net/kubernetes-app-developer/articles/kubernetes-ingress-guide-nginx-example.html.

[93] A. Bhuyan, "Externalizing Configurations in Kubernetes Using ConfigMap and Secret." [Online]. Available: https://faun.dev/c/stories/aditya-bhuyan/externalizing-configurations-in-kubernetes-using-configmap-and-secret/.

[94] J. Shah and D. Dubaria, "Building modern clouds: using docker, kubernetes & Google cloud platform," in *2019 IEEE 9th Annual Computing and Communication Workshop and Conference (CCWC)*, IEEE, Jan. 2019, pp. 0184–0189.

[95] Red Hat, "Stateful vs stateless." [Online]. Available: https://www.redhat.com/en/topics/cloud-native-apps/stateful-vs-stateless.

[96] L. A. Vayghan, M. A. Saied, M. Toeroe, and F. Khendek, "A Kubernetes controller for managing the availability of elastic microservice based stateful applications," *J. Syst. Softw.*, vol. 175, p. 110924, 2021.

[97] Techopedia, "Apache Mesos." [Online]. Available: https://www.techopedia.com/definition/31935/apache-mesos.

[98] O. Pandithurai, M. Poongodi, S. P. Kumar, and C. G. Krishnan, "A method to support multi-tenant as a service," in *2011 Third International Conference on Advanced Computing*, IEEE, Dec. 2011, pp. 157–162.

[99] Intel, D. P. D. K., "DPDK Documentation." [Online]. Available: https://doc.dpdk.org/guides/prog_guide/.

[100] J. Sherry, S. Hasan, C. Scott, A. Krishnamurthy, S. Ratnasamy, and V. Sekar, "Making middleboxes someone else's problem: Network processing as a cloud service," *ACM SIGCOMM Comput. Commun. Rev.*, vol. 42, no. 4, pp. 13–24, 2012.

[101] T. Barnett, S. Jain, U. Andra, and T. Khurana, "Cisco visual networking index (vni) complete forecast update, 2017–2022," Americas/EMEAR Cisco Knowledge Network (CKN) Presentation, 2018.

[102] J. Martins et al., "ClickOS and the Art of Network Function Virtualization," in *11th USENIX Symposium on Networked Systems Design and Implementation (NSDI 14)*, 2014, pp. 459–473.

[103] N. McKeown et al., "OpenFlow: enabling innovation in campus networks," *ACM SIGCOMM Comput. Commun. Rev.*, vol. 38, no. 2, pp. 69–74, 2008.

[104] T. Zhang, "NFV Platform Design: A Survey," *ArXiv Prepr. ArXiv200211059*, 2020.

[105] R. Mijumbi, J. Serrat, J. L. Gorricho, N. Bouten, F. De Turck, and R. Boutaba, "Network function virtualization: State-of-the-art and research challenges," *IEEE Commun. Surv. Tutor.*, vol. 18, no. 1, pp. 236–262, 2015.

[106] Y. Xu and V. P. Kafle, "An availability-enhanced service function chain placement scheme in network function virtualization," *J. Sens. Actuator Netw.*, vol. 8, no. 2, p. 34, 2019.

[107] L. Qu, C. Assi, K. Shaban, and M. Khabbaz, "Reliability-aware service provisioning in NFV-enabled enterprise datacenter networks," in *2016 12th International Conference on Network and Service Management (CNSM)*, IEEE, Oct. 2016, pp. 153–159.

[108] G. Venâncio et al., "Beyond VNFM: Filling the gaps of the ETSI VNF manager to fully support VNF life cycle operations," *Int. J. Netw. Manag.*, vol. 31, no. 5, p. e2068, 2021.

[109] V. G. Nguyen, A. Brunstrom, K. J. Grinnemo, and J. Taheri, "SDN/NFV-based mobile packet core network architectures: A survey," *IEEE Commun. Surv. Tutor.*, vol. 19, no. 3, pp. 1567–1602, 2017.

[110] Cisco, "The Zettabyte Era Officially Begins (How Much is That?)." 2023.

[111] S. Lange et al., "A network intelligence architecture for efficient vnf lifecycle management," *IEEE Trans. Netw. Serv. Manag.*, vol. 18, no. 2, pp. 1476–1490, 2020.

[112] T. A. Khan, K. Abbass, A. Rafique, A. Muhammad, and W. C. Song, "Generic intent-based networking platform for E2E network slice orchestration & lifecycle management," in *2020 21st Asia-Pacific Network Operations and Management Symposium (APNOMS)*, IEEE, Sep. 2020, pp. 49–54.

[113] A. Leivadeas and M. Falkner, "VNF placement problem: A multi-tenant intent-based networking approach," in *2021 24th Conference on Innovation in Clouds, Internet and Networks and Workshops (ICIN)*, IEEE, Mar. 2021, pp. 143–150.

[114] T. Soenen et al., "Insights from SONATA: Implementing and integrating a microservice-based NFV service platform with a DevOps methodology," in *NOMS 2018-2018 IEEE/IFIP Network Operations and Management Symposium*, IEEE, Apr. 2018, pp. 1–6.

[115] K. Kaur, V. Mangat, and K. Kumar, "Towards an Open-Source NFV Management and Orchestration Framework," in *2022 14th International Conference on COMmunication Systems & NETworkS (COMSNETS)*, IEEE, Jan. 2022, pp. 251–255.

[116] A. Gulenko, M. Wallschläger, F. Schmidt, O. Kao, and F. Liu, "A system architecture for real-time anomaly detection in large-scale NFV systems," *Procedia Comput. Sci.*, vol. 94, pp. 491–496, 2016.

[117] J. Kim et al., "Service provider DevOps for large scale modern network services," in *2015 IFIP/IEEE International Symposium on Integrated Network Management (IM)*, IEEE, May 2015, pp. 1391–1397.

[118] A. Rao, "Choosing a VNF lifecycle management solution: Key challenges and crucial considerations for CSPs." [Online]. Available: https://www.acca ntosystems.com/~accantosystems/wp-content/uploads/2018/05/Analysys-Mason-Whitepaper.pdf.

[119] C. Sieber, R. Durner, M. Ehm, W. Kellerer, and P. Sharma, "Towards optimal adaptation of NFV packet processing to modern CPU memory architectures," in *Proceedings of the 2nd Workshop on Cloud-Assisted Networking*, Dec. 2017, pp. 7–12.

[120] S. Lal, T. Taleb, and A. Dutta, "NFV: Security threats and best practices," *IEEE Commun. Mag.*, vol. 55, no. 8, pp. 211–217, 2017.

[121] G. Sun, G. Zhu, D. Liao, H. Yu, X. Du, and M. Guizani, "Cost-efficient service function chain orchestration for low-latency applications in NFV networks," *IEEE Syst. J.*, vol. 13, no. 4, pp. 3877–3888, 2018.

[122] N. F. S. De Sousa, D. A. L. Perez, R. V. Rosa, M. A. Santos, and C. E. Rothenberg, "Network service orchestration: A survey," *Comput. Commun.*, vol. 142, pp. 69–94, 2019.

[123] J. Obstfeld, S. Knight, E. Kern, Q. S. Wang, T. Bryan, and D. Bourque, "VIRL: the virtual internet routing lab," in *Proceedings of the 2014 ACM conference on SIGCOMM*, Aug. 2014, pp. 577–578.

[124] J. Batalle, J. F. Riera, E. Escalona, and J. A. Garcia-Espin, "On the implementation of NFV over an OpenFlow infrastructure: Routing function virtualization," in *2013 IEEE SDN for Future Networks and Services (SDN4FNS)*, IEEE, Nov. 2013, pp. 1–6.

[125] C. Sun, J. Bi, Z. Zheng, H. Yu, and H. Hu, "NFP: Enabling network function parallelism in NFV," in *Proceedings of the Conference of the ACM Special Interest Group on Data Communication*, Aug. 2017, pp. 43–56.

[126] A. V. I. Networks, "Virtual Load Balancer Definition." [Online]. Available: https://avinetworks.com/glossary/virtual-load-balancer/.

[127] M. Savi, M. Tornatore, and G. Verticale, "Impact of processing-resource sharing on the placement of chained virtual network functions," *IEEE Trans. Cloud Comput.*, vol. 9, no. 4, pp. 1479–1492, 2019.

[128] A. K. Alnaim, A. M. Alwakeel, and E. B. Fernandez, "Towards a security reference architecture for NFV," *Sensors*, vol. 22, no. 10, p. 3750, 2022.

[129] J. Frahim, O. Santos, and A. Ossipov, *Cisco ASA: All-in-one Next-Generation Firewall, IPS, and VPN Services*. Cisco Press, 2014.

[130] Ž. Bojović, D. Vukobratović, and J. Šuh, "Računarske mreže zasnovane na Internet protokolu," *Fak. Teh. Nauka U Novom Sadu*, 2018.

[131] J. Šuh, Ž. Bojović, M. Despotović-Zrakić, Z. Bogdanović, and A. Labus, "Designing a course and infrastructure for teaching software-defined networking," *Comput. Appl. Eng. Educ.*, vol. 25, no. 4, pp. 554–567, 2017.

[132] D. Kreutz, F. M. Ramos, P. E. Verissimo, C. E. Rothenberg, S. Azodolmolky, and S. Uhlig, "Software-defined networking: A comprehensive survey," *Proc. IEEE*, vol. 103, no. 1, pp. 14–76, 2014.

[133] K. Kirkpatrick, "Software-defined networking," *Commun. ACM*, vol. 56, no. 9, pp. 16–19, 2013.

[134] B. A. A. Nunes, M. Mendonca, X. N. Nguyen, K. Obraczka, and T. Turletti, "A survey of software-defined networking: Past, present, and future of programmable networks," *IEEE Commun. Surv. Tutor.*, vol. 16, no. 3, pp. 1617–1634, 2014.

[135] Ž. Bojović, P. Bojović, and J. Šuh, "The implementation of software defined networking in enterprise networks," *J. Inst. Telecommun. Prof.*, 2018.

[136] Sdxcentral, "What Is Open SDN? A Definition." [Online]. Available: https://www.sdxcentral.com/networking/sdn/definitions/what-the-definition-of-software-defined-networking-sdn/what-is-openflow/open-sdn/.

[137] T. Malbašić, P. D. Bojović, Ž. Bojović, J. Šuh, and D. Vujošević, "Hybrid SDN Networks: A multi-parameter server load balancing scheme," *J. Netw. Syst. Manag.*, vol. 30, no. 2, p. 30, 2022.

[138] Y. Sinha and K. Haribabu, "A survey: Hybrid SDN," *J. Netw. Comput. Appl.*, vol. 100, pp. 35–55, 2017.

[139] S. Vissicchio, L. Vanbever, and O. Bonaventure, "Opportunities and research challenges of hybrid software defined networks," *ACM SIGCOMM Comput. Commun. Rev.*, vol. 44, no. 2, pp. 70–75, 2014.

[140] J. He and W. Song, "Achieving near-optimal traffic engineering in hybrid software defined networks," in *2015 IFIP Networking Conference (IFIP Networking)*, IEEE, May 2015, pp. 1–9.

[141] M. Canini, A. Feldmann, D. Levin, F. Schaffert, and S. Schmid, "Software-defined networks: Incremental deployment with panopticon," *Computer*, vol. 47, no. 11, pp. 56–60, 2014.

[142] H. Xu, J. Fan, J. Wu, C. Qiao, and L. Huang, "Joint deployment and routing in hybrid SDNs," in *2017 IEEE/ACM 25th International Symposium on Quality of Service (IWQoS)*, IEEE, Jun. 2017, pp. 1–10.

[143] D. J. Casey and B. E. Mullins, "SDN shim: Controlling legacy devices," in *2015 IEEE 40th Conference on Local Computer Networks (LCN)*, IEEE, Oct. 2015, pp. 169–172.

[144] GeeksforGeeks, "Types of Software Defined Networks Implementation." [Online]. Available: https://www.geeksforgeeks.org/types-of-software-defined-networks-implementation/.

[145] N. F. Mir, *Computer and communication networks*. Pearson Education, 2015.

[146] Statista, "Number of internet and social media users worldwide as of October 2023." [Online]. Available: https://www.statista.com/statistics/617136/digital-population-worldwide/.

[147] M. K. Shin, K. H. Nam, and H. J. Kim, "Software-defined networking (SDN): A reference architecture and open APIs," in *2012 International Conference on ICT Convergence (ICTC)*, IEEE, Oct. 2012, pp. 360–361.

[148] Z. Latif, K. Sharif, F. Li, M. M. Karim, S. Biswas, and Y. Wang, "A comprehensive survey of interface protocols for software defined networks," *J. Netw. Comput. Appl.*, vol. 156, p. 102563, 2020.

[149] B. Pandya, S. Parmar, Z. Saquib, and A. Saxena, "Framework for securing SDN southbound communication," in *2017 International Conference on Innovations in Information, Embedded and Communication Systems (ICI-IECS)*, IEEE, Mar. 2017, pp. 1–5.

[150] O. N. Foundation, "OpenFlow Switch Specification." [Online]. Available: https://opennetworking.org/wp-content/uploads/2014/10/openflow-switch-v1.5.1.pdf.

[151] B. Pfaff and B. Davie, "The open vSwitch database management protocol," rfc7047, 2013.

[152] Huawei, "What Is NETCONF?" [Online]. Available: https://info.support.huawei.com/info-finder/encyclopedia/en/NETCONF.html.

[153] "RESTCONF Protocol." [Online]. Available: https://datatracker.ietf.org/doc/html/rfc8040.

[154] R. Narisetty et al., "OpenFlow configuration protocol: Implementation for the of management plane," in *2013 second GENI research and educational experiment workshop*, IEEE, Mar. 2013, pp. 66–67.

[155] D. L. Tennenhouse, J. M. Smith, W. D. Sincoskie, D. J. Wetherall, and G. J. Minden, "A survey of active network research," *IEEE Commun. Mag.*, vol. 35, no. 1, pp. 80–86, 1997.

[156] D. Sheinbein and R. P. Weber, "Stored program controlled network: 800 service using spc network capability," *Bell Syst. Tech. J.*, vol. 61, no. 7, pp. 1737–1744, 1982.

[157] L. Yang, R. Dantu, T. Anderson, and R. Gopal, "Forwarding and control element separation (ForCES) framework," rfc3746, 2004.

[158] M. Casado, M. J. Freedman, J. Pettit, J. Luo, N. McKeown, and S. Shenker, "Ethane: Taking control of the enterprise," *ACM SIGCOMM Comput. Commun. Rev.*, vol. 37, no. 4, pp. 1–12, 2007.

[159] M. Paliwal, D. Shrimankar, and O. Tembhurne, "Controllers in SDN: A review report," *IEEE Access*, vol. 6, pp. 36256–36270, 2018.

[160] S. A. Shah, J. Faiz, M. Farooq, A. Shafi, and S. A. Mehdi, "An architectural evaluation of SDN controllers," in *2013 IEEE International Conference on Communications (ICC)*, IEEE, Jun. 2013, pp. 3504–3508.

[161] Z. Cai, A. L. Cox, and T. S. Ng, "Maestro: A system for scalable OpenFlow control," 2010.

[162] S. Shin et al., "Rosemary: A robust, secure, and high-performance network operating system," in *Proceedings of the 2014 ACM SIGSAC Conference on Computer and Communications Security*, Nov. 2014, pp. 78–89.

[163] M. N. A. Sheikh, M. Halder, S. S. Kabir, M. W. Miah, and S. Khatun, "SDN-Based approach to evaluate the best controller: internal controller NOX and external controllers POX, ONOS, RYU," *Glob. J. Comput. Sci. Technol.*, vol. 19, no. 1, pp. 21–32, 2019.

[164] S. Asadollahi and B. Goswami, "Experimenting with scalability of floodlight controller in software defined networks," in *2017 International Conference on Electrical, Electronics, Communication, Computer, and Optimization Techniques (ICEECCOT)*, IEEE, Dec. 2017, pp. 288–292.

[165] NetworkStatic, "Floodlight OpenFlow Controller: Using the Static Flow Entry Pusher." [Online]. Available: http://networkstatic.net/floodlight-openflow-controller-using-the-static-flow-entry-pusher/.

[166] T. L. Foundation, "OpenDaylight Project." [Online]. Available: https://opendaylight.org/about/platform-overview.

[167] J. Networks, "What's Behind Network Downtime?" [Online]. Available: https://cdn2.hubspot.net/hubfs/2581329/Tellabs_Feb2017%20Theme/pdf%20files/200249.pdf.

[168] S. Matsumoto, S. Hitz, and A. Perrig, "Fleet: Defending SDNs from malicious administrators," in *Proceedings of the third workshop on Hot topics in software defined networking*, Aug. 2014, pp. 103–108.

[169] A. Tootoonchian and Y. Ganjali, "Hyperflow: A distributed control plane for OpenFlow," in *Proceedings of the 2010 internet network management conference on Research on enterprise networking*, Apr. 2010, pp. 10–5555.

[170] GeeksforGeeks, "Open Networking Operating System (ONOS) in Software Defined Networks." [Online]. Available: https://www.geeksforgeeks.org/open-networking-operating-system-onos-in-software-defined-networks/.

[171] L. Peterson, C. Cascone, and B. Davie, "Software-defined networks: a systems approach," *Syst. Approach LLC*, 2021.

[172] Z. Shu et al., "Traffic engineering in software-defined networking: Measurement and management," *IEEE Access*, vol. 4, pp. 3246–3256, 2016.

[173] G. Han, J. Jiang, N. Bao, L. Wan, and M. Guizani, "Routing protocols for underwater wireless sensor networks," *IEEE Commun. Mag.*, vol. 53, no. 11, pp. 72–78, 2015.

[174] G. Swallow, "MPLS advantages for traffic engineering," *IEEE Commun. Mag.*, vol. 37, no. 12, pp. 54–57, 1999.

[175] Paloalto, "What Is SD-WAN?" [Online]. Available: https://www.paloaltonetworks.com/cyberpedia/what-is-sd-wan.

[176] Z. Yang, Y. Cui, B. Li, Y. Liu, and Y. Xu, "Software-defined wide area network (SD-WAN): Architecture, advances and opportunities," in *2019*

28th International Conference on Computer Communication and Networks (ICCCN), IEEE, Jul. 2019, pp. 1–9.

[177] M. S. Bonfim, K. L. Dias, and S. F. Fernandes, "Integrated NFV/SDN architectures: A systematic literature review," *ACM Comput. Surv. CSUR*, vol. 51, no. 6, pp. 1–39, 2019.

[178] G. Carella et al., "Cross-layer service to network orchestration," in *Proceedings of the 2015 IEEE International Conference on Communications (ICC'15)*, 2015, pp. 6829–6835. doi: 10.1109/ICC.2015.7249414.

[179] R. Cziva, S. Jouet, K. J. S. White, and D. P. Pezaros, "Container-based network function virtualization for software-defined networks," in *Proceedings of the 2015 IEEE Symposium on Computers and Communication (ISCC'15)*, 2015, pp. 415–420. doi: 10.1109/ISCC.2015.7405550.

[180] I. Cerrato, A. Palesandro, F. Risso, M. Suñé, V. Vercellone, and H. Woesner, "Toward dynamic virtualized network services in telecom operator networks," *Comput. Netw.*, vol. 92, no. 2, pp. 380–395, 2015, doi: 10.1016/j.comnet.2015.09.028.

[181] J. Schulz-Zander, C. Mayer, B. Ciobotaru, S. Schmid, and A. Feldmann, "OpenSDWN: Programmatic Control over Home and Enterprise WiFi," in *Proceedings of the 1st ACM SIGCOMM Symposium on Software Defined Networking Research (SOSR'15)*, New York, NY: ACM, 2015, pp. 16:1–16:12. doi: 10.1145/2774993.2775002.

[182] ETSI, "Mobile Edge Computing (MEC): Technical Requirements," Technical report ETSI GS MEC 002, Mar. 2016.

[183] ETSI, "Mobile Edge Computing (MEC): Framework and Reference Architecture," ETSI, ETSI GS MEC 003 v1.1.1, Mar. 2016.

[184] R. Roman, J. Lopez, and M. Mambo, "Mobile Edge Computing, Fog et al., A Survey and Analysis of Security Threats and Challenges," *Future Gener. Comput. Syst.*, vol. 78, no. 2, pp. 680–698, 2018, doi: 10.1016/j.future.2016.11.009.

[185] EU SELFNET Project, "Framework for Self-Organized Network Management in Virtualized and Software Defined Networks." 2016.

[186] Ž. Bojović, P. D. Bojović, D. Vujošević, and J. Šuh, "Education in times of crisis: Rapid transition to distance learning," *Comput. Appl. Eng. Educ.*, vol. 28, no. 6, pp. 1467–1489, 2020.

[187] R. Nageswara, R. V. Srinivasa, and E. K. Kumari, "Cloud computing: An overview," *J. Theor. Appl. Inf. Technol.*, vol. 9, no. 1, pp. 71–76, 2009.

[188] W. Odom, *Cisco CCNA Routing and Switching ICND 200-101: Official Cert Guide*. Pearson Education, 2013.

[189] P. Mell and T. Grance, "The NIST definition of cloud computing," 2011.

[190] N. B. Ruparelia, *Cloud computing*. Mit Press, 2016.

[191] P. Golding, *Cloud Computing, Saas and PaaS*. 2011.

[192] S. Bhardwaj, L. Jain, and S. Jain, "Cloud computing: A study of infrastructure as a service (IAAS)," *Int. J. Eng. Inf. Technol.*, vol. 2, no. 1, pp. 60–63, 2010.

[193] O. I. Guide, "OpenStack Installation Guide – Installation Guide documentation." [Online]. Available: https://docs.openstack.org/install-guide/.

[194] O. Sefraoui, M. Aissaoui, and M. Eleuldj, "OpenStack: toward an open-source solution for cloud computing," *Int. J. Comput. Appl.*, vol. 55, no. 3, pp. 38–42, 2012.

[195] F. Hsu, M. S. Malik, and S. Ghorbani, "OpenFlow as a Service." 2014.

[196] R. Hat, "Red Hat OpenStack's History, Community, and 7 of its Core Projects," *Journal/Source*.

[197] T. Tsuboi, "OpenStack Heat." Accessed: Jan. 14, 2024. [Online]. Available: https://qiita.com/ttsubo/items/92b41155fa8f6a639f2c.

[198] M.-H. Tsai, H.-T. Liang, Y.-H. Wang, and W.-C. Chung, "Enhanced OpenStack cloud for network function virtualization," in *2020 International Computer Symposium (ICS)*, IEEE, Dec. 2020, pp. 185–190.

[199] P. Patel, V. Tiwari, and M. K. Abhishek, "SDN and NFV integration in openstack cloud to improve network services and security," in *2016 International Conference on Advanced Communication Control and Computing Technologies (ICACCCT)*, IEEE, 2016, pp. 655–660.

[200] W. P. de Jesus, D. A. da Silva, R. T. de Sousa, and F. V. L. da Sousa, "Analysis of SDN contributions for cloud computing security," in *2014 IEEE/ACM 7th International Conference on Utility and Cloud Computing*, IEEE, Dec. 2014, pp. 922–927.

[201] R. Munoz et al., "Integrated SDN/NFV management and orchestration architecture for dynamic deployment of virtual SDN control instances for virtual tenant networks [invited]," *IEEEOSA J Opt Commun Netw*, vol. 7, no. 11, pp. B62–B70, Nov. 2015, doi: 10.1364/JOCN.7.000B62.

[202] K. Kaur, V. Mangat, and K. Kumar, "A comprehensive survey of service function chain provisioning approaches in SDN and NFV architecture," *Comput. Sci. Rev.*, vol. 38, p. 100298, 2020, doi: 10.1016/j.cosrev.2020.100298.

[203] A. M. Medhat, T. Taleb, A. Elmangoush, G. A. Carella, S. Covaci, and T. Magedanz, "Service function chaining in next generation networks: State of the art and research challenges," *IEEE Commun. Mag.*, vol. 55, no. 2, pp. 216–223, 2016.

[204] K. Watsen, M. Richardson, and L. Jalil, "Network Service Header (NSH)," Internet Engineering Task Force, RFC 8300, 2018. [Online]. Available: https://www.rfc-editor.org/info/rfc8300.

[205] M. Kucherawy and A. Sullivan, "SMTP MTA Strict Transport Security (MTA-STS)," Internet Engineering Task Force, RFC 9451, 2021. [Online]. Available: https://www.rfc-editor.org/info/rfc9451.

[206] A. Haider, R. Potter, and A. Nakao, "Challenges in Resource Allocation in Network Virtualization," in *20th ITC Specialist Seminar*, ITC, 2009, p. 20.

[207] A. Fischer, J. F. Botero, M. T. Beck, H. de Meer, and X. Hesselbach, "Virtual Network Embedding: A Survey," *IEEE Commun. Surv. Tutor.*, vol. 15, no. 4, pp. 1888–1906, 2013, doi: 10.1109/surv.2013.013013.00155.

[208] J. Sun, Y. Zhang, F. Liu, H. Wang, X. Xu, and Y. Li, "A survey on the placement of virtual network functions," *J. Netw. Comput. Appl.*, vol. 202, p. 103361, 2022, doi: 10.1016/j.jnca.2022.103361.

[209] N. M. K. Chowdhury, M. R. Rahman, and R. Boutaba, "Virtual network embedding with coordinated node and link mapping," in *IEEE INFOCOM 2009*, IEEE, 2009, pp. 783–791.

[210] N. Laoutaris, I. Stavrakakis, and G. Smaragdakis, "On minimizing the cost of virtual network embedding," in *IEEE INFOCOM 2008-The 27th Conference on Computer Communications*, IEEE, 2008, pp. 1–9. doi: 10.1109/INFOCOM.2008.290.

[211] T. Guo, S. Subramaniam, and Z. Liu, "A Survey on Virtual Network Embedding: Taxonomies, Challenges, and Solutions," *IEEE Commun. Surv. Tutor.*, vol. 20, no. 1, pp. 726–750, 2018, doi: 10.1109/COMST.2017.2763720.

[212] N. Siasi, M. A. Jasim, A. Yayimli, and N. Ghani, "Service Function Chain Survivability Provisioning in Fog Networks," *IEEE Trans. Netw. Serv. Manag.*, vol. 19, no. 2, pp. 1117–1128, 2021, doi: 10.1109/TNSM.2021.3063423.

[213] Y. Xie, Z. Liu, S. Wang, and Y. Wang, "Service Function Chaining Resource Allocation: A Survey," *ArXiv Prepr.*, 2016.

[214] D. Bhamare, R. Jain, M. Samaka, and A. Erbad, "A survey on service function chaining," *J. Netw. Comput. Appl.*, vol. 75, pp. 138–155, 2016.

[215] J. Halpern and C. Pignataro, "Service Function Chaining (SFC) Architecture," Internet Engineering Task Force (IETF), RFC 7665, Jan. 2015. [Online]. Available: https://tools.ietf.org/html/rfc7665.

[216] Q. Zhang, L. Cheng, and R. Boutaba, "Cloud Computing: State-of-the-Art and Research Challenges," *J. Internet Serv. Appl.*, vol. 1, no. 1, pp. 7–18, 2010, doi: 10.1007/s13174-010-0007-6.

[217] A. Luigi, A. Iera, and G. Morabito, "The Internet of Things: A Survey," *Comput. Netw.*, vol. 54, no. 15, pp. 2787–2805, 2010, doi: 10.1016/j.comnet.2010.05.010.

[218] S. Zhang, "An overview of network slicing for 5G," *IEEE Wirel. Commun.*, vol. 26, no. 3, pp. 111–117, 2019.

[219] J. Ordonez-Lucena, P. Ameigeiras, D. Lopez, J. J. Ramos-Munoz, J. Lorca, and J. Folgueira, "Network slicing for 5G with SDN/NFV: Concepts, architectures, and challenges," *IEEE Commun. Mag.*, vol. 55, no. 5, pp. 80–87, 2017.

[220] 3rd Generation Partnership Project (3GPP) and Maurice Pope, "3GPP TR 23.799," Dec. 2016. [Online]. Available: https://portal.3gpp.org/desktopm odules/Specifications/SpecificationDetails.aspx?specificationId=3008.

[221] A. A. Barakabitze, A. Ahmad, R. Mijumbi, and A. Hines, "5G network slicing using SDN and NFV: A survey of taxonomy, architectures and future challenges," *Comput. Netw.*, vol. 167, p. 106984, 2020.

[222] P. D. Bojović, Ž. Bojović, D. Bajić, and V. Šenk, "IP Session Continuity in Heterogeneous Mobile Networks Using Software Defined Networking," *J. Commun. Netw.*, vol. 19, no. 6, pp. 563–568, 2017.

[223] NGMN Alliance, "NGMN Alliance." [Online]. Available: https://www.ng mn.org/.

[224] R. M. Sohaib, O. Onireti, Y. Sambo, and M. A. Imran, "Network slicing for beyond 5G systems: An overview of the smart port use case," *Electronics*, vol. 10, no. 9, p. 1090, 2021.

List of Acronyms

A

AKS	Microsoft Azure Kubernetes Service
AMQP	Advanced Message Queuing Protocol
AP	Access Point
API	Application programming interface
App	Application
ASIC	Application-specific integrated circuit
AMQP	Advanced Message Queuing Protocol

B

BGP	Border gateway protocol
BSS	Business support system

C

CapEx	Capital expenditures
CCE	Huawei cloud container engine
CDN	Content delivery networks
CIFS	Common internet file system
CLI	Command-line interface
CNCF	Cloud-native computing foundation
COE	Central office equipment
CORD	Central office re-architected as a data center
COTS	Commercial-Off-The-Shelf

CPU	Central processing unit
CR	Container runtime
CRI	Container runtime interface
CRM	Customer Relationship Management

D

DAL	Data abstraction layer
DDoS	Distributed denial of service
DPDK	Intel's data plane development kit
DPI	Deep packet inspection
DPU	Data processing unit
DSL	Digital subscriber line

E

EC2	Elastic Compute Cloud
EII	Enterprise Information Integration
EKS	Amazon elastic Kubernetes service
EM	Element manager
eMBB	enhanced mobile broadband
ERP	Enterprise Resource Planning
E2E	End-to-End
ETL	Extracts, transforms, and loads
ETSI	European Telecommunications Standards Institute
ETSI ISG	ETSI Industry Specification Group

F

FCAPS	Fault, configuration, accounting, performance, and security
FCoE	Fiber channel over ethernet
FPGA	Field-Programmable Gate Array

G

GKE	Google Kubernetes engine
GPU	Graphics processing unit
GUI	Graphical user interface

H

HOT	Heat orchestration template
HPA	Horizontal Pod Autoscaler
HRM	Human Resources Management

I

IaaS	Infrastructure-as-a-Service
ICN	Information-centric networking
ICT	Information and Communication Technology
IDS	Intrusion detection system
INT	In-band network telemetry
IoT	Internet of Things
IPC	Inter-process communications
IPS	Intrusion prevention systems
IS-IS	Intermediate System to Intermediate System
ISO	International organization for standardization

K

KPI	key performance indicator

L

LBaaS	Load balancing as a service
LCM	Lifecycle manager
LLDP	Link layer discovery protocol
LSP	Label-switched path
LVAP	Light Virtual Access Point
LVM	Logical Volume Manager
LXC	Linux container

M

M2M	Machine-to-Machine
MANO	Management and network orchestration
MD-SAL	Model-driven service abstraction layer
MEC	Mobile edge computing

MIB	Management Information Base
MME	Mobility Management Entity
mMTC	massive Machine Type Communication
MPLS	Multiprotocol label switching
MSO	multidomain SDN orchestrator

N

NAS	Network-attached storage
NAT	Network address translation
NETCONF	Network configuration Protocol
NFP	Network forwarding path
NFS	Network file system
NFV	Network function virtualization
NFVI	Network function virtualization infrastructure
NGMN	Next-generation mobile networks
NIC	Network interface card
NIST	USA National Institute of Standards and Technology
NMS	Network management system
NOS	Network operating system
NS	Name server
NSD	Network service descriptor
NSH	Network Service Header
NSO	Network service orchestration
NUMA	Non-uniform memory access
NVGRE	Network virtualization using generic routing encapsulation

O

OCI	Open Container Initiative
ODL	OpenDaylight
OF-CONFIG	OpenFlow configuration and management protocol
ONAP	Open Network Automation Platform
ONF	Open Networking Foundation
ONOS	Open network operating system
OpEx	Operational expenditures
OPNFV	Open Platform for NFV
OS	Operating system
OSGi	Open Service Gateway interface
OSI	Open Systems Interconnection

OSM	Open-Source MANO
OSPF	Open shortest path first
OSS	Operation Support Subsystem
OTT	Over-The-Top
OVF	Open virtualization format
OVSDB	Open vSwitch database management protocol

P

PaaS	Platform-as-a-Service
PANE	Policy-based architecture for networked environments
PCEP	Path computation element communication protocol
PCRF	Policy and charging rules function
PE	Provider edge
PGW	Packet data network gateway
PID	Process ID
PMI	Parallel method invocation
pNIC	physical Network Interface Cards
PON	Passive optical network
PoP	Point of Presence
POX	Pythonic network operating system
PXE	Preboot Execution Environment client-server interface

Q

QoE	Quality of Experience
QoS	Quality of Service

R

RAID	Redundant array of inexpensive disks
RAM	RAM
RAN	Radio access network
RDP	Remote desktop protocol
Rkt	Rocket
RL	Resource Layer
RO	Resource orchestration
RPC	Remote procedure call
RSM	Replicated state machine

S

SaaS	Software-as-a-Service
SAN	Storage area network
SDK	Software development kit
SDN	Software-defined networking
SEBA	SDN-enabled broadband access
SF	Service Function
SFC	Service function chaining
SFF	Service Function Forwarder
SFI	Service Function Instance
SG	Serving gateway
SIL	Service Instance Layer
SLA	Service Level Agreement
SNMP	Simple network monitoring protocol
STP	Spanning tree protocol

T

TKE	Tencent Kubernetes engine
TOR	top-of-the-rack

U

U/C	User/control
UE	User equipment
URLLC	Ultra-reliable low latency communication
UTS	Unix time-sharing

V

VDI	Virtual desktop infrastructure
VDI	Virtual disk image
vEPC	virtual Evolved Packet Core
VIM	Virtualized infrastructure manager
VIO	Virtual infrastructure orchestration
vLB	virtual Load Balancers
VM	Virtual machine
vMB	Virtual middlebox

VMDK	Virtual machine disk
VMM	Virtual machine manager
VNC	Virtual network computing
VNE	Virtual Network Embedding
VNF	Virtual network function
VNFD	VNF descriptor
VNF-FG	VNF Forwarding Graph
VNFM	VNF Manager
vNIC	virtual Network Interface Card
VHD	Virtual hard disk
VoIP	Voice over Internet Protocol
VPA	Vertical Pod Autoscaler
vPE	virtual Provider Edge
VPN	Virtual private network
vRR	virtual Route Reflectors
vSwitch	virtual switch
VTN	Virtual Tenant Network

X

XML	Extensible markup language

Y

YAML	Yet another markup language

About the Author

Professor Dr. Živko Bojović, born in 1967 in Peć, has had a serious journey in the field of computer communications. He completed his primary and secondary education in his hometown before pursuing higher education at the Universities of Pristina, Belgrade, and Novi Sad. In 2011, he obtained his doctorate in computer communications, marking a significant milestone in his academic journey.

During his career, Professor Bojović has held important roles in prominent organizations. Notably, he played a pivotal role as the main organizer of the information system at BK Group from 1992 to 1994. Subsequently, he contributed greatly to the telecommunications sector as a director and engineer at 'Telekom Srbija a.d.' from January 1995 to December 2014.

Professor Bojović's influence in the academic sphere has been significant and emphasizes his commitment to advancing the field of computer communications. His career progression is a clear reflection of his continuous professional growth. He was appointed as an assistant professor at the Faculty of Technical Sciences, University of Novi Sad, in January 2015, a role that allowed him to share his knowledge and passion with students. His subsequent promotion to associate professor at the Department of Telecommunications and Signal Processing five years later further underscored his dedication and contributions to the field.

Professor Bojović's expertise spans various crucial areas, including computer networks, cloud computing, software-defined networking, the Internet of Things, and Big Data. His contributions to these domains are evident through his numerous publications in SCIe-listed journals, along with presentations of academic papers at over 15 conferences. Moreover, his authorship of four textbooks and a practicum for laboratory exercises in the field of computer networks reflect his commitment to knowledge dissemination and academic excellence.

Milton Keynes UK
Ingram Content Group UK Ltd.
UKHW020616110724
445220UK00001B/8